ARE OUR KIDS ALL RIGHT?

ARE OUR KIDS ALL RIGHT?

ANSWERS TO THE TOUGH QUESTIONS ABOUT CHILD CARE TODAY

Susan B. Dynerman

Peterson's
Princeton, New Jersey

The author gratefully acknowledges permission to reprint excerpts from the following previously published material:

"A Woman's Work," copyright © 1993 by Louise Erdrich. Reprinted with the author's permission.

The chart "Infant Behavior: When to Be Concerned," by Justin D. Call, M.D., reprinted by permission of Justin D. Call, M.D. Copyright © 1989 by the *New York Times*. Reprinted by permission.

The Preschool Years, by Ellen Galinsky and Judy David. Copyright © 1988 by Ellen Galinsky. Reprinted by permission of Times Books, a division of Random House, Inc.

Solve Your Child's Sleep Problems. Copyright © 1985 by Richard Ferber, M.D., and Martha J. Cochrane. Reprinted by permission of Simon & Schuster, Inc.

Safe & Sound: Choosing Quality Child Care (videotape). Copyright © 1991 by Baxley Media Group (110 W. Main St., Urbana, IL 68101). Used by permission.

Sharing the Caring. Copyright © 1991 by Amy Laura Dombro and Patty Bryan. Reprinted with the authors' permission.

"Family Day Care: Discrepancies Between Intended and Observed Caregiving Practices," by Brenda Krause Eheart and Robin Leavitt. Copyright © 1986, Ablex Publishing. Used with permission.

Developmentally Appropriate Practice in Early Childhood Programs Serving Infants, 1989, Washington, D.C.: NAEYC. Copyright © 1991 by the National Association for the Education of Young Children. Adapted by permission.

Infants: Their Social Environments (pp. 25-26), B. Weissbourd and J. Musick (eds.), 1991, Washington, D.C.: NAEYC. Copyright © 1991 by the National Association for the Education of Young Children. Reprinted by permission.

Nothing But the Best: Making Day Care Work for You and Your Child. Copyright © 1992 by Diane Lusk and Bruce McPherson. By permission of William Morrow & Company, Inc.

The Dragons Are Singing Tonight. Text copyright © 1993 by Jack Prelutsky. By permission of Greenwillow Books, a division of William Morrow & Company, Inc.

"The White Seal," by Rudyard Kipling, appeared in *Rudyard Kipling's Verse*, Doubleday, New York, 1940.

Bare det var sondag altid, by Niels Lund, is used with the permission of Abra Cadabra Musikforlag International APS.

The poem by Justin Taylor on page 293 originally appeared in *Expressions 1992* and is used with the author's permission.

Copyright © 1994 by Susan Dynerman

Library of Congress Cataloging-in-Publication Data
Dynerman, Susan Bacon
        Are our kids all right? answers to the tough questions about child care today / Susan B. Dynerman.
        p. cm.
        Includes bibliographical references.
        ISBN 1-56079-334-1 (hc) : $19.95
        1. Child care—United States. 2. Day-care centers—United States. 3. Children of working parents—United States. 4. Child rearing—United States. I. Title.
HQ778.7.U6D96 1994
649'.1—dc20   94-28670
                                                                                    CIP

Cover design: Circa 86, Inc.

Interior design: Greg Wozney Design, Inc.

Printed in the United States of America
10 9 8 7 6 5 4 3 2 1

To Alex, Max, and, of course, Alan

If It Were Only Sunday All The Time
An old Danish Folk Song

I have a father and mother
Who both must go to work
Because they must earn money
For the benefit my brother and me

But when my Dad comes home
My mother has just left
And when my Mom returns
My father is asleep

I have a father and mother
Who are almost never home
Because our family needs the money
To benefit my brother and me

But when my Dad comes home
My mother has just left
And when my Mom returns
My father is asleep

I have a father and mother
Who I barely even see
They work all the time
To benefit my brother and me

But when my Dad comes home
My mother has just left
And when my Mom returns
My father is asleep

I have a mother and father
Who would do anything for me
So that we can have a better life
Both my brother and me

But when my Dad comes home
My mother has just left
And when my Mom returns
My father is asleep

I have a father and mother
Who, when Sunday comes around
Take us out on trips
Both my brother and me

And when they take time off
We do things together
And that's what I prefer
Most of all

—Niels Lund

TABLE OF CONTENTS

ACKNOWLEDGMENTS

I have far too many people to thank for helping me with this book, including scores of parents, caregivers, family day-care providers, and people in the day-care field who took the time to talk with me. Many are not named on these pages, at their request. They shared personal stories about their experiences and those of their children and, in some cases, the children they care for. Some sat for more than one interview; some talked with me for many hours; others welcomed me into their child-care programs and homes. My special thanks to Maryanne Lazarchick, president of the Montgomery County family day-care association, and Anne Durso and Laura Hubert of Broadcasters' Child Development Center in Washington, D.C.

The first part of this book represents my effort to distill the research on child care and our children. Naturally, whatever conclusions I have drawn are based on the work of many, many researchers, some of whom I also interviewed. For their time, their help, and their frankness, I particularly want to thank T. Berry Brazelton, Edward Zigler, Ellen Galinsky of the Families and Work Institute, Deborah Vandell of the University of Wisconsin, Deborah Phillips of the University of Virginia, Carollee Howes of the University of California at Los Angeles, Jay Belsky of Pennsylvania State University, Ellen Greenberger of the University of California at Irvine, Deborah Belle of Boston University, Ellen Gannett of the Wellesley School-Age Child Care Project, Sarah Friedman of the National Institutes of Child Health and Human Development, and Barbara Willer of the National Association for the Education of Young Children. In addition, my thanks to Amy Dombro of the Families and Work Institute, Tracey Ballas of the National School-Age Child Care Alliance, and Linda Creighton of *U.S. News & World Report* for sharing their knowledge with me.

On a more personal note, I thank my friends and fellow writers Susan and Tom Price for their immeasurable support and my editors, Carol Hupping and Kitty Colton, for their patience, intelligence, and support beyond the call of duty. For help in gathering research materials, I am indebted to computer data-bases, my research assistant, Marsha Berg, and my very busy brother, Alfred Bacon, and his office staff.

This was not an easy project. I wouldn't advise any parent to immerse him or herself in child-rearing books while at the same time trying to raise children. A little constructive advice is helpful; a lot of extraneous advice can't help but cause confusion. I am most grateful to those people who, over the past year, offered me solace from too much reading and too much writing—to my parents and my sister, Abby, and to my friends Jody Jaffee and Charlie Shepard, Frank and Draga Schlesinger, and Catherine Cotter.

There are never enough opportunities to acknowledge the people who have done the most. Without my husband, Alan, and my sons, Alex and Max, there would be no books and no reason to celebrate once they are written.

PART I

What the Research Tells Us

CHAPTER ONE

The Minotaur in the Maze: The Search for Answers

As a society, our attitudes about how children should be raised have changed remarkably little since the 1950s. As a result we are at war with ourselves, even within ourselves, over the fact that in America today, fewer and fewer mothers are at home full time with their children. Despite the fact that most mothers now work, we seem to believe that employment is incompatible with parenthood; that by working we are shortchanging, even endangering, our children. Our ideals about how children should be raised are hopelessly out of sync with reality. And as a result, we are frozen in an ideological debate over what to do about it.

In 1987, for the first time in history, more than half of all American mothers with infants and toddlers—children one year old or younger—were working or looking for work.[1] In 1992 that figure hit 54 percent. In the 20-year period from 1970 to 1990, the number of mothers with preschool-age children in the labor force increased from 32 percent to 58 percent.[2] Employment levels are even higher among mothers with older children. In 1990, according to the Report of the National Commission on Children, 74 percent of women whose youngest child was between 6 and 13 years old were either working or looking for work.[3]

Those rather remarkable statistics carry a lot of messages. One of the most obvious is this: Our child-care needs are enormous, and they are also diverse and complex, running the age gamut from infancy through adolescence. But as a society we appear to be unable to come to grips with these needs. It's as if we're just not quite ready to admit how important child care is and how dependent we are on people outside our families to help us with our families.

When I began my research for this book, I knew from hundreds of conversations with women, and from researching an earlier book, how ambivalent, even torn, many mothers feel about working while raising their children. I wanted the answer to the question that lies at the root of that ambivalence: Are our kids really all right?

The three biggest issues raised by parents when they talk among themselves, by mothers in an implicit tug-of-war within themselves and among each other, by experts in the fields of education, psychology, and sociology, and—with relentless persistence—by the media, are these: Is day care harmful? Are babies somehow irreparably damaged by the fact that their mothers work? And are working parents, by being absent during most of the day, neglecting the needs of their children?

Despite the fact that mothers are working in record numbers, our society is still deeply divided over the answers to these questions—a conflict reflected in the war over family values that surfaced during the 1992 presidential campaigns and in recent public opinion polls. Most child-rearing books still advise mothers to stay home for the first three years of their children's lives. In her 1994 book, *Children First*, Penelope Leach—one of our most popular child-rearing experts—argues that full-time child care is inappropriate for preschoolers and full-time work is incompatible with parenthood. Leach is not alone in her beliefs. Most pediatricians, according to a 1989 survey, feel that having a full-time working mother may "have a harmful effect" on infants (68 percent) and on children under age three (52 percent).[4] One in four American teachers feels that mothers shouldn't work.[5] When polled in 1990 by the Roper Organization, American youths—kids between the ages of 8 and 17—were far more likely to say that having both parents work outside the home was bad for kids (46 percent) than good for them (18 percent). And most family day-care providers, who represent one of the most popular child-care choices for America's infants and toddlers, appear to believe that those children would be better off at home with a parent.

If you're a working parent, you'd have to have been on assignment in Siberia to have not noticed the attention these subjects have received over the past decade.

The controversy over the role of attachment in child development and the impact of a mother's employment on infants, once restricted to academic journals like *The Early Childhood Research Quarterly* and *Child Development*, went public in the mid-80s. In 1986, Jay Belsky, a psychologist from Pennsylvania State University, announced that nonmaternal care in infancy might put children at risk for later problems, because of the importance of infant-mother attachment to later development. Given the speculative nature of some of his claims and the methodology he used, Belsky's work set off a firestorm of controversy within the academic community. Nevertheless, his findings and opinions were picked up and replayed like gospel over and over in the mainstream press.

The debate in Congress over parental-leave legislation, which stretched on for nearly a decade as President Bush vetoed one version after another before it was finally passed in 1993, drew an outpouring of supportive testimony from popular child-rearing experts and developmental psychologists, who argued with compelling certainty that new babies need their mothers *at home*. The subtext of the discussion was pretty clear: Having a working mother may be harmful to babies.

By the end of the decade, articles in popular magazines and newspapers were raising another specter: Day care itself may be harmful to young children. Back in the 70s, when much of the research on day care was being conducted in high-quality university centers or on low-income kids who stood to benefit the most from such early intervention programs, we heard a lot of good news about day care. The effects on children's cognitive and social development appeared to be almost uniformly positive. Joan Lynch, director of a Washington, D.C., child-care center, told me that back then she was getting calls from mothers who weren't employed but wanted to put their children in the center so they could take advantage of the spectacular benefits of day care. But she's not getting those calls anymore.

As researchers ventured out into the real world of day care—which includes all kinds of day-care centers, family day care, unlicensed care, and in-home care of varying quality—the findings on the effects of child care became much less consistent, although not uniformly negative. The press picked up on the negative studies and produced a spate of articles with headlines such as "Can Your Career Hurt Your Kids?" "The Day-Care Generation" and "Do Kids Need a Stay-at-Home Mom?" That, combined with highly publicized charges of sexual abuse in child-care centers in New Jersey, California, and North Carolina, led to rising concerns among working parents. Suddenly, day care didn't seem like such a safe bet anymore.

The Great American Day-Care Debate

Before I began researching this book, I had read the contradictory studies on the effects of child care, on the importance of attachment, and on maternal employment in snippets—a piece here, a piece there—all trumpeted with equal fervor in the mainstream press, all seeming to raise more questions than they answered. Is day care good or bad? Is home rearing better for kids? Is a mother hurting her baby by going back to work after six weeks or three months or a year?

Much of what I'd read on the subject of child care seemed to be shrouded in rhetoric. A series of articles published in 1993 in *The Utne Reader,* a relatively obscure digest, captures the character of the debate over our values, our changing lifestyles, and how our children are being raised. At one extreme, Susan Faludi, feminist and author of the best-selling *Backlash*, contributed an article titled "The Kids Are All Right," in which she tells us that, contrary to popular belief, the long-term effects of day care are almost uniformly positive; studies show that day care "has made [children] somewhat more social, experimental, self-assured, cooperative, creative." Despite all the negative publicity surrounding abuse in day care, she writes, research shows that child abuse is much more likely to occur at home—a documented fact. Our misconceptions about day care, she argues, are the product of our cultural biases toward home rearing, reinforced by "years of relentless anti-day-care and anti-working-mother rhetoric from the Reagan and Bush administrations and from the media, where bashing day care seems to be a sanctioned sport."[6]

On the pages of the same digest, I found an excerpt from a 1993 book entitled *The Spirit of Community: Rights, Responsibilities and the Communitarian Agenda*, by Amitai Etzioni,[7] an eminent sociologist and advocate for the renewal of community values. He hits all the hot buttons. Our values are askew, he argues: " . . . many parents have a choice between enhanced earnings and attending to their children," he writes, claiming that two-income couples are working to buy VCRs and $150 sneakers. Calling day care "kennels for kids," Etzioni adds, "Unless the parents are absent or abusive, children are better off at home. Older children, between 2 and 4, may be able to handle some measure of institutionalization in child care centers, but their personalities often seem too unformed to be able to cope well with nine-to-five separation from a parent." He insists that parents are working at their children's expense and ultimately at the expense of society as a whole, an argument I heard numerous times while researching this book. "We must all live with the consequences of children who are not brought up properly," he writes.

Is day care itself harmful? Truth is, it's pretty easy to make the case either way. Consider these conflicting conclusions about the effects of day care, from which any writer is free to pick and choose—all supported by valid research conducted in the 1970s and 80s:

The good. Day care–reared children are more independent, outgoing, cooperative, empathetic, and considerate. Day-care kids do better in school, behave more maturely with adults, and do better on cognitive tests. You name it, they achieve it.

The bad. Day-care kids are more competitive, more aggressive, less interactive, louder, less cooperative with adults, less compliant with their mothers, and generally all-around bad apples.

The indifferent. Home-reared children and center-reared children are no different on measures of cooperativeness, sociability, aggression, the ability to focus on a task, frustration tolerance, and overall emotional well-being.[8]

Confusing? That's an understatement.

It's no wonder Edward F. Zigler, Sterling Professor of Psychology at Yale University, says simply, "Ignore the research, because you can pick any position that you would like . . . everything from if you put your child in day care the child will turn to dust, to if you don't put your child in day care you're costing the child a growth catalyst."

Ultimately, though, all roads lead to the same logical conclusion: There's no evidence that day care is inherently bad for children or that home rearing is inherently better for kids. But the research makes it clear that *good* day care can be good for kids and, conversely, *bad* day care can be bad for them. The quality of care, says Zigler, is the issue.

Kids from day-care programs that are rated high in quality, not by parents but by independent observers, tend to do better than all right. They seem to come out pretty much the way Susan Faludi describes them—although I haven't seen the studies that suggest day-care kids are more "experimental" or "creative."

Unfortunately, in defending child care as we know it, the feminist position may be a particularly dangerous one. I'm concerned that in an effort to zealously protect the interests of working mothers and minimize maternal guilt, feminists like

Faludi paint a misleading picture of American child care. When she asserts that the children are doing fine, she's making a case for the idea of day care—the idea that day care can be just as good as mother care. But if she's making a case for day care as we know it, her position is indefensible. Because child care in America should come with a warning label. It is substandard, it is inadequate; it is the kind of care that is more apt to produce kids with behavior problems, poor peer relations, and lower achievement in school than kids who are sociable, creative, and cooperative.

Mary Francis Berry, in a complex and compelling 1993 book, *The Politics of Parenthood*, argues that it's time to take sole responsibility for child rearing off the backs of American mothers; she argues for child-care reforms and creative strategies for supporting working parents. But then she seems almost unaware of the enormity of the task at hand when she offers this astonishingly simplistic view of a child's needs: "All experts agree that the most important ingredient for a child's healthy psychological development is non-abusive and consistent care, whether from a parent, a nanny or a child-care worker in a center."[9] That's rather like saying all pediatricians agree that the most important ingredient for a child's physical growth is food, whether animal, vegetable, or mineral.

Children need much more than "non-abusive and consistent care." Unless advocates for day care like Faludi and Berry stop simplifying the needs of children for rhetorical purposes, the children in this country are not going to get the kind of care they need. Socializing and nurturing young children, like educating older ones, requires certain very specific skills (and personality characteristics), a good deal of commitment, and an understanding of children that is generally acquired through training, education, or reading. Caring for America's children, from birth through adolescence, is a big job. And until we get past the idea that mother care is the best or the only way, just because it's mother, we're not going to be able to address head-on the issue of what child care can and should be.

Our Kids Aren't All Right

In the course of researching this book, I've spoken with some of the top people in the child-care field, people who believe in the idea of child care, who don't believe home rearing is the only option. And they tell me our children aren't doing fine. Why? Because of the dismal state of child care in America. It's not a matter of abusive and neglectful care, although by some estimates as much as 10 percent of America's child care may fall into that category. Rather, it is a matter of inferior care. Yale's Edward Zigler tells me "70 percent of the child care in America is substandard." T. Berry Brazelton, the preeminent child-rearing expert of our time, points out that at least 50 percent of the child care in America is inadequate. And Deborah Phillips, director of the Board on Children and Families at the National Academy of Sciences, whose area of expertise is the quality of child care in America, tells me *most* child care in America falls below the threshold of acceptable care. These people are not suggesting that most American child care is "abusive" or even "inconsistent." They're saying most American child care does not foster the healthy development of children; they're saying that finding someone to help raise your children is not as simple as finding a good babysitter; and they're saying that the components of good care go well beyond the need for consistency and "non-abuse." These people are saying that child care in the United States in the 1990s is not good enough; that our children are not all right.

The Minotaur in the Maze

By now, I have read many of the hundreds of studies that serve as fuel for the day-care debate. I have talked with more than a hundred researchers, educators, and experts in the field of child development, family day-care providers, day-care workers, and working parents with children of all ages. Much of my research was concentrated in Washington, D.C., northern Virginia, and Montgomery County, Maryland—an area with the highest concentration of dual-income couples in the United States. But I've also interviewed parents, providers, and people who run child-care referral services in Louisiana, Washington State, Maine, New Jersey, Delaware, Pennsylvania, Tennessee, and Illinois—all in an attempt to determine what we've learned over the past two decades and whether there's evidence in favor of scrapping our old child-rearing models and instituting some new ones.

Coming up with new child-rearing models involves answering questions that, two decades ago, appeared irrelevant to most American parents, questions such as:

- What's the optimal parental leave—not from the perspective of an employer but from the perspective of babies *and* parents?
- What is this thing called attachment? And should we pay homage to it?
- What are the optimal child-care arrangements at what ages?
- How do you evaluate the quality of child care? Is group care okay? Is one-on-one care really essential? How can we make sure that our kids will be all right in child care?

In 1994, there's no lack of research on these subjects. But social scientists didn't begin exploring these issues in earnest until women began entering the workforce in droves in the 70s. So theirs are only first-generation findings, and as such they raise as many questions as they answer. Not surprisingly, the studies and their findings are complex and sometimes contradictory. There's not a lot of what researchers call "clean data."

What did I find? There is no evidence in the research that having a working mother is harmful to children. There *is* evidence, however, that when and how much parents work, their child-care choices, and how they deal with their kids can have an enormous impact on how those kids grow up and turn out. That's the story all these studies, and all these people, have to tell. And that's the story that appears on these pages.

But there's a bigger story here that begs to be told. I found that looking for the answers to all these questions was rather like being trapped in a maze with a Minotaur. No matter what path I took, I ran into the same monster. That monster is child care in America. Ultimately, all the research on infants and attachment, on children in child care, and on maternal employment leads to the inevitable conclusion that the kids are only going to turn out all right if their child care is all right—and that child care in America is not all right.

***

In April 1994, as this book was going to press, the results of a new wave of studies on children and child care began to surface, lending further support to the idea that American child care is in drastic need of reform. The Carnegie Corporation released a major study on infants and toddlers in America, implicating poor-quality child care as a risk factor for millions of American children of all social classes. The Families and Work Institute in New York released the first major study of family day care and relative care in America, and the results were disturbing: Only 9 percent of the providers studied were deemed high quality. Judging from the research I've seen and the experts I've inter-viewed, it's likely that at least half the kids in child care in America today are in substandard arrangements—including chil-dren in center care, family day care, and before- and after-school programs, those in the care of an in-home sitter or relative, and those in what is euphemistically labeled "self-care."

Given that, isn't it time we shelved our ambivalence and accepted the fact that child care is here to stay? Isn't it time we turned our attention away from mothers and what they should and shouldn't do and toward the issue that demands our attention—that of improving child care in America?

CHAPTER TWO

The Quality of Child Care in America

I can remember, vividly, the moment when my first child made it clear that he didn't want me to go to work. It was a warm morning in the early spring of 1980. He was just over a year old, a happy, curly-haired cherub of a kid. I said good-bye and breezed out the front door just like every other weekday, closing the screen door behind me. But this time he followed. I can still see him, dressed only in a diaper, his hands and face pressed up against the screen, screaming bloody murder. "Mamaaaaaaa."

His sitter, Letha, who had been with us since he was three months old, followed, picked him up, and began waving, a broad smile on her face. "Bye-bye. Mommy's going to work," she said cheerily, encouraging me to push on. "Bye-bye." She was a wise lady, loving and warm. "Bye-bye." I must have taken her cue and walked on, waving in response. But it was as wrenching a moment for me, I have no doubt, as it was for my son.

Letha left us within a few weeks of that day, over some disagreement about going against doctor's orders and feeding my son solids in the wake of a stomach virus. A small matter, in retrospect, that at the time seemed monumental.

If I had known then what I know now, I would have held on to Letha with every ounce of my being. I had no idea how hard it would be on my son to make not just one change but all the changes that followed as a result of her departure. And I had no idea how hard it would be for me to replace her, because she had dropped into my lap like a gift from heaven. She was, it turned out, irreplaceable.

Caregiver number two lasted about a week. She arrived one morning, not long after I had hired her, slurring her words and moving with a sloppy slowness. Instead of rushing off to work, I decided to hang around—a judgment call that, admittedly, didn't require any kind of special intuition. When she picked my son up in her arms, she very nearly dropped him on his head. She claimed to be a diabetic but appeared to be drunk. I offered to get her medical care, and when she protested too much I took her home. That night I had the first and only migraine I have ever had in my life. I took a leave of absence from my job and began, in earnest, the search for child care.

I tell this tale because it marks the moment when I first became aware of the Child-Care Problem, the moment when my—and my son's—child-care woes began. He would soon have to adjust to caregiver number three, followed by one day-care center and then another—changes that would be largely beyond my control.

I know from experience how hard it is to find—and keep—good child care. I've had my name on waiting lists for top-quality centers, with no apparent hope of getting in when the time came around. I've placed ads in the newspapers for in-home caregivers and screened literally dozens of applicants by phone, only to have just one of the five prospective candidates show up for the interview. I've watched as my son's day-care center closed, suddenly, with only a few weeks' notice. And I've settled on child-care arrangements that have ranged from good to merely acceptable to downright bad. Once, I dropped in unexpectedly at a family day-care home—a temporary arrangement recommended by a friend—to find 20 toddlers and preschoolers lying on the floor sucking on lollipops, having what was euphemistically labeled "nap time"—although only a handful of them appeared to be sleeping. One of these children, sprawled out on the dirty carpet, was my own child.

That was my first child, born in the late 70s. With my second, born more than ten years later, I elected to stay home and work out of an upstairs room; as a family, we could afford it. I made that decision not because I felt my working outside the home would be harmful to my child, not because I thought day care (in its many forms) was inherently bad, but because I couldn't bear the knowledge of what lay ahead—the prospect of negotiating my way through a child-care system that doesn't work, the uncertainty of knowing an arrangement might fall through any day, and the feeling that such a system couldn't possibly serve the best interests of a child, not to mention the interests of anyone to whom I might obligate myself as an *employee*.

Times Have Changed, but Not Enough

My personal odyssey through the child-care universe began 15 years ago. But it might as well have been a century. Back then, the child-rearing books offered little, if any, advice to people in my situation. Is an 18-month-old ready for group care? Will the readjustment cause permanent trauma? Should I take time off, try to find someone else, quit my job? All I knew from the child-rearing books I'd read was that if I had my head screwed on straight, I'd be home with that child, not running around doing some job.

I couldn't look to other mothers for support because, believe it or not, I didn't know any other working mothers with toddlers, although I know now that they were out there, determined to work, struggling privately with the same problems I faced. Nor did I know anyone who'd already been through what I was going through. For educated, professional women, this was a first-generation phenomenon.

There was nowhere to turn for help. No child-care networks, no child-care referral agencies or nanny placement services—at least not where I lived, in Memphis. Family day care? I don't think I'd ever even heard the term used. But I know there were no licensed family day-care homes back then, because a license wasn't required by law until 1989—and then only for homes keeping five children or more. What about day-care centers? In 1980, no more than a dozen day-care centers in this city of 800,000 people accepted infants. Today, nearly 200 day-care centers in Memphis take infants; the total number of centers has doubled, from about 200 to close to 400.[1]

Today you'd have to live in near-isolation not to know at least one new mother who is working. Indeed, it's much harder to find a new mother who *isn't* going back to work. The standard questions for a new mother these days are: Is it a boy or girl? How much does he/she weigh? When do you have to go back to work? What did you name him/her? A phenomenal 59 percent of American mothers now return to work after the birth of their first child.[2]

Vast changes have taken place in the child-care system. Networks of referral agencies, nanny placement firms, and more than a dozen nanny schools have sprung up around the country. The au pair program, established as a cultural exchange program, primarily between Europe and the U.S., has been in place since 1986, bringing nearly 8,000 young women and men to U.S. families for one-year stints as live-in babysitters. Employers, motivated to improve productivity and enhance benefits, have gotten into the act. Workplace consultants hand out brochures on how to find child care, and sick child–care centers have begun to appear here and there. Big corporations, even some small firms, offer on-site child care and child-care referral services and sponsor support groups and bag lunches for parents to talk about child-rearing issues. That's a far cry from my experience. In the early 80s, nobody in American companies wanted to talk about child rearing, much less make an event out of it.

The 80s saw the birth of the National Association for Child Care Resource and Referral Agencies (NACCRRA) and the National Association for Family Child Care (NAFCC). In 1985 the National Association for the Education of Young Children (NAEYC) began a program for accrediting day-care centers, using standards that go well beyond licensing requirements. Advocacy groups such as the National School-Age Child Care Alliance and the Child Care Action Campaign opened their doors. Most of these networks, which link providers, offer training, educate parents, and promote child-care reform, didn't exist even a decade ago.

We may have come a long way since 1980, but we haven't even begun to solve the problems of child care in America. We have barely scratched the surface when it comes to the issue at hand: the quality of child care. The child-care community and the corporate community are moving forward. The amount of child care available has skyrocketed along with the number of children in care. The supports for American parents are improving. But despite all that, the quality of care, the real measure of what's happening out there, is *declining*. Since 1980, the quality of American child care has gotten worse, despite enormous efforts on the part of child-care advocates and the dedication of a growing number of child-care professionals[3]—and despite the fact that more than seven million infants and preschoolers are in some form of supplemental care while their parents are at work.[4]

In truth, the American child-care system isn't a system at all; at least not yet. It is a patchwork of licensed and unlicensed, regulated and unregulated, profit and nonprofit, trained and untrained, monitored and unmonitored sitters, converted homes, day-care centers, and school-based programs. Consider these facts:

Most of America's day-care centers are **not** *accredited by the National Association for the Education of Young Children.* NAEYC's accreditation program, which aims to establish nation-wide standards for high-quality center care, is just too new, and when parents don't even ask about it, there's little incentive to shoot for accreditation. There are 90,558 regulated day-care centers and preschool programs in the U.S.[5] Of these, only 2,500—that's 2 percent—are certified by NAEYC.[6]

Most family day-care programs operate illegally. Somewhere between 500,000 and two million family day-care homes are neither licensed nor registered.[7] No one monitors this care but the parents. There's no telling how many children are cared for in unlicensed homes; it may be as many as three to four million.[8] Some of these kids are in situations that are genuinely frightening. Unlicensed providers aren't required to meet fire safety codes, to have a TB test, or to know CPR; nor do they need training in child development. And they don't have to comply with mandated ratios or group sizes.

Yale psychologist Edward Zigler has called family day care the great "cosmic crapshoot." Of the 273,926 family day-care providers in the U.S. who are licensed or registered, only 708—next to none—are accredited by the National Association for Family Child Care.[9]

At this writing, there are no federal guidelines to help states set licensing requirements. The result: standards that are inconsistent and, at best, minimal. Research has uncovered some of the most important components of good child care—including high staff-child ratios, small group sizes, and trained teachers—but those standards are not being implemented nationwide, although many states have improved their licensing requirements in recent years. Still, referral agencies are quick to counsel parents that a license offers no guarantee of quality, and in the worst states, referral agencies simply tell parents that a license means next to nothing.

For example, it's widely agreed that the minimal acceptable standard for infant care is one caregiver for three, or at the very most four, infants. But in family day care, when other children are present, a 1:2 caregiver-to-infant ratio is considered optimal. In North Carolina, in large family day-care homes, it's legal for one adult to care for up to six infants. In South Carolina, in group day-care homes, a single adult can care for up to eight infants. And in Idaho it's legal for one adult to take on up to 12 infants. Such regulations border on the absurd. But even in the best states, regulations seem curiously lax. In Maryland a licensed provider can care for up to eight children in her home, including two infants.[10] That may not be absurd. But is it humanly possible for one adult to take good care of two babies and six other children? "It's ridiculous," says one Maryland family day-care provider. "I'd never consider taking on two babies with my other children here."

There are serious gaps in the child-care system—particularly for infants and toddlers (the most expensive and labor-intensive forms of care) and for school-age children (the most overlooked market for care). It's extremely difficult for most parents to find sick care, night care, and odd-hours and seasonal care in farm-cropping states and oil-rig states and areas where major employers operate around the clock. There are major gaps in the before-school, after-school, and summer programs for school-age kids. But only a handful of studies examine this network's impact on the school-age kids it serves, or underserves. Estimates of the number of children, ages six and up, who care for themselves while their parents work range from 2 to 15 million.[11] Despite a growing interest in part-time and flexible schedules, there's little evidence that the child-care network can serve the needs of part-timers. In-home caregivers don't want part-time jobs; many centers don't accept part-time children; and many family day-care providers prefer full-timers.

Although there are more than 400 referral agencies nation-wide, the vast majority of child-care placements occur outside this network. As of 1991, the agencies affiliated with the National Association of Child Care Resource and Referral Agencies (NACCRRA) reportedly "helped" 750,000 parents a year and listed 250,000 providers. But in fact only 10 to 15 percent of child-care placements nationwide come through these agen-cies.[12] Says Sarah Nordmann, coordinator of membership services and technical assistance for NACCRRA, "One of the most critical issues is funding. A lot of agencies don't receive public funding through city, county, or state governments." Referral agencies can provide names, addresses, and phone numbers of providers and centers, a service they generally offer free of charge. If they operate under contract with a corporation, they offer employees the added service of confirming vacancies. But they cannot list in-home providers, because these providers are not covered by state licensing requirements. Nor can they legally offer any kind of quality ratings, recommendations, or stamp of approval.

Referral agencies can't even tell you if they've received complaints about a provider or center, unless a formal complaint—say, of abuse or neglect—has been filed with state authorities. "As phone counselors we try to make humane judgments about the quality of care," says Elizabeth Thompson of Washington State Resource and Referral. "But legally we cannot stop making referrals to a family day-care home, even if we know a child is being beaten at that home, unless an action is being taken [by the licensing office]." So while they routinely hear complaints about cleanliness, nutrition, a "harried" caregiver, or someone who has too many kids in care, they can't legally pass any of that information along to consumers. As a result, they see their role as one of education: training providers and educating parents. Parents, they say, must learn how to judge—because a referral is not a reference, a distinction of which many parents are unaware.

All of this, of course, puts an enormous burden on working parents—to find, evaluate, and monitor their children's care.

Child care is not babysitting; it is more like education. Anyone who thinks otherwise is misinformed. What are the lessons of early childhood? Between birth and age five, children are learning social skills: how to get along with others and how to treat others; how to get attention and show affection; how to share and negotiate. They're learning what they need to know before they begin school: how to focus on a task; how to solve a problem without getting frustrated; how to exercise patience and self-control. They're learning about themselves in relation to the world, about autonomy and trust, about separating from those they love—one of the biggest lessons of early childhood.

Consider the phenomenal lessons children learn before they're ready to take on the lessons of the classroom: how to cooperate, how to wait their turn, how to sit and listen. The little sponges are soaking up everything that's going on around them: the uses of language, the value of books, how the world works and what's in it. They're learning all these lessons through the environment and the people who care for them. Make no mistake about it: Child care involves education, but not education as we know it or imagine it.

Given that, imagine if only 1 or 2 percent of all the schools in America were accredited by their local Board of Education, because nobody really thought it mattered. What if most American children were in schools that did not meet minimal safety standards or fire codes? What if the teachers changed periodically throughout the year, they were paid even less than the janitors who cleaned their buildings, and parents didn't expect them to have any training whatsoever? What if all schools charged tuition and you were forced to weigh the cost of your child's education against your annual income? That gives you some insight into where child care stands in America today.

Ultimately, any child-care choice is up to the parents. But the sad truth is, choosing child care today is like selecting a pickle from a bad barrel: There aren't too many good options. Worse still, parents are often ill-equipped to judge. Could you march into a second-grade class and evaluate the teacher and the curriculum based on what you know as a parent? And yet American parents are expected to make decisions regarding the care and socialization of their young children with little or no guidance on how to make that choice, aside from the presence of a "license," maybe a brochure on choosing care, and their own good judgment. Worse still, they're operating in a universe where what they're looking for may not even exist in their community or near their job site.

What Does "Quality" Mean?

Some people imagine that the problems of child care in America today are associated with poverty—that only poor kids are getting poor care, as if that's to be expected. But this is a problem that affects all of us. "There is a wide range of quality of care, and that range is reflected across social class," says Deborah Vandell, a psychologist at the University of Wisconsin and one of the most prominent researchers in the child-care field. "Wealthy families are using poor-quality care, but they have high-quality care available to them as well. The same holds true for families living in poverty. There are not high correlations between quality of child care and income."

Other people imagine that bad child care means abuse and neglect, crowded and unsafe conditions, and unregulated care. Sadly, such care exists. But the problems with the American child-care system are much broader and much deeper. I've talked to caregivers who were not allowed to hug the children—toddlers and young threes—at their day-care center for fear of projecting favoritism; tragically, according to news reports, some caregivers are being trained not to hug or hold children, even when they're looking at a picture book together, in order to guard against charges of sexual abuse.[13] I've met day-care teachers who are actively discouraged from communicating with parents. I've watched a group of three-year-olds wait in line to paint at a single easel at a for-profit center—an absurd exercise for children of that age.

Referral agencies report that there are centers and family day-care homes where children three and four years old are expected to sit at desks and perform written lessons for much of the day—an equally absurd exercise for preschoolers. Every evening these kids are expected to do their homework. I've seen children, the offspring of high-powered professionals, in family day-care homes—or rather apartments—spending their days in a single crowded room dominated by a television set. In another suburban home, eight toddlers and preschoolers share a box of toys and a handful of books; most mornings, however, are spent walking to a nearby shopping mall, and most afternoons are spent sleeping.

I've heard tales that make me wince—of in-home caregivers who spend their time on the phone while their charges watch TV or play video games, of unlicensed family day-care providers with no training, no space, dime-store toys, and houses jammed with kids.

Is this the kind of care that dominates what can, sadly, be called the child-care *market?* Are these stories the exception or the rule? The answer, of course, is that we have no way of knowing, because the care in this country is not adequately monitored and regulated, and parents don't have the means or the time to find out. But plenty of evidence indicates that there's more poor care than excellent care, more mediocre care than good care.

The Child-Care Research: Disturbing Findings on Quality

Released in 1989, the National Child Care Staffing Study evaluated the nation's day-care centers on a variety of measures —including the extent to which programs had appropriate materials and spaces, how well they were tailored to the needs and abilities of age groups, and how providers actually talked to the kids. The study of more than 200 centers even included a measure of "staff sensitivity." The findings were disturbing, suggesting that most center care in America is barely adequate. Only 12 percent of classrooms achieved a good score on "developmentally appropriate activities." Only 30 percent of classrooms achieved good or better scores on caregiver behavior. The study also found that "children from middle-income families were enrolled in centers of lower quality than were children from low- and high-income families."[14] Training, according to the study, was the single most important predictor of how well a caregiver interacted with kids. Despite that, most parents still feel training is irrelevant and are ill-equipped to judge whether a program is age-appropriate.

In 1994, the Families and Work Institute released the most comprehensive study to date of family day care in America. Called the Study of Children in Family Child Care and Relative Care (and hereafter referred to as the 1994 family day-care study), it looked at family day care of all types, including large and small group care, one-on-one family day care, and care by a relative. The findings were as disturbing as those of the National Child Care Staffing Study. Only 9 percent of family day-care arrangements surveyed fell in the "good" range on standard measures of quality. Thirty-five percent of the care was rated "poor." Fifty-six percent fell in the range of "adequate" or "custodial."[15]

Commenting on the findings, Carollee Howes of UCLA, one of the researchers on the study, said, "The median level of quality of care in this country is adequate. It does not harm children, but it doesn't enhance development. Some people would argue that providing adequate child care is good enough. I would argue that our society's responsibility is to provide child care that enhances child development. When we have children who are doing well in child care, benefiting in positive ways, we're all going to benefit from that, eventually." Howes is not talking about child care that promotes intellectual development; she's talking about care that promotes healthy social and emotional development.

The 1994 family day-care study and the National Child Care Staffing Study are remarkable in their consistency. There's no proof that either form of care is generally better—or generally worse—than the other. Center-based and home-based providers received comparable average scores on sensitivity; centers and home-based providers received comparable average scores on measures of overall program quality. And both studies identified a clear link between caregiver training and sensitive, responsive, and nurturing care. In family day care, the least nurturing, least sensitive providers (relatives included) were those who were *unlicensed and untrained.*[16]

Parents Know About the Quality Problem

Sixty-two percent of the more than 3,000 parents surveyed for the National Study of the Changing Workforce[17] said finding high-quality care was the biggest child-care problem they face. Not convenience, not even affordability, but simply finding good enough care. In that study, 58 percent of the parents surveyed felt they essentially had no choices. According to the 1994 family day-care study, among parents who looked for alternatives to their current child-care arrangements, 65 percent found nothing else and more than one-fourth would have put their children in better care if they had been able to find it.[18]

The difficulty of finding good care is magnified by the fact that many parents have to go through the process of finding child care again and again and again. When the Child Care Action Campaign, an organization for child-care research and education, conducted consumer research in nine U.S. cities in 1991, the results were similar. They found that because of problems related to quality, most parents end up trying two or three arrangements before they find "one that works."[19]

Change is endemic to the American child-care system.

My own, and my son's, experience with child care back in the early 80s was not—and is not, even today—unique. Stability, the steam that should drive this whole system, the characteristic of child care that children may well need the most and parents crave, is missing from the American child-care system. Problems related to quality and instability are inextricably linked. Consider the child-care options one at a time.

In-Home Care

When most people begin their child-care odyssey, they are looking for in-home sitters, often for their new babies. The vast majority of calls coming into referral agencies are from first-time mothers with newborns, who don't want to put their children in day-care centers or family day-care homes. A nanny, a mother substitute, an affordable Mary Poppins is what most parents want. But as I mentioned, referral agencies don't really handle these calls, although some provide lists of employment agencies in the area and guidance on how to select an in-home caregiver.

Theoretically, in-home care is considered the best possible form of child care for newborns and infants up to age one or even, as some experts maintain, up to age three. But in-home care offers the perfect example of just how dramatically theory diverges from reality. In-home care is the most unstable and hardest to monitor form of child care there is. There's no evidence that in-home care beyond infancy is better for children than any other form of child care; and during infancy, the emotional impact of losing an in-home caregiver may pose problems. Although few studies of in-home care have been conducted, what little research exists suggests that in-home care may be the worst possible form of child care.

There's no telling how many in-home caregivers there are in America today, because there's no way of counting them. They move in and out of middle-class and affluent households as if through a revolving door. Are most of these people trained? Again, there's no way of knowing, but empirical evidence suggests that most in-home caregivers have little or no training; and training has been found to be the single most important determinant of how nurturant, attentive, and competent the caregiver is.

Given the wages, the lack of benefits, the working conditions, and the extent to which the job of caregiver is undervalued in our society, most in-home sitters are drawn from the ranks of the underclass. Lucky parents find caregivers who are overqualified for the job, trained in another field—often in another country— and unable to find other employment here; they are committed, responsible, trustworthy, and, in some cases, good with children. But the good fortune of such parents depends on their caregiver's misfortunes. Writes an anonymous caregiver in an article entitled "Nanny: Confessions of an 'Illegal' Caregiver": "They hire us and because we hunger, we work. Maybe, in our countries, we were secretaries, accountants—and here, maids. What I wouldn't do to work in an office with a computer in front of me! That's what I did in El Salvador."[20]

Take the case of Jennifer Williams, who has spent the past two years caring for a toddler while the child's parents, a lawyer and a journalist, are at work. A woman of striking dignity, Williams studied nutrition in her home country of Jamaica before she moved to America. She considers herself a professional. "When I'm caring for a child, I portray them as my own," she says of her relationship with her charge, a two-year-old girl who has obviously thrived in her care. But Williams's own son, Adrian, has experienced the worst of American child care. He has been in unlicensed family day care ranging from good ("She treated him the way I would treat him") to poor ("There was this child with a runny nose. She said, 'Come here, boy,' very roughly, and wiped it so hard that he began to cry") to downright disturbing. At three, Adrian was enrolled in a day-care center that, at the rate of $75 a week, Williams could afford. First, he got sick on the center's food. "He was picking up parasites," she says. "Apparently they weren't cooking the food properly." So she started sending a bag lunch with him. Then she arrived ahead of schedule one day and found Adrian sitting in a corner with his eyes closed and his hands on his head. "I don't know how long he'd been sitting there," said Williams. The infraction: He wanted to play at nap time.

Not long afterwards, Williams was boarding a bus after the morning drop-off, and a woman stopped her in the aisle and warned her about the center. "She said that when the children misbehave, they don't feed them. Their punishment is, they don't get any lunch. Those children are dropped off at 8 in the morning and picked up at 6 P.M.," says Williams. Adrian is now cared for by a relative while his mother works—one of the most common arrangements for women in the lowest income brackets.

In the pyramid of American child care, the people at the top have access to better care. But money offers no guarantee of high quality.

Can Money Always Buy Good Care?

Lest you imagine that affluent, two-income families have homes staffed by efficient, professional, well-trained nannies, consider Zoë Baird's testimony before the Senate Judiciary Committee in 1993. Here is a woman, married to an academic and surely earning a six-figure income as a corporate attorney, who felt compelled to hire an illegal immigrant, one she apparently had to hand-hold through a series of marital problems, because that was the best care she could find. Not the only care she could find, not the best care she could afford, but, according to her testimony before the U.S. Senate, the *best care available* for her child.

Zoë Baird was no anomaly. Says one attorney, "In Washington, D.C., it's almost impossible to find a good sitter who speaks English well, who's legal, who can drive, and who wants to be a sitter."

Parents with years of experience with in-home caregivers tell me you're lucky if a sitter stays a year and even luckier if you find someone who's interested in your child. "In a bad year," says JoAnn Zuercher, a Washington attorney who is now at home with her children, "we used to go through two or three people." I have interviewed people who've held on to caregivers for five, even ten years, but they are the exception, not the norm. In fact, one 1984 study, the only such study of in-home care I encountered, found turnover rates for in-home caregivers of 59 percent, meaning more than half leave their jobs each year—a rate that is "twice the average for all employed persons," according to one report and "comparable to the rates for gas station attendants,"[21] and worse than turnover rates for family day-care providers or center staff.

There's plenty of anecdotal evidence to suggest that little has changed in the past ten years. I've interviewed families who've had four, five, or six such caregivers during their children's preschool years. Another Washington lawyer, who worked for ten years before throwing up her hands in frustration, estimates that she had 12 in-home caregivers over the course of a decade. The problem, she says, is that you're drawing from a pool of unskilled, unstable workers. "A lot of them are doing this because it's the quickest way to make money," she says. "They have no interest in children. The people who were good with children tended to not stay very long, because they were good at a lot of things and they wanted to go on to other things."

This isn't a supply problem. Anyone who places an ad in the paper in search of an in-home caregiver can tell you they will get plenty of phone calls. It is a quality problem. The pool of truly qualified in-home caregivers is minuscule. Certainly there are problems inherent in any form of child care. With in-home care, the built-in problem is that it's difficult for parents to monitor the kind of care their child is getting, which makes the need for safeguards particularly acute.

There is no national certification program for in-home caregivers. There's no nationwide network for screening out criminals, although you can hire a detective to do a thorough check. Parents must go through nanny placement firms, which are often nothing more than glorified employment services for the barely qualified and may charge upwards of $2,000 per referral. "If someone could drive and they knew how to microwave a dinner, they were presented by the agency as being skilled," says one parent.

In-home care is plagued by the same problem that plagues all child care in America. It's not considered a profession; it's a job, and a low-ranking one at that. Consider this tale told by another Washington lawyer, who has had four caregivers over the past four years. When caregiver number two got pregnant and left, the lawyer went through a placement firm, paid a hefty $2,000 fee, checked references and resumes, and thought she'd found a real professional. Three months later, the woman left for a job with the postal service, which she considered to be a step up professionally.

The U.S. government considers in-home care an unskilled occupation. According to the *Directory of Occupation Titles* published by the U.S. Employment Services, which is used by the U.S. government to set policies, an in-home caregiver—called a "child monitor"—is an unskilled occupation. The requirements for the job are up to three months of experience. The government's definition of in-home care is used, among other things, to set immigration quotas. If you want to sponsor someone to come into the country to do a job, any job, you first have to advertise the job in the paper to make sure you can't get a U.S. citizen. If you're looking for an in-home caregiver, you have to first prove that you can't find a qualified applicant with three months' experience. Three months. That's not even long enough to watch a child move from infancy to toddlerhood.

In reality, studies show that most in-home caregivers have little or no training,[22] that children in sitter care during their preschool years spend more time alone or with a relatively uneducated, untrained adult than children in any other form of child care, that these children watch more television, and that they are less competent—at the ages of two and three—than young children in any other form of care, despite the fact that they get more attention and more nurturing than children in group care.[23]

All of this may be a moot point, since most Americans can't afford in-home care anyway. Nanny care is the rarest form of child care; only about 3 percent of children under five with working mothers are cared for in their own homes by a nonrelative.[24] But lest you think the affluent have easy access to quality child care, think again. There are 14 accredited nanny schools in the U.S. today; they've graduated about 3,000 nannies over the past ten years. The demand, in this case, far outpaces the supply.

Family Day Care

Family day care is the least expensive and most popular form of group care for infants and toddlers. In theory, family day care may be the best possible arrangement for young children: Groups tend to be small, affording more chances for interactions between children and caregivers; there's more opportunity for peer play; the homelike setting promotes a variety of learning experiences; and the family-like setting provides for a mix of ages and plenty of opportunity for nurturing. In her 1994 book, *Children First*, Penelope Leach argues that family day care is more likely to meet the needs of infants than "institutional group care" or what she calls "pseudo-professional care by nannies and their like," noting that many family day-care providers are in business specifically so they can stay home and care for their own children.

Yet family day care is as variable in terms of quality, and nearly as volatile in terms of turnover, as in-home care. Certainly, your friendly neighborhood provider isn't going to up and move anytime soon. No, but she may close her doors. Family day care, particularly in states with less-than-stringent licensing requirements, is easy to open up and easy to close down. It's not uncommon for referral agencies to recruit new providers from the ranks of mothers who call their agencies looking for child care. But these mothers get a quick lesson in the realities of group care—what it means to spend 10 to 12 hours a day with small children, isolated from the outside world, working for less than minimum wage and no benefits, lunch breaks, or breaks from harried parents.

Says a woman I'll call Mary Rose, who took in another baby shortly after her first child was born, "It was horrible. The two of them never slept at the same time. I never got a break, and I felt totally isolated." Many of these providers drop out. Rose cracked after a few months, although she went back into family day care a few years later because she couldn't afford not to work and didn't want to leave her own children with anyone else all day. When asked her preferences, however, she said she'd rather find part-time office work.

In all fairness, there are providers in the family day-care business who've been doing it for 5, 10, even 20 years, and there have been serious efforts to make the job more professional, spearheaded by referral and licensing agencies and spurred in part by a major family day-care initiative sponsored by a $10 million grant from the Dayton Hudson Foundation. But we aren't there yet. One survey in Denver found that during the first five months of 1990, 250 new family day-care homes opened their doors and "almost that many closed their doors."[25] With each of those closings, hundreds of children had to make a change.

New providers are not hard to come by. Sharon Strauss, who teaches an orientation program for new providers in Montgomery County, Maryland, reports that in her area alone about 50 new people show up every six weeks to find out how to become family day-care providers. Some, she says, have just arrived in America and have no other means of support. Others are new mothers who imagine that family day care will provide the dual opportunity to make money and stay home with their new babies. Some have quit their jobs because of bad experiences with child care for their own children. But most of these people have no training or experience working with groups of children or, in some cases, even raising a child of their own. Again, this is not a supply problem, it's a quality problem.

Center Care

Center care is not immune to the general instability that characterizes American child care. Indeed, staff turnover is one of the biggest problems facing day-care centers in America today. And it's getting worse. According to the 1989 National Child Care Staffing Study, "nearly half of all child-care teachers leave their jobs each year, many to seek better paying jobs."[26] Equally disturbing is the study's finding that "turnover has nearly tripled in the last decade, jumping from 15 percent in 1977 to 41 percent in 1988"[27]—which means that, on average, 41 percent of the staff leaves a center every year. But that's the average. In Headstart programs, for example, where teachers are well paid and well trained, turnover is relatively low (averaging 20 percent). People who've worked in for-profit centers tell me about phenomenal rates of turnover—centers in which the entire staff changes in a given year. For-profit and chain-operated centers, which make up a growing share of the child-care market, tend to have the highest turnover rates and the lowest salaries in the industry—which means middle-class children, the likely candidates for chain-operated centers, may be hardest hit by high turnover in American day-care centers.

The Impact of Instability on Kids

If there's one thing children need, it's constancy—someone to whom they can relate when Mom and Dad are absent, an anchor away from home. Changing the caregiver, even in a day-care center, is tantamount to changing the care. And it has disturbing effects on children.

Take the case of Adrian Shaw, age four. His mother reports that initially, at least, he loved his day-care center, situated in the upscale suburb of Bethesda, Maryland, and one of a network of private, nonprofit centers. The network promotes caregiver training, closely monitors its centers, and has a fairly good reputation. But salaries are low, and by the time Adrian left, after 16 months, the head teacher in his room had changed three times.

"He was really attached to each of his teachers. I was attached to them. They were great," says Lori Shaw, Adrian's mom. "Every time one of them left, he'd have a problem. He seemed to regress. He'd wet his bed or his behavior would change." With each successive change, his difficulties in day care increased. With the last teacher, he was spending more and more time in the director's office in what the center called "time-out," a punitive approach to handling behavior problems that's practiced by some centers and frowned on by others. He started complaining every morning about day care. Then, after 16 months in care, he reached the point where he was clinging to his mother, hysterically, refusing to go into the center. At age four, when most children are more able to let go, he was holding tighter than ever. Baffled at his behavior and upset by the frequent turnover, Adrian's mother quit her job and pulled him out of the center.

Staff changes may appear minor, but they can mean a major change in the feel of a program. For two years, a Memphis couple I'll call Bunny and Jeff were perfectly happy with the Montessori program in which both their preschool-age sons were enrolled. But with staff changes came major changes in how the teachers handled the children. Bunny saw the first signs of trouble on Mother's Day. The children had made sachets for their mothers, tied with colored ribbon and stuffed with potpourri. After the exercise, the staff dumped all the sachets in a big box, and then randomly handed one to each child at the end of the day. The children were distraught. One after another, they looked at the sachets and pronounced them frauds. "This one isn't mine," said one three-year-old. "I didn't make this," protested another. Children, after all, are not stupid. They'd invested a fair amount of time and energy in stuffing these sachets and selecting the colors they wanted. And this was a gift for Mother—one of the most important people in their lives. Insensitive, thought Bunny, who trudged back into school with her two kids and stood by as they rustled through the box until they found the sachets they had made.

But that was just a small sign, a tip-off that maybe these teachers didn't know what they were doing. The next time Bunny picked her kids up at school, she came into the room and spent a few minutes observing the scene. One of the children wanted something and was badgering a teacher, as children will do. The teacher turned around and screamed, "Can't you see I'm busy?"

"That was it," says Bunny. "I pulled them out. Look, if I want my kids to get yelled at, I am perfectly capable of keeping them home and yelling at them myself. I'm not paying someone to stand there and yell at my kids."

Child Care and Abuse: A Red Herring

In the course of researching this book, I heard some horror stories: one tale of children left alone in a house while a *licensed* family day-care provider made a trip to the post office (she was discovered by a licensing agent doing a routine drop-in visit); another about an in-home caregiver who left the children under her care to go to a doctor's appointment (the children were discovered by their father, who came home to fetch a forgotten wallet). I heard tales of young children subjected to physical punishment and neglect by family day-care providers. One mother told me her two-year-old son was required to sit on a sofa all day and was not allowed to get up. The mother didn't discover this until she pulled him out and he described his "last babysitter" to his new babysitter. Not far from my own home, an infant was killed a few years ago when her babysitter banged the child's head against a wall.

Child abuse happens in day care, but studies have consistently found that physical and sexual abuse are far more likely to occur at home than in child care. As an example, in a study of physical and sexual abuse in Iowa, more than 8,000 cases of both types of abuse were reported statewide between 1985 and 1986. Of these, only two involved child-care programs. According to a North Carolina study of complaints coming into the Office of Child Care Licensing, 17 percent involved charges of abuse or neglect, of which one-third were judged to be "severe" cases. Severe cases of physical or sexual abuse, according to one North Carolina study, are more likely to be reported for unlicensed homes or centers that meet only the minimal licensing standards.[28] A nationwide study of sexual abuse in day care estimated an annual rate of 5.5 sexually abused children per 10,000 enrolled in child care—lower than the annual rate of sexual abuse in the U.S., which is 8.9 per 10,000 children under the age of six.[29]

Certainly, we'd all prefer that no children were ever sexually or physically abused. But the studies suggest that our fears about abuse in child care are unwarranted.

Caregivers tell me that when a new person joins the staff, most kids shy away, demanding attention from the adults they know. Even so, it can be—and has been—argued that turnover in center care is *less* detrimental to kids than the process of changing child-care arrangements. After all, in the former situation the environment, the other children, and the other teachers remain constant. In fact, some studies of the effects of turnover on kids reveal that center turnover has no long-term effects on a child's competence—a limited measure to be sure.[30] Others suggest that the effects on children of caregiver instability disappear over time—a finding that tells us children are resilient creatures. But what parents want to test the boundaries of their child's resilience?

Moving a child from one care arrangement to another is viewed as the most disruptive child-care change of all. In fact, numerous studies suggest that the children with day-care experience who are most well-adjusted are those who have been in the same stable, high-quality child-care arrangement from infancy through the preschool years (a subject discussed in more detail in subsequent chapters). For example, one study of first graders found that the more often children's care arrangements changed, the less well they did in first grade. Studies of infants and toddlers show that those who experienced frequent changes in child-care arrangements were less competent in playing with peers and with objects.[31]

It doesn't take a developmental psychologist to figure out that instability and discontinuity are bad for children, and some kids find it more disturbing than others. When turnover runs high, children don't have the opportunity to build long-term relationships with the people who care for them. They have to cope with the changes brought about by a rotating staff who may have different styles, different approaches, different attitudes about children. The net result of high turnover in child-care centers is that a center that may have been terrific in 1993 is lousy in 1994. The net result of turnover in the family day-care field and in in-home care is that children have to go through change after change throughout the course of their young lives.

But instability is a symptom of a bigger problem: America's caregivers are overworked, underpaid, and severely undervalued—a concept repeated over and over and over to me by parents, providers, and child-care advocates. Says Sally Haggerty, project manager of a child-care resource and referral program in Maine, "The hardest job in the world is to be a parent. The second hardest job is to care for someone else's children. We need to support everybody who's caring for children. I don't think people honor children and the people who care for them enough."

What Needs Fixing: The Money Issue

The problems with the American child-care system are not about child abuse or neglect. They are much less sensational. According to child-care advocates, they're about money. As such, they're easy to understand but incredibly difficult to solve. It is impossible, they argue, to operate a system that provides for training, recruitment, competitive salaries, competitive benefits, and national networks for screening caregivers without some form of subsidy. It is impossible, they argue, to raise the salaries and status of American caregivers in a system that's completely funded by parent fees.

Look at it this way: How can almost any working parent afford to pay a competitive salary, benefits, and taxes for an in-home caregiver without eating up most of his or her own income? How can a day-care center pay competitive wages—on par, say, with what we pay teachers in the public school system—without putting the cost of care outside the reach of most American families? How can a family day-care provider operate what is essentially a small-scale, home-based day-care center—purchasing equipment and supplies, complying with state regulations, paying self-employment taxes, purchasing health benefits, buying backup care for vacations, paying for workshops and seminars— and still keep enrollment low enough to offer high-quality care?

According to day-care advocates, funding high-quality child care nationwide is an economic impossibility without child-care subsidies. Deborah Phillips, director of the Board on Children and Families at the National Academy of Sciences, puts the problem simply: "There's not enough high-quality child care to go around, and even if there were, most parents couldn't afford it anyway."

The cost of child care is, essentially, the cost of paying caregivers. Even in day-care centers, the biggest item on the operating budget is caregiver salaries, a cost that's raised by the fact that most centers are open not eight hours but ten, so centers need a rotating staff. Our entire economy is dependent on these people—fully 38 percent of the American workforce is made up of working parents, many of whom need some form of substitute care for their kids.[32]

Caregivers should be regarded as saints, yet their stature and wages suggest that they are treated like something more nearly resembling another *s* word. The good news is that caregivers are actually better qualified than ever before. Says one report, "The average levels of education and training received by both regulated family day-care providers and center staff have increased substantially over the past fifteen years."[33] But caregivers' real wages have declined. Between 1977 and 1988, day-care "teachers' earnings fell by 27 percent and assistants' earnings by 20 percent."[34] As a result, turnover rates are up dramatically. What good is a qualified caregiver if he or she leaves?

How Much Do These People Make?

Even center directors may earn as little as $12,000 a year. "Parents are shocked to see how little the center staff and director earn," says Barbara McCreedy, director of the Montgomery County Day Care Association. Average wages at private, nonprofit centers range from $7.40 to $8.46 an hour. For-profit centers pay less; the average hourly rate at chain-affiliated centers is $5.43.[35]

Family day-care providers earn even less than center staff, on average bringing in $10,000 a year minus costs (for toys, equipment, and food). Even in high-priced markets, family day-care providers may gross as little as $20,000 a year, and many work 9, 10, even 12 hours a day without a break. One nationwide survey found that more than half of all licensed family day-care providers bring in less than $8,000 a year.[36] Studies of unregulated providers suggest absurd earnings in the range of $1.25 an hour.[37]

In-home caregivers may earn anywhere from $150 a week in rural areas and in the South to $300 a week or more in the Northeast. But again, they may work nine or more hours a day on weekdays. Nanny-school graduates command salaries in the range of $225 to $350 a week, but many of them are on call round-the-clock.

These people need a raise. According to child-care advocates, some form of subsidy is essential to raise wages, raise standards, reduce turnover, and ensure some measure of professionalism. But where is that subsidy going to come from? And is it really necessary? Are parents able to pay more? On average, a family with one child in care devotes 10 percent of its income to child care, making it one of the largest line items on the family budget. More kids obviously mean higher costs. But child-care costs vary widely, ranging from $3,000 to $15,000 a year, and the relationship between quality and the cost of care is not always clear-cut. Consider the child-care options one at a time:

In-home care. Right now, in-home caregivers are employed, primarily, by affluent parents. According to parents I interviewed, those who are most able to hold on to trusted caregivers are those who treat their caregivers as professionals. They pay well (including overtime hours), find ways to offer benefits, put the job description in writing, sign contracts, and treat their employees as they themselves would like to be treated. Right now, in-home, one-on-one care—considered by many to be the optimal child-care situation for infants—is out of the reach of most American parents. If, as a society, we decide that one-on-one care is essential for healthy infant development, a subject explored in chapter four, we have two choices: *(a)* We can provide a subsidy (in the form, say, of a tax exemption for in-home caregivers) and health insurance coverage (through a national program); we can create a nationwide certification program and an accessible nationwide network for screening out criminals. (This is no small issue. I heard tell of a federal judge with access to the FBI's computer system who decided to run a check on his own caregiver and found she had 17 aliases.) Or *(b)* we can legislate paid leave policies that allow parents to take more time off to care for their own children during infancy.

Family day care. In family day care, studies show, high-quality providers tend to be better trained, more professional, and better compensated. According to the 1994 study conducted by the Families and Work Institute, in family day care, quality *is* directly

Child Care for Preschoolers:
What Does It Cost?

The price of child care varies dramatically from one place to another and across types of care:

- In Baltimore City, a small town near Baltimore, the median income lingers below $30,000 a year. Here, family day care costs about $85 a week, in-home care averages $6.50 an hour (about $250 a week), and center care costs around $130 a week for a two-year-old.

- Not far away, in upscale Montgomery County, family day care costs about $95 to $110 a week, centers average $195 to $225 a week, and in-home sitters might cost upwards of $300 a week.

- In nearby Washington, D.C., a privately run center that caters to low-income families costs about $75 a week, or $3,900 a year, and a top-notch day-care center might run about $200 a week, which translates into $9,000 or $10,000 a year—as much as nine months in the city's most exclusive private kindergartens. In-home care in a city like Washington costs about $300 a week ($15,000 a year); family day care costs $100 to $150 a week.

- Contrast those numbers with what you'd pay in Louisiana. The going rate for licensed child care, statewide, is $60 a week—$55 a week for family day care and $25 for school-age kids.

Based on personal interviews with referral services in 1993.

related to cost. That study, which cut across all income groups, found that parents who paid more for care had more sensitive caregivers, and upper-income families had access to higher-quality care.

Interestingly, the 1994 family day-care study found that the vast majority of parents (92 percent) who pay for family day care, regardless of their level of income, *would be willing to pay more—*

anywhere from $5 to $50 more a week. Overall, parents using family day care were willing to pay 22 percent more for child care.[38]

Improving family day care involves training and education—educating parents on the relationship between training, a license, and good care; educating providers on what they can and must charge to raise program standards; subsidizing training programs; and subsidizing fees for families who can't afford to pay what quality care costs.

Center care. The National Center for the Early Childhood Work Force, an educational and advocacy organization, claims that the relationship between turnover and training, salaries, and working conditions is the crucial problem facing center-based programs. Salaries and training are directly related to turnover, which is directly related to the quality of care and even to the establishment of developmentally appropriate programs. To attack the problem of high turnover and low quality, we have to pay caregivers more, we have to give them benefits, and we have to improve their working conditions.

The costs of such employment practices would raise expenses beyond the reach of most parents. Barbara Willer, author of *Reaching the Full Cost of Quality in Early Childhood Programs*, a 1990 report that analyzes precisely this issue, maintains that if caregivers were paid competitive wages, the cost of center care in America would *double*. Right now, nonprofit centers rely on foundation grants, donations, sponsorship by a church or temple, or high weekly rates to keep standards up. Centers serving low-income children are eligible for federal funds, including Title XX money and community-development block grants—but even so, many are ill-equipped. For-profit and chain-operated centers, the only forms of center care that operate on "free market" principles and have no access to outside funds, have the lowest wages and highest turnover in the industry—although economies of scale and an emphasis on marketing mean these centers are filled with bright, shiny toys.

Across all these programs caregivers are paid wages that should put our society to shame. Child-care advocates argue that caregivers are, in effect, subsidizing the system by working for substandard wages. Their pitiful incomes reflect our values as a culture.

Staffing Child-Care Programs

One night not long ago, as my four-year-old sat next to me on his bed, his lower lip began to quiver and he looked positively bereft. "Shannon is leaving," he said. "She's leaving the day after tomorrow." And then the tears came. For whatever reason—a sick day, a missed newsletter—we had missed the announcement that one of the teachers in his after-school program had gotten another job. "I love her," he said. "I'll miss her."

Shannon, trained as an elementary school teacher, had finally found a teaching job, so she would no longer be working from noon to six in my son's preschool child-care program.

Teachers, people trained in the field of education, often take short-term child-care jobs until new opportunities open up. But they're not interested in child care or trained in the field. People who run outstanding child-care programs tell me that they don't choose their caregivers from the ranks of the education profession. They find people who genuinely like young children, who are natural with them, and they train them to be caregivers. Says Tiffany Field, a psychologist and day-care researcher who turns out some of the most positive findings in the day-care field from three university-based child-care centers in Miami, "A lot of people seem to have the notion that you should have master's-level people in the classroom and doctorate-level people directing the programs. Those people are expensive, and they're not generally very happy doing this kind of work." Her caregivers have high school degrees, and her head teachers have college degrees. "These people stay longer, and they're more involved with the children," she explains. The key, though, is that they're trained.

At one of the best day-care centers in Washington, D.C., Anne Durso, the program's director, adopts the same approach to caregivers. "You can't learn to be natural with children," she says, so she hires caregivers who relate well to kids, and if they don't have some training in early-childhood development, she makes sure they get training.

Truth is, caregivers are not teachers. These may be parallel professions, but they are not the same. When people talk about training caregivers and raising caregiver salaries, they are not talking about drawing from the pool of teachers with master's degrees. They are talking about raising salaries to reasonable levels, raising standards to suit the profession, and creating an army of caregivers—people who genuinely enjoy working with young children.

And when child-care advocates talk about reforms, they are, by and large, addressing people who manage center-based programs. Because it's management practices, as much as wages, that drive the turnover in center-based care.

A Teacher's View

In 1991, a woman I'll call Roberta Marshall went to work for a day-care center operated by a small, regional, profit-making chain. She had no experience and joined the staff as an aide; simultaneously, she enrolled in a training course. Six months later Marshall was promoted to head teacher of the youngest group, age two and under, despite the fact that she had no experience working with that age group. Why? "They had hired a teacher, and on the first day it became evident that she wasn't going to work out. So they pulled me out of another room and put me in charge," says Marshall.

Most of the teachers at the for-profit center were "wonderful," she says, but they didn't stay long enough to benefit the children. During that year, turnover at the center was 100 percent. Every-one on staff was replaced. Explains Marshall, "The staff don't agree with the policies, which is why most of them don't stay. Anyone who's a professional recognizes that that kind of a center doesn't really put the children first." But the salary and benefits package might have had something to do with it as well. Marshall began working at the center for $4.50 an hour; by the time she left, she was making $7.50 an hour, with seven personal days a year (meaning sick *and* vacation days). At the nonprofit center where she's now employed, she's paid the same but has four weeks' annual leave and 10 to 12 days' sick leave.

The aides at the for-profit center were untrained, many of them "high school girls," says Marshall, and "they had inappropriate ways of handling children." She adds, "I had a lot of trouble convincing them that at lunchtime they should sit down and interact with the kids." In some cases, people were laid off because enrollment dropped. "Morale would get low when staff was fired for no apparent reason; they'd cut people's hours because of quotas—drop-offs in enrollment."

Teachers were discouraged from communicating with parents; all parent contacts had to go through the director's office. "I had a little boy who transferred in from another center," says Marshall. "He was very aggressive. So we had a problem that needed to be addressed." She told the director, who waited six weeks to call the parents. "If I'd been able to do that in the beginning, we could have worked together. There was a good possibility some of the behavior would have diminished. When we finally talked, the parent said, 'Why didn't I hear about this before?' The answer was basically because of the center policy."

In the center where Marshall now works, they don't even use "time-out" because "it's so punitive." But at the chain-affiliated center, children were sent to the office "like schools use the principal." At her current center, parents are actively involved in setting policy. Parents and teachers talk regularly, every room has a parent representative, and the center has a parent council. "We make a terrific effort to make sure everyone on the staff is aware of anything important that's going on at home," Marshall says.

She talks at length about the art projects at her old center, which were fashioned by adults and put together by the children— work that impresses parents but is of little value to children.

"They spend a lot of time cutting out heads and tails and bodies and so forth and push the kids into putting it together properly. That's not necessarily high on a parent's list, but it makes so much difference to the children if you give them all kinds of materials and let them create whatever they want to create."

What difference does it all make? Marshall maintains the turnover, the lax attitudes, the punitive approach to teaching social skills, and the lack of communication with parents at her old center have a cumulative effect on the kids. The children at the two centers sound very different. At the for-profit center, "the older they got, they became more unmanageable," she says. The kindergartners at the first center she describes as "resistant to any kind of authority" and "hard to control." By comparison, she maintains, the kids at her current center are "interested in the program" and "socially, pretty well-adjusted."

I was struck after my conversation with Marshall by how closely her experience, in two years of working in child care, reflected the views of people researching the field. The keys to evaluating a program often bear no relationship to what you'll see on that first one-hour visit. The for-profit center is beautifully equipped, professionally run, convenient, and staffed by trained teachers. What you don't see, though, is what you get: high turnover, inappropriate policies, and an approach that's motivated more by the bottom line than anything else. That's not to say that all for-profit centers are bad, but a lot depends on the director's ability to stay focused on the most important goal: the children. And that, apparently, is the big difference between good and bad child care.

What's a Parent to Do?

I don't mean to suggest that all American child care is substandard, that every child-care arrangement is unstable, or, more important, that all caregivers are incompetent. There are extraordinary people working in the child-care field. I met a lot of them while researching this book, and many of them appear on the pages that follow. Nor do I mean to suggest that it's impossible to find quality child care. What I am saying is this:

Parents must be alert to the problems associated with child care as it exists in America today. They should be aware that when they look for child care, they must look with a discerning eye. Some naively assume, as I did 15 years ago, that they're operating in a system that can be trusted. Says Judy Montgomery, who runs a referral service in Baton Rouge, "When we first opened up, three or four years ago, parents were highly critical of the agency because of the poor quality of care they encountered." Louisiana has notoriously lax child-care regulations. So Montgomery realized they had to explain to parents that a license is no guarantee of quality, that parents have to be discriminating. "We still get feedback that the referrals are horrible, maybe 20 to 25 percent of the time. But we're not getting criticized anymore, because we advise parents that that might be the case. Before, parents didn't have a clear picture of licensing."

Parents need to know that a referral is no guarantee; a license is no guarantee; a friend's recommendation is no guarantee.

Parents must become educated consumers. In study after study, parents tell researchers they are satisfied with their child-care arrangements—even arrangements that researchers consider low-quality. In the 1994 family day-care study, 92 percent of parents said that if given the chance to choose child care again, they'd stick with their current arrangement—yet only 9 percent of the arrangements studied were rated "good."[39] In a recent study of 46 day-care centers in Atlanta, the level of care generally fell in the range of poor to adequate, and only one of the 46 centers met recommended levels for group size, ratios, and staff training. Yet when asked, 80 percent of the parents who used those centers said they'd enroll their children again "without hesitation."[40] And a parent/teacher study undertaken as part of the National Child Care Staffing Study found that "parents were quite satisfied with programs deemed low in quality by independent researchers."[41] Does that mean parents don't know any better? Or that researchers are setting standards that are higher than those of American parents? What it may mean is that parents don't know what they cannot see. That parents forced to choose between the lesser of evils are happy to find a place where their child will not be harmed, instead of one in which their child will grow and thrive.

As parents, we must revise our notions about what makes for good child care. Research has confirmed the link between training—in child development and in how to deal with young children—and the ability to provide sensitive, nurturing care. They've found that far from being irrelevant, a license, accreditation, course work, membership in professional associations, and evidence of a commitment to the child-care profession make an enormous difference.

We must begin to believe in the idea of child care. Many parents, raised in our American culture, genuinely believe day care is second best, a poor substitute for mother care. Our expectations are low, so we don't demand the best. Some parents believe center care is bad for kids; they put their children in unregulated family day-care homes because they're after that homelike environment, or they hire underqualified in-home sitters in a quest for a mother substitute. In such cases, our own assumptions can work against us. But good child care exists; I've seen it. It's just hard to find. And many parents just haven't the vaguest notion of what good child care even looks like (a subject discussed in chapter eight).

Parents must become advocates for better child care. First, they must demand the most from their program. But it's time, too, for working parents to join hands with advocates for better child care—that means demanding subsidies, demanding stringent licensing standards, demanding excellence. The beauty of the kind of structures—for regulating, accrediting, and training—that came into place in the 1980s is that there's a genuine opportunity for reform here. The systems are in place. Where licensing offices exist, the challenge is to raise standards. Where mechanisms for accreditation and certification exist, parents have to put pressure on providers to earn accreditation and get certified. (See page 212.) Where training programs are in place, again, parents need only demand that the people they hire be trained. Creating a system is the first step; improving child care is the next.

Right now, advocacy groups are asking questions like: How can we raise wages in the industry to reduce turnover, increase stability, improve provider status, and attract people to the field of child care? They're promoting training programs and exploring funding strategies. Parents should be asking: What can *we* do?

Toward that end, I offer a list of advocacy groups and organizations that are hell-bent on improving child care in this country. But for starters, concerned parents should send a postcard to the White House. Just tell them you think it's time we addressed the issue of child-care reform head-on. The address is 1600 Pennsylvania Avenue NW, Washington, DC 20500. After all, this administration, more than any that has come before, has expressed a genuine interest in addressing the needs of children.

Resources for Parents

Child Care Action Campaign
330 Seventh Ave., 17th Fl.
New York, NY 10001-5010
212-239-0138

Promotes quality, affordable child care through public education, research, and advocacy and provides information to parents, employers, and policymakers, including free information for parents on choosing child care.

National Center for the Early Childhood Work Force
733 15th St. NW, Suite 800
Washington, DC 20005
202-737-7700

Formerly known as the Child Care Employee Project, this advocacy and research organization was founded in 1977 to promote better wages, working conditions, benefits, and access to training for child-care teachers and providers.

National Association of Child Care Resource and
Referral Agencies
319 F St. NW, Suite 810
Washington, DC 20004
202-393-5501

NACCRRA supports the growth of local child-care resource
and referral agencies and acts as an advocate for high-quality child
care. *The Complete Guide to Choosing Child Care* is available through
NACCRRA for $12.95 plus $2 shipping and handling. To locate
the referral agencies in your area, call the Child Care Aware line
(below).

Child Care Aware
800-424-2246

A nationwide campaign for parent education, funded by the
Dayton Hudson companies and operated in cooperation with
prominent national child-care advocacy groups, Child Care Aware
provides free information for parents on finding and evaluating
quality child care and refers callers to community-based child-
care resource and referral agencies in their area.

National Association for the Education of Young Children
1509 16th St. NW
Washington, DC 20036
800-424-2460 or 202-232-8777

NAEYC provides information for parents and educators on
quality child care, including videotapes, pamphlets (50 cents
each) and books on early childhood topics. (Ask for their catalog.)
NAEYC has developed the largest nationwide accreditation process for early childhood programs, including day-care centers.
(See page 215.)

National Association for Family Child Care
1331A Pennsylvania Ave. NW, Suite 348
Washington, DC 20004
800-359-3817

Founded in 1982, this national association of family day-care providers, with some 4,000 members, began a program for accrediting providers in 1988. Local associations are not affiliated with this national group, although NAFCC plans to evolve into an umbrella for local associations. NAFCC is not designed to offer parent assistance, but it can give you the names of accredited providers in your area.

National School-Age Child Care Alliance
c/o Tracey Ballas, President
614-338-8855

The National School-Age Child Care Alliance was formed by school-age child-care professionals to advocate for and support the development and expansion of high-quality, affordable, and accessible school-age child care nationally.

Parent Action
2 North Charles St., Suite 960
Baltimore, MD 21201
410-727-3687

While not exclusively concerned with the issue of child care or issues facing working parents, Parent Action is the only nationwide association for parents, designed to lobby for their interests and disseminate information to them about pending legislation, grass-roots activities, and helpful resources.

School-Age Child Care Project
Wellesley College Center for Research on Women
Wellesley, MA 02181-8295
617-283-2547

Initiated in 1979 in response to the latchkey crisis, the School-Age Child Care Project researches and develops school-age child-care options and policies. The project provides training, technical assistance, needs assessment, and evaluation for school-age programs. (See page 308 for information on a related publication.)

School of the 21st Century
Bush Center in Child Development and Social Policy
Yale University
310 Prospect St.
New Haven, CT 06511-2188

Yale University Bush Center faculty members are helping schools set up preschool child-care centers that are affiliated with the public school system. Federal funding—in the form of Child Care and Development Block Grants—is available to subsidize the cost of care for some low-income children attending these programs. Contact the School of the 21st Century at Yale University for information on how to establish such a program.

***

In the 50s, American mothers who could afford to stay home subsidized the education of America's young children. They raised us free of charge. Today, America's caregivers are essentially subsidizing the education—or, more aptly, socialization—of America's children by working for peanuts. If we expect them to work well, we are going to have to offer them creative supports. If we expect professionalism, and indeed we should, we are going to have to rely on more than caregivers' dedication and goodwill. As a society, we're going to have to put our money where our kids are.

We need to provide an incentive for caregivers to get trained, through the channels that already exist, by *demanding* that our caregivers be trained. If parents demand trained caregivers—if they demand a license and ask about accreditation and spend ample time observing child-care programs before signing up—then parents will be playing an active role in a reform movement that is already under way.

But more than anything else, Americans are going to have to start believing in the idea of child care. Child care is not a second-best substitute for full-time care by a mother. We must recognize that while bad child care is bad for kids, there's ample evidence that good child care is good for them—a subject that's explored in the next chapter.

CHAPTER THREE

The Day-Care Studies

"When my daughter reaches adulthood, I'm afraid she won't be able to find anyone who's capable of forming a close relationship with her," Karla Harris told me a few years ago. Harris, who had elected to stay home after her daughter was born, in 1987, was concerned not about her daughter but about her daughter's generation. At the time, she was living in Washington, D.C., and actively involved in an organization called Mothers-at-Home, which, among other issues, opposed child-care legislation and instead favored legislation that might enable more American mothers to stay home with their kids. "I've read the research on day-care kids, and I think they're going to grow up with serious problems in the trusting category," said Harris.

Around the same time, a neighbor of mine, a Vassar-educated mother of three, voiced similar concerns about the generation of children we are raising. "I think one of the reasons kids are so aggressive is because mothers are working. They don't have any time for their kids. They're being raised in day-care centers," she volunteered.

Day-care *centers* seem to take the rap for just about every negative finding on the effects of day care on children. That's not surprising. For one thing, in the minds of many Americans, day care *means* center care. Yet in America today, center care is actually one of the least-used forms of child care. It is also the most regulated form; teachers in centers appear to have more training than those in family day care, and the studies of children in high-quality centers suggest that not only do they do all right but the experience itself may be beneficial.

Center Care: The Numbers

There are more than seven million preschool-age children in some form of child care while their parents work.

The number of infants enrolled in day-care centers is relatively small, although it's growing. Children under two whose mothers work are most likely to be cared for by their fathers, a relative, a friend, or a neighbor. According to 1991 Census data, about 20 percent are cared for in family day-care homes;[1] only about 16 percent are cared for in day-care centers.

Once kids hit the age of three, there's a big shift toward center care; by some estimates, 43 percent of three- and four-year-olds with employed mothers are in day-care centers.[2] These tend to be kids at the upper and lower ends of the economic spectrum.

A case could be made that for families with access to good center care, the period when their kids are between three and five represents a kind of window, a welcome breather, during which parents can rest assured that their kids are in good hands and are freed up from the concerns that plague the infant/toddler years (when center care is less available and less appealing, particularly because of the illness that runs rampant through day-care centers) and the school years (when issues like transportation, scheduling, homework, before-school care, self-care, and the quality of after-school care can make child care a nightmare for parents and children alike).

Despite all that, many of the middle-class parents I spoke with were uncomfortable with the very idea of center care, a discomfort that's reflected in the numbers. We have a strong cultural bias against institutional care. Day-care centers are alien to the American Way; they smack of sovietization and collectivism, Brave New Worlds and Israeli kibbutzim.

It's not surprising that when parents look for justification for their own child-rearing decisions, center care becomes an easy target. One parent told me he suspected that a friend's child, a four-year-old, was unable to ride a bicycle without training wheels because he had been in center care. Another shared her observations with me regarding a handful of youngsters encountered at a playground during a family vacation. "None of them could speak as well as my son, and they were all about the same age. Then I discovered they'd been in a day-care center," she said, as if that explained it.

In fact, some of the most positive findings on the impact of child care on young children are those on kids who have attended high-quality day-care centers—the salient phrase here being *high quality*; certainly, some of the best child-care programs I encountered while researching this book were organized centers. Child care is extraordinarily inconsistent in our society; but for parents who are very selective and live in states with strict licensing requirements, center care may be the best option.

Certainly, there's nothing inherently wrong with it. Cross-cultural studies tell us that. For example, studies of center care in Sweden have found that kids in full-time day care are more cooperative and less aggressive than their home-reared counterparts, and they tend to be more advanced cognitively and socially, more verbal, less anxious, and more persistent. Studies of children who've attended top-notch U.S. centers reveal similar results.

The Day-Care Debate Revisited

The trouble with the day-care debate in this country is that both extremes of the debate are hopelessly reductive.

One side maintains that full-time group care can never be as good as mother care, that kids cannot be socialized in a group setting, and that center care is inherently bad. It's too stressful. The day's too long. Toddlers and preschoolers, who exist in a kind of presocialized state, are unready for the demands of the group situation. Day-care kids, the critics argue, have all kinds of behavior problems because they're being socialized by other children.

The other side argues that day care is good for kids, that it promotes sociability and cognitive development, that day care creates better kids, and that, not incidentally, kids really enjoy it. Advocates of day care point out that kids learn self-control—to stand in line, take turns, follow directions, cooperate—just as well in group care as at home. They are as well-adjusted and well-socialized as home-reared kids—if not better.

People are still arguing over whether day care is preferable to mother care, but the real issue is not whether it is better or worse but whether it is an acceptable alternative—whether it can be as good as mother care.

Day care is not about intellectual development. Except as an intervention program for low-income children, it is not about education; it's about social, emotional, physical, *and* cognitive development. There's little evidence that any particular form of child care, except perhaps long-term exclusive care with an in-home sitter who is much less educated than the parents, has any measurable effect—either positive or negative—on a child's cognitive or language development. Center care does not produce geniuses or inhibit intellectual development, although studies of kids with extensive experience in high-quality, university-based programs suggest that these programs can enhance development.

The studies reveal that children in better centers are better socialized. They learn how to interact with adults and their peers; they're more cooperative, more compliant, less aggressive, and less impulsive. Children from poor child-care programs emerge with a cluster of bad behaviors—aggression, noncompliance, poor peer relations, conduct problems. In other words, they don't relate as well to other kids or to adults, they're less responsive to authority, and they show signs of being less happy with themselves.

This is no small matter. Conduct plays a central role in early education, and as any teacher will tell you, a child who is disruptive, distracted, and defiant alienates teachers and students alike. When children hit first grade with these characteristics, they are not as school-ready as their peers. More important, they have difficulty learning in traditional classroom settings. Sadly, difficult kids can be the products of bad, even mediocre, day care—particularly boys and particularly, *but not exclusively*, those who come from stressed-out home environments and low socio-economic groups.

The big issues raised by the day-care research are behavioral. And the biggest question raised is this: Does group care produce children with behavior problems? Consider what the research has to say:

The consequences of good child care. Tiffany Field, a researcher at the University of Miami, consistently comes up with astonishingly heartening findings on the positive effects of day care. Her studies are conducted at three day-care centers based at the university. In 1991, Field published a study of grade-school children who had graduated from her three centers. She looked at kids who had started care before age two and spent their remaining preschool years in these centers, full time, until they entered school, and she found "no undesirable outcomes for those children . . . during the grade school period." In fact, the findings show that the more time they spent in care, the more sociable, emotionally stable, and socially competent these kids were. More than half the group (19 out of 28) were in gifted programs, and "the number of months spent in day care was positively related to the number of friends and the number of extracurricular activities."[3] All of this suggests that full-time care in a high-quality center, started early and maintained throughout the preschool years, can be good for kids. Field's studies of children who've begun high-quality care in infancy—even during the first six months of life—are just as optimistic.

The consequences of poor child care. Researchers who have studied middle-class children with extensive experience in low-quality child care, starting in infancy, tell us these kids have poor work habits, poor academic performance, poor conduct, poor peer relationships, and emotional maladjustments.[4] Kids who spend many hours a week for many years in substandard American child-care settings may wind up with all kinds of problems. Regardless of their socioeconomic class, they are disadvantaged when compared to children from better child-care programs, children with part-time child-care histories, and children raised at home by their parents.

Consider a study conducted in Texas, where day-care licensing standards are lax. In a 1990 study, Deborah Vandell and Mary Anne Corasaniti, psychologists and day-care researchers at the University of Wisconsin and the University of Texas at Dallas, looked at more than 300 eight-year-old white, middle-class school-children in Texas. Their results are particularly enlightening—and disturbing. They compared these school-age kids, with different child-care histories, and found that the more time spent in child care (over 30 hours a week) from infancy on, the more likely a child was to receive poor ratings from parents, teachers, and other children on a variety of measures, including cognitive, social, behavioral, and emotional. They were less compliant, more difficult to discipline, and had poorer conduct grades and lower academic performance.

The researchers looked at whether these characteristics were associated with social class, parents' education, the child's gender, birth order, and other family characteristics. Boys with extensive day-care experiences had the poorest interpersonal relations; children with extensive day-care experience from infancy and divorced parents had the lowest IQ scores. But overall, although family factors played a major role as well, child-care history was the single most important predictor of a slew of negative outcomes in these children.

What conclusions did Vandell and Corasaniti draw? They didn't conclude that child care is inherently bad, because their findings in Texas are contradicted by studies of children who have spent many years in high-quality child care, both in the U.S. and elsewhere. Nevertheless, they concluded that middle-class children in child care in Texas are not doing all right; they're doing very poorly. Wrote the researchers, "These results are in marked contrast with Andersson's (1989) findings of positive social and cognitive development associated with early, extensive child care in Sweden (a country characterized by high child care standards and opportunities for paid parental leave during early infancy)."[5]

Day Care and Behavior Problems

There is a whole body of research suggesting that children who spend a lot of time in group care are more aggressive, more assertive, and less compliant, both with their mothers and with other adults. For parents, these may well be the most troubling findings from the day-care studies.

For families who can afford it and mothers or fathers who want to stay home, there's no question that home rearing, particularly when combined with preschool at age two and a half or three, is good for kids. Full-time care by a competent and loving parent is a model that seems to work pretty well; of that there's little doubt. It's consistent, it's reliable, it's customized, it provides continuity, and, ideally, it's loving, warm, and nurturing.

Some psychologists believe that children raised at home by their mothers—or fathers—are more responsive to authority (compliant), less aggressive, and better socialized because they get constant monitoring from a trusted authority figure. They internalize their parents' own values—about aggression, manners, sharing, and playing by the rules—and they learn to control their own impulses. Kids who attend group day care are socialized in a very different setting, one full of other kids, and by adults who may or may not have a handle on how to teach children in large groups. Generally, regardless of the quality of the program, kids with extensive experience in day-care centers tend to be more independent and more assertive.

But the issue that really haunts the subject of center care is the widespread assumption that center care produces aggressive children who don't respond to adult authority. Researchers have been focusing on that issue for 20 years.

One of the earliest long-term day-care studies, which followed two groups of children from early childhood through the school years, was begun in London in 1964 by a British researcher named T. W. Moore and was published in 1975. Moore followed these two groups of kids—one with child-care experience (at least 25 hours a week), one in exclusive mother care in early childhood—up to age 15. The biggest difference among these kids (and it was far more pronounced among the boys) was this: Those with extensive day-care experience (including sitter care) were more assertive, less conforming, and "less impressed with punishment" as children; as teenagers, they were more rebellious, more peer-oriented, and more antisocial than their home-reared counterparts.

Moore's research was done in another time, another place, so the findings can't really be generalized to modern-day America. Yet his work sparked a good deal of interest and is examined in some detail in an influential 1977 book written by American psychologist Uri Bronfenbrenner called *The Ecology of Human Development*, a critique of standard research practices. Bronfenbrenner focused, among other things, on the conclusion that boys may be more vulnerable to the effects of day care than girls. Boys are more prone to aggression; in group child-care situations, studies show that boys tend to gravitate toward other children, while girls are more drawn to adults (facilitating relationships with caregivers and increasing the likelihood that girls will internalize adult values); as a result, boys appear to be more likely to emerge from group care with problems in the behavior department. The subject calls to mind a kind of *Lord of the Flies* effect, in which male impulses are set free within the context of group care, and aggressions, left unchecked, run wild. Since 1976, numerous psychologists have attempted to replicate Moore's findings, with mixed results. For example:

- Some researchers have found that boys who attended low-quality day-care programs full time, particularly from infancy, are more likely to graduate with behavior problems and that when other factors—like poverty or parents' divorce—come into play, boys are even more prone to conduct problems, poor peer relations, and aggression.

- Other researchers have failed to confirm the link between substitute care and behavior problems of any kind in middle-class boys. Certainly, there's no evidence that high-quality group care leads to anything other than prosocial behaviors. At least one study of middle-class U.S. kindergartners, published in 1988, compared boys and girls with a variety of child-care histories, including exclusive mother care, and found that the group of children with the most impulse control (ego-resilience) were boys with working mothers, lending credence to the view that good day care might help children develop self-control. Argues the University of Miami's Tiffany Field, "There are more directives in the school situation than in the home. There's more discipline and more structure, and there are more demands placed on the children."

Day Care and Aggression

It appears that children from low-income homes, in programs that stress cognitive development, may emerge from child care more aggressive than low-income kids from other kinds of child care. The research linking aggression—meaning hitting, pushing, kicking, swearing, threatening, and arguing—to child care generally involves kids in poverty.

A study by Ron Haskins of the University of North Carolina, which received a lot of play in the mainstream press following its release in 1988, was conducted on a group of kids from families with "very low education and income" who were enrolled in an intervention program at birth because they were "at risk for developmental problems." Hardly your typical middle-class sample. Haskins found that when these kids entered kindergarten they were significantly more aggressive than their class-mates.[6]

In fact, researchers at the Frank Porter Graham Child Development Center, where Haskins conducted the study, found similar results years earlier when they began measuring aggression among the center's children. So they changed the program, emphasizing prosocial behavior and social skills training and de-emphasizing cognitive development. Their graduates then entered kindergarten less aggressive, with better social skills—which suggested that day-care programs can be developed that promote social skills.[7]

What about assertiveness and noncompliance? The words "assertive," "noncompliant," and "aggressive" come up a lot in the literature on day care. While to the typical parent they may sound almost interchangeable, all drawn from the big pot called misbehavior, they are, in fact, quite different. Increasingly, researchers are making a distinction between hostile aggression (hitting, kicking, pushing, fighting) and assertiveness, defined in one report as "refusal to cooperate with others or ignoring the requests of others; assertive noncompliant behavior which does not directly injure another person."[8] A handful of studies suggest that so-called day-care kids are more assertive, particularly when data is based on *teacher* evaluations; but studies using *direct observations by social scientists* say it just ain't so, "that day care children display higher frequencies of social behaviors but no higher percentages of aggressive behaviors than do home-reared children."[9]

The distinction between who's doing the evaluating—psychologists or teachers—is no small issue. One study that attempted to take into account the role played by teachers' perceptions looked at middle-class preschoolers who attended day care and compared them with home-reared kids. They found no differences in either social or antisocial behaviors between groups of children. They did, however, find that teachers tended to describe children who "assert their own rights" and don't "comply with the teacher's requests" as more aggressive—a tip-off that teacher ratings of aggression may not be an appropriate methodology for studying aggression. This is an esoteric point. But it gives you some insight into the fine points of social science research: How can we possibly know whether day-care kids are more aggressive if researchers are still in the process of determining how to measure aggressive behavior? Or looking at it another way, how can we consider assertiveness a positive trait if teachers tend to view it negatively?

Ultimately, though, researchers maintain that aggression, a lack of self-control, a lack of responsiveness to authority, and problems with relating to other kids are symptoms of experience in poor-quality child care. Says Carollee Howes of the University of California, talking about her observations of low-quality center care, "One of the images that stays with me is an asphalt playground filled with a bunch of kids with not much to do. They've been put out to play. There's no teacher there to guide their play; instead, they stand by just watching. The biggest, bossiest kids rule over the playground. Combine that setting with the tendency for four-year-old boys to be assertive and aggressive, and you can imagine the consequences."

Says Deborah Vandell of the University of Wisconsin, "There are two types of problematic behavior that you see in poor-quality care. One is what people call aimless wandering. The other is acting out—out-of-control kind of behavior. Both of these behaviors are serious problems. Both of them speak to subsequent developmental problems . . . I tie both of them back to the quality of the caregiving."

Quality Care and Child Development

When you look at the studies comparing home-reared kids with day-care graduates, many of which make no distinction between kids from family day care or center-care graduates, you find few differences between these groups of children. But when you look at studies that compare middle-class kids from high-quality child-care programs (a rare bird in America today) and kids from lower-quality child-care programs (a much more common animal), significant differences do emerge.

Without question, the most consistent and compelling studies in the field of child-care research today concern the quality of care and how it relates to child development. These studies take the issue well beyond the debate over home care versus child care and into the realm of how to raise children successfully within the context of child care. For example, when Tiffany Field of the University of Miami compares graduates of the high-quality programs there with graduates of other, lower-quality day-care programs, she finds that the latter group is not as sociable, as cooperative, and as high achieving as her "cohort," in the lingo of the trade.

There is now an entire body of literature in the day-care field that supports the view that children in high-quality child-care programs—programs with stable staffs, trained caregivers, high ratios (more adults per child), small group sizes (particularly for infants and toddlers), and competent caregivers who stress problem-solving over discipline as a way of fostering social skills— are not only less aggressive, more cooperative, and less impulsive than those reared in lousy child-care situations[10] but may also be more emotionally and socially competent and higher achieving, even when compared to their home-reared counterparts.[11]

At least a dozen studies confirm that children in higher-quality day-care centers "exhibit more advanced cognitive and social development during the preschool years and afterwards" when compared to low-quality child-care situations.[12] For example, a 1989 study of 100 four-year-olds found that kids in high-quality child care did better on language comprehension and vocabulary tests than children in low-quality care.[13]

Study after study reveals that the quality of care is determined, in large measure, by the quality of the caregiver. Indeed, for preschool-age children, the degree to which teachers talk to, encourage, nurture, and just plain interact with kids may be the single most important determinant of the quality of a child-care arrangement.[14] The extent to which infants, toddlers, and preschoolers are able to form relationships with their caregivers determines, to some extent, their future social competence.[15] And across all types of child care, studies show that caregiver education and knowledge of child development determine how nurturing and attentive the care is and how well-adjusted the children will be.[16] These findings have been generated for family day care and center care.

Finally, it appears that poor care produces lasting consequences and, not surprisingly, that the single most important determinant of poor care is the quality of the caregiver. In 1983, Deborah Vandell and her colleagues studied and observed four-year-olds in three kinds of centers in Texas.[17] The good centers were "well-equipped, spacious centers with good adult-child ratios, well-trained teachers, and small classes." The bad centers were "large, crowded, poorly equipped centers with poor adult-child ratios, untrained teachers, and large classes." The researchers sat there and watched the children; they counted the number of times the adults talked to the children; they recorded how the children were engaged or whether they were engaged at all. They found, not surprisingly, that the adults in the better centers interacted more with the kids. The children in the poor-quality centers spent more time wandering around aimlessly, uninvolved and disengaged.

Four years later, the researchers went back and looked at the same kids, by then eight years old and attending elementary school. Their findings were significant. Children who graduated from the poor-care situations didn't relate well to their peers, were less competent socially, and were "unhappy." They had, in the words of these psychologists, "more problematic behavior." The good-care graduates were more cooperative and empathic and "better able to negotiate conflicts." These kids were, at least in part, the products of their child-care environments.

Most interesting, however, was this fact: The eight-year-olds from poor-quality centers who turned out "best," from a behavioral standpoint, were the ones who had the most direct, positive interaction with their caregivers. Meaning that if a kid in a poor day-care center has a good caregiver, it can make all the difference.

Family Day Care vs. In-Home Care vs. Center Care

Most books about choosing child care will tell you about the types of child care that are out there—day-care centers, family day-care homes, in-home caregivers, and care by a relative. They'll talk about the pluses and minuses of each form of care, which, in most cases, are fairly obvious. The best options for infants and toddlers, for example, are widely considered to be in-home care, because it offers the advantage of one-on-one interaction, and family day care, which is touted as the closest thing to being home with Mom. But such perfunctory advice is of little use in the real world, where finding consistent, reliable, long-term care, in which the caregivers are actually trained and qualified to deal with young children, is a pretty tall order.

I found that many of the child-care decisions parents make are based on assumptions that have little or no foundation in reality. While many parents assume that a grandmother's loving care, or that of a trusted friend, is the best child care for children under three, the research to date on middle-class kids largely contradicts that notion. And while family day care is the dominant form of group care for children three and under, the studies on the variability and character of family day care are deeply troubling.

In the real world, what are the differences between various types of child care? What have researchers learned by observing children in child care?

In-Home Care: Not Necessarily the Best

There have been few observational studies of in-home child care, and given that only 3 percent of the parents who use child care for preschoolers hire a sitter to come to their own home, there's been little incentive to make a study of it. It's widely assumed that one-on-one care is the best form of care for infants. But other research suggests that in-home care may not, in fact, be so great.

Turnover is higher than for any other type of child care, a subject discussed in chapter one. And the growing recognition that children can and do form attachments to their caregivers leads to the obvious conclusion that turnover among in-home caregivers may pose problems for kids—although no studies directly address this question.

Evidence of the importance of training to good caregiving suggests, as well, that in-home care might be the least optimal form of care. The 1994 family day-care study found that kids do less well in settings with very few children, because caregivers don't organize and plan activities and are less invested in child-rearing—suggesting that a caregiver/housekeeper is not necessarily the best arrangement. Going about your daily activities, when you're a housekeeper as opposed to a mother with a strong emotional link to a child, may not be good child care.[18]

The Chicago Study, conducted in the 1980s by researchers at the University of Chicago, was one of the first comparative studies of the impact of different forms of child care on children. Researchers looked at 80 two- and three-year-olds from mixed-income groups—primarily middle-class and upper-class—in what were reportedly "better than average day-care arrangements" in nursery schools, center care, family day care, and sitter care at home. The researchers evaluated the children's social and cognitive development and found that the nursery school children (who were also least likely to have an employed mother) scored consistently higher on just about every measure, "especially on assessments of cognitive ability, social knowledge, and sociability with an adult stranger." They were the "most developmentally advanced." The kids in sitter care at home scored least well; as a group they didn't score highest on any of the tests, making them, overall, the least developmentally advanced. Kids with in-home sitters were more likely than kids in group care to behave negatively toward a peer and less likely to interact positively, and they were "significantly lower in competence overall" than the nursery school kids. The children in full-time center care appeared to be the most independent (they maintained the greatest distance from their mothers) and scored highest on verbal sociability toward their mothers in lab assessments and at home at dinnertime. The kids in family day care scored highest on staying close to their mothers ("least independent") and on social competence with peers.[19]

Family Day Care: Another World

Maryanne Lazarchick has been in the family day-care business for nearly three decades. She started taking in children so she could be home with her own kids; the first child she was ever paid to care for is now 27 years old. In her split-level suburban home, she takes care of eight children. Four part-timers (including an infant) come in the morning, and four school-age kids arrive in the afternoon. She's licensed to care for two infants and up to eight children, full time, but she says she'd never care for more than one infant at a time. And she doesn't keep eight full-time kids. "That's what licensing allowed. I'm registered for eight. I have room for eight. But I have enough common sense to know what I'm able to handle. I'm not 30 years old," she says. "I don't have the energy for eight kids."

Lazarchick is the epitome of a committed family day-care provider. She's president of the Family Day Care Association in Montgomery County, Maryland. She's one of only eight providers in the entire county who have achieved accreditation by the National Association for Family Child Care and one of only about 700 in the entire nation. She attends workshops and seminars and is still active in the local family day-care network.

Lazarchick is a pro. She has a resume that she presents to prospective parents, outlining the hours of course work she's taken.

She publishes a booklet detailing the rules of her program, as a typical preschool does. She has expanded her house to accommodate her profession: Two family rooms in her basement, stocked with toys, games, puzzles, bristle blocks, dolls, and Legos, all neatly organized, open up to a backyard filled with riding toys and climbing equipment.

Some of the parents who enroll their kids in Lazarchick's program are themselves professionals in the day-care field. They work for referral agencies or conduct workshops for providers. They are hooked in. Lazarchick's is like the hub of the family day-care world. She spends a lot of time with other providers.

She genuinely likes the parents whose children are in her care, which isn't the norm among family day-care providers. Most studies suggest that half of family day-care providers harbor anger, resentment, and negative feelings toward the parents who use their care. And unlike many providers, Lazarchick believes day care is not just all right but can be good for kids. Lazarchick believes the parents who bring their children to her care about their kids, which changes the dynamic of the relationship.

Says Mitzi Ross, a social worker whose son is in Lazarchick's care, "It's like here's this other adult who's significant in your child's life, who is interested in your child's development, is fascinated by what your child does, reports the funny and nice things your child does, and lets you know 'We need to work on this together' or 'Such and such seems to be going on. What do you think?' It's like having an extended family." Or a partner.

Lazarchick knows what's out there. She bemoans the poor quality of family day care in general, feels strongly that providers need training, and has no kind words for unlicensed family day-care providers, who undercut the market by charging less and offer what she feels is substandard care. "I've been in homes where there's one basket of toys in the corner for six or seven children," she says. "Of course, you're going to have behavior problems when you have six books, two trucks, a television, and a couple of tapes."

What's life like at Maryanne's? A sense of levelheadedness and order pervades the place. She knows what to do with these kids. She's big on setting limits (30 minutes of television—public television—a day before lunch), on manners (there are a lot of pleases and thank yous), and on teaching negotiating skills— "Timmy had it first; when he's finished, you can have a turn"— and social skills: "When the baby's crying, the kids gather round. They offer toys; they try to help," she says, and she encourages that empathy. She keeps a lid on things. "If a child is giving me a rough time, I say, 'That's your second warning. Three strikes, you're out.'" Meaning they're in time-out—and the kids know she means it.

Lazarchick takes two months off—July and August—every year. "In September," she says, "I'm rejuvenated, recharged." Many of her kids are the children of teachers, so taking off is no problem. She helps the others adapt to her absence: I visited her program in June, while she was preparing two three-year-olds for their first camp experience; during her vacation, they would be attending day camp together. She took them to the store to buy backpacks and lunch boxes. And she started teaching them how to deal with their lunch. "Monday they were so proud. They walked in with their lunches and backpacks. They practiced unwrapping the Saran Wrap, eating from a lunch box, dealing with the thermos. It's practice week for them." Her idea of an outing for three-year-olds is a trip to the supermarket followed by a picnic in the park.

Kids who begin care with Lazarchick stay with her, often through after-school care and into adolescence. The continuity, the consistency, the character of Lazarchick's family day-care program stand in striking contrast to what's available in most of the country.

Lazarchick registers high on what researchers have labeled "intentionality," an umbrella term for all the characteristics that are identified with high-quality family day-care providers.

Defining Quality in Family Day Care

When I had finished researching this book, I sat down one night to review some of my preliminary notes on the subject of choosing child care. Scrawled in the margin of an article on how to choose child care was this note to myself: "Training. Ridiculous. It's unrealistic to expect most caregivers to be trained." Like most parents, I imagined that what a good caregiver needs is simply experience with children; that what children need is a "mother substitute"; that personality means more than training. One-on-one care, I assumed, was the best arrangement for an infant or toddler, in a setting that most nearly resembles one's own home. Like most American parents, I have been brainwashed by a culture that assumes mother care is best and that the best child care is care that serves as a mother replacement. But, I find now, that couldn't be further from the truth.

Child care isn't, and can't be, mother care. As Carollee Howes, one of the preeminent researchers in the field, points out, "If you're not going to have that deep emotional bond that a parent has with a child, you'd better do something like give the person some training and as much formal education as you can get, because that's what correlates with responsive care." People who are good at dealing with kids, at providing that mother-loving care, are people who are trained for the job.

Many, many studies have confirmed that the best child care occurs when a provider is professional, possesses knowledge of child development, and has a positive, nurturing attitude toward children. The 1994 family day-care study,[20] conducted by the Families and Work Institute, was the first study to link training and nurturing behavior among family day-care providers to that list of attributes they define as "intentionality."

Who were the most caring and nurturing providers?

- People with training—formal and informal—in child development. Says Ellen Galinsky, co-president of the Families and Work Institute, "A parent might imagine that someone with training would be more bureaucratic and formal, but in fact they're more warm, caring, and responsive."

- Providers who participate in local associations and provider networks, who get informal training through workshops, conferences, and family day-care associations, and who socialize with other providers. All this suggests a commitment to their field as a profession.
- Providers who initially went into the business because they wanted to be in the business, stayed with it, and, like Lazarchick, became professionals.
- People who plan activities for kids. Ellen Galinsky says, "A lot of providers didn't give any thought to what kids would be doing all day." Those were the providers, too, who tended to be less warm and responsive.
- People who say that child care is their chosen occupation as opposed to a temporary situation or even a way to be with their own children.
- Regulated, licensed, and registered family day-care providers. These caregivers tended to be more "intentional," more committed to child care as a profession, more sensitive to the children, and more nurturing and caring.
- Providers with more children (three to six) as opposed to fewer children, within the legal limits. These caregivers tended to be more sensitive to the children's needs. Providers with more than a few children appear to invest energy in planning activities, engaging the children rather than simply "going about their normal business." This was a surprise finding. Many parents imagine that family day care is like home, and mothers doing family day care should pretty much be doing what they do anyway: the laundry, shopping, housework, and child rearing. But family day-care providers are not mothers. They don't have an inherent, long-term investment in how the kids do. They don't have a natural, ongoing relationship with the children unless they make an effort to establish such a relationship.

- Providers who charge more and follow standard business practices—pay taxes, give parents their social security number, have a written contract. These caregivers were found to deliver higher-quality, more sensitive, more nurturing care.

Who delivered the poorest care, on standard global quality measures? Who were the least nurturing, the least attentive?

- Relatives, neighbors, and friends who take care of children out of an obligation to the parents. They have little or no commitment to child care as a profession. According to Galinsky, "Relatives by and large provided lower-quality care, which busts the stereotype straight in the face. Our feeling is that a lot of them don't want to be doing child care." The researchers were "startled" to find that care by relatives is the least sensitive and least responsive. A full 69 percent of the relatives studied delivered substandard care. However, the researchers urge caution in interpreting these findings. A full two-thirds of the relatives providing child care were also living in poverty.
- Unlicensed providers. Half of the unlicensed providers studied delivered substandard or inadequate care; only 13 percent of the licensed and regulated providers delivered inadequate or substandard care.
- People with many years of experience. Here Lazarchick bucks the trend. Providers with many years of experience were more likely to be "more detached and more harsh" with the kids and less likely to have training. Yet mothers surveyed believed experience was more important than training.

What about the kids? Did nurturance and sensitivity make a difference? The kids with sensitive, responsive, nurturing providers—as measured by observations in the child-care setting—tended to be securely attached to their providers. They played more with other children and with objects, they engaged in more high-level and complex play, and they were more securely attached to their parents. The kids in good family day care were not just doing all right, they were doing great. The kids in poor family day care were not.

While in center care quality is not necessarily related to price, studies show a direct correlation between quality and price in family day care. Parents who can afford better family day care appear to consistently get better care for their kids.

What Bad Family Day Care Looks Like

The idea of family day care is appealing to a lot of parents; it offers a "homelike" setting, plenty of mother (substitute) love, and good old-fashioned unstructured play. But what does that mean? In 1989, researchers at the University of Illinois conducted a study of how family day-care providers *perceive* what goes on in their homes versus what actually goes on in their homes. They began by interviewing 31 providers, most of whom talked about providing a "home atmosphere" where kids get "a lot of attention and a lot of love"; they said they did "what parents would do for their children at home" and let the kids "just kinda run around and do what they please." Following that, the researchers spent ten months observing in six family day-care homes, making 20 two-hour visits to each home. To offer a "slice of life" in family day care, they published an article in which they described some of the typical behavior they saw in these homes. Herewith, a few examples:

> The caregiver had seven children in her care, all under age four. Two of the children, Jessie (three) and Lani (24 months), were new. When I arrived at 9 A.M., Lani was sitting very quietly, with tears in her eyes. The caregiver's dog walked into the front room, and both Jessie and Lani started crying. The caregiver made no effort to comfort them. Eventually they stopped crying but still looked distressed. Lani hugged a doll she had brought. . . . Around ten the caregiver carried on a lengthy phone conversation. About 10:30 she turned the TV off and told the children to lie down on the blanket that was on the front room floor. Again Jessie and Lani cried. The caregiver went into the kitchen and remained there during the rest of the time I was there, except once when she came in with a switch and tapped one of the children a bit to remind him to lie quietly.

Here's another example of the homelike care offered by one family day-care provider:

> The caregiver told Sam (30 months), "You go to the bathroom and don't wet your pants." As he went off, she reminded him to pull his pants down. "You can do it by yourself." He came back and apparently had dirtied his pants. The caregiver spanked him and made him go back into the bathroom with her. She was yelling at him for getting his pants dirty. He came out with no pants on. The caregiver found another pair of pants and put them on him. She then put him in a crib and told him to "get to sleep!" She seemed angry with him and was not gentle at all.

And another:

> The children were dancing to music. The caregiver decided to initiate a game of Simon Says. She had Sally (four years) and Stuart (28 months) stand in front of the bookshelf. They did not understand the game and followed *all* her directions, whether "Simon" said to or not. The caregiver laughed and said, "You guys don't listen very well."

According to the report, the provider said she was frustrated "trying to keep the children entertained. She said she had been letting them watch more TV, even though she did not like it, because she had done everything she could think of to entertain them."[21]

Not a particularly heartwarming picture of a homelike setting. These were all untrained providers; none of them belonged to their area day-care association; none had any formal or informal training in child development. It's not that they were lying about the kind of environment they provide; the problem, according to the researchers, is that their definition of a loving, warm environment—based on how they were raised or what they've seen—is very different from what researchers, or parents, might imagine to be a loving, warm environment.

Concludes the report: "This study suggests that the world of family day care for some children may be one that is void of toys, where commands and demands are more prevalent than questions and comments, where negative affect is commonplace, where children repeatedly experience favoritism, and where the caregiver is emotionally uninvolved with the children." If that's the case, then, indeed, family day care can be a terribly damaging environment.

Why Training Matters: Dealing With Children

Consider the kind of knowledge typical family day-care providers or in-home caregivers should possess, relative to the knowledge of child development they actually may possess. Ask yourself these questions:

- When is a child generally ready to start using a cup? To try finger foods? To manipulate objects? To walk? To tie shoes? What about stand in line? Take turns? Follow two, three, or four directions in sequence? Or understand Simon Says?
- How old is a child before he is able to share, to negotiate, or to actually play with another child? And how can you encourage cooperation and discourage aggression in young children?
- What about discipline? What forms of discipline elicit the best results—at what ages?
- How does your average two-year-old spend a day? What about an 18-month-old or a 13-month-old?
- When is it hardest for children to say good-bye to their parents? What makes it easier?
- How can you encourage a parent to work out a behavior problem in their child that's causing a problem in your program?
- What's the best way to get a toddler to do what you wish? Or a three- or four-year-old?
- What do you do if a one-year-old throws food? A two-year-old pitches a fit? A three-year-old says "shut up"? A four-year-old sticks out his tongue?

- How do you soothe a wounded child? Draw out a shy one? Make an anxious one feel safe? Ever had to do CPR? Or guess what ails a child who's not your own?
- How about this one: How do you stay attentive, alert, and responsive when you may be completely isolated from other adults and outside stimuli all day long?

It doesn't take a master's degree to know the answers to all these questions. But I've raised two children, and I'd still have a good deal of trouble coming up with the answers to all of them off the top of my head. But whoever is taking care of your children, regardless of the setting, should know the answers to the questions that apply. How can anyone imagine that taking care of children is an unskilled job, that it doesn't require training, that three months of experience is enough?

In the child-care business, the buzzword for knowing the answers to all these questions is knowing what's developmentally appropriate—what's age appropriate. What should you expect from kids ages zero to five, and how should you respond to them? There are libraries full of books on child rearing, and not all of them are in agreement about how to handle what when. But that's what choosing child care should be about: selecting a program that conforms to your attitudes about child rearing. Instead, today in America, choosing child care means finding a place that's safe, convenient, affordable, and, if you're lucky, lasting.

Why Training Matters: Dealing With Parents

One afternoon I sat down with a group of day-care center directors and listened to a discussion that I think might have surprised many parents. They bemoaned the lack of quality staffers, the high turnover in their programs. They brainstormed ways to find people to staff part-time after-school programs. They talked about how to keep the physical spaces they are in, negotiating with churches and schools. They discussed strategies for in-house training. "When attendance is down," said one director, "I have my teachers and assistants observe in other rooms. It sharpens their skills." These are issues most parents don't even think about. Then, toward the end of the discussion, they began talking about "difficult" parents. "I get so I can recognize their footsteps," said one day-care director. "They come in all brusque and demanding: 'Where are Joshua's socks? Did he sleep today? Why isn't his coat in his cubby?'"

Said the facilitator, a parent educator with 30 years' experience, "Some of these people are really stressed out. You have to be patient with them. That's part of your job."

Not long afterward I spent an evening with a group of family day-care providers, who talked with me about their concerns—which, quite naturally, were completely different from those of day-care directors. They talked about budgeting and even about asking parents to pay for new equipment ("Should I mention that we need a stroller in the Christmas newsletter?"), about area training programs, and about unlicensed providers—one of their biggest beefs was with unlicensed providers who offer substandard care and below-market prices and with licensed providers who are ill-equipped for the job of child care.

But they reserved their strongest words for parents—parents who plop down on their sofas at 6 P.M. for a visit; parents who ask to bring their kids by on the day after Thanksgiving; parents who pay late, arrive late, or appear not to know how to manage their kids.

When providers in Montgomery County, Maryland, were surveyed in 1993, the majority said that a parent's number one concern when choosing child care was price.[22] When parents are surveyed, they consistently say their number one concern is program quality. Why the difference? "I think, unfortunately, it's indicative of the tension that often exists in the relationship between parents and providers; that's due in part, I think, to the fact that neither side is fully respected as much as they need to be," says Barbara Willer, director of public affairs for the National Association for the Education of Young Children. "Providers often feel dumped on because parents may not pick their children up on time or they may feel like they're being viewed as a babysitter, almost like a dry-cleaning service—you drop your kids off and that's it."

Parents, on the other hand, may feel jealous or resentful of the relationship between the caregiver and their children; uncomfortable with what can be a poorly defined relationship (who's in charge here?); even timid about approaching caregivers. Many parents have little or no idea how demanding a job they are leaving to day-care teachers, family day-care providers, and in-home sitters. "We work hard to train our caregivers in how to deal with parents," says Pamela Ward, a day-care director in Maryland. "But nobody's teaching the parents how to deal with caregivers."

There's a gap between most parents and providers, through which the children's needs sometimes fall. The studies on the subject are pretty consistent:

- Studies show that family day-care mothers are more stressed than either mothers at home caring for their own kids or employed mothers with kids in child care. They have longer hours and lower incomes than their clients and significantly lower levels of education.[23] That gap in itself creates tension, although a study conducted by the Families and Work Institute suggests that higher levels of stress may be associated with better—not poorer—care for children. These, it appears, are the caregivers who genuinely care.[24]

- Other studies show that family day-care providers as a group tend to be more traditional than mothers who work outside the home. Many enter the field so they can be home with their own kids, and many family day-care providers seem to feel that working parents are neglectful; they are particularly judgmental about working parents. One 1989 study of family day-care providers and parents revealed deep ideological differences between the two. Providers couldn't imagine how parents could leave their kids all day; parents couldn't imagine how provider's could deal with "all those children" all day.[25]

- A 1988 study found that most problems reported by family day-care providers center around difficulties with parents, such as "anger, resentment, and disapproval" of their behavior—issues like late pick-ups, late payments, and unsupportive attitudes.[26]
- Research suggests that parents and caregivers communicate less than they should and less than they *think* they communicate, and researchers speculate that "parents may limit communication with caregivers to avoid being aware of differences in their values about child-rearing."[27]
- One 1984 study grouped family day-care providers as either "mothers," "grandmothers," or "teachers" based on the providers' own perceptions of their roles. They found that 42 percent of all caregivers "expressed hostility towards parents for neglecting their children." And while many of them felt child care was adequate, only 3 percent thought day care was beneficial to children. Those classified as "mothers"—who saw themselves as mother substitutes—tended to feel the most hostility toward parents; "grandmothers" seemed to feel day care was okay, but only if the mother had to work; and "teachers" seemed to be more concerned with whether parents used appropriate styles at home.

If you think about it, these are not surprising findings. Caregivers are not immune to the general attitude in our culture that mother care is best for kids; they may be more susceptible to that view since they themselves have chosen this occupation so they can be home with their own kids. Obviously such perceptions are going to color these relationships, and ultimately, where tensions arise, children will be aware of them.

It's widely accepted in the field of education that teachers tend to be judgmental of parents, and when they judge, they judge harshly. This is less true, according to the research, when teachers are more educated, have more experience, and are themselves parents. Parenthood, after all, is a lesson in humility. But it's also widely accepted that clear boundaries should exist between home and school. Ongoing communication between parents and teachers, unless there's a serious problem, is generally discouraged. What parents would march their seven-year-old into class and announce to the teacher that Johnny had a bad night? But with a toddler, that's precisely what a parent must and should do, because in all likelihood, if Johnny had a bad night, he's going to have a bad day.

The parent-caregiver relationship is central to good child care. One environment acts as an extension of the other. Issues related to socializing young children are quite different from issues related to educating them, so it stands to reason that any good child-care environment fosters parent-caregiver interaction. Training can play a role in resolving some of these hostilities. Training programs aimed at helping providers set limits and rules with parents are crucial to promoting a kind of professionalism—e.g., putting a "no late payments" policy in writing, setting firm rules about drop-offs and pick-ups. Day-care centers report success in teaching caregivers how to deal with parents more effectively and how to be more sensitive to the pressures that come with their jobs.

***

As I've endeavored to show in this chapter, we know from research that day care can be good for young children—if it's good child care.

Social scientists are not so sure, however, about the effects of group care on babies, about the impact on babies (and mothers) of absurdly short parental leaves, and about how much children need their mothers during the first year of life.

Some of the most negative—and most controversial—studies to come out of the field of child-care research over the past decade concern infancy. Given the fact that some experts define "infancy" as the first *three* years of life, these studies address the two questions that are really central to this whole discussion: Is exclusive mother care the best child-rearing model? Or is it just one option among many? These are questions to which the next two chapters are devoted.

CHAPTER FOUR

The Attachment Controversy

obin Parker is looking directly into the camera and talking like a media-trained pro. Surrounded by a handful of other women, mothers and experts in the field of child development, she's speaking to the audience about her son, adopted when he was five years old. "At age nine, he was diagnosed with an attachment disorder," she says. "Basically, he has no conscience. He is not bonded. He is not attached." Her two daughters, on the other hand, were both adopted at birth. In both cases, she was present in the delivery room. "They are very attached children," she says. "They're emotionally healthy children. They are just real secure in who they are."

Live, from Chicago, it's *Phil Donahue*. It's April 5, 1993, and the subject is bonding. Today's special guest is Diane Eyer, a psychologist from the University of Pennsylvania and author of *Mother-Infant Bonding: A Scientific Fiction.*

"How does a nine-year-old manifest his absent conscience?" asks the talk-show host.

"Lying, stealing—pathological lying and stealing . . . fire starting," says Parker. Her child, in short, is every parent's nightmare. But this is no bad seed, according to Parker. The problem, according to her, is this: Her adopted son didn't have a chance to form a close relationship with anyone at infancy.

Of course, there's no way of proving or disproving her point, that this child suffers from an "attachment disorder." Was her son neglected or abused in childhood? Shuffled from one foster home to another? Was he born of a mother or father with sociopathic tendencies, the victim not of insufficient nurturing but of nature itself? Nobody raises these questions. Her testimony is taken at face value.

More testimony is offered up by callers and members of the audience. We hear from a working mom, probably in her early 30s, who travels extensively. Quality time, she says with a broad grin—perhaps aware that she is a walking cliché—is what counts. We hear from another mother, a middle-aged woman seated beside her grown daughter; they were separated for a year following the daughter's birth because Mom had tuberculosis and had to live in a sanitarium. Both of these mothers—the young working mom and the middle-aged parent—say that despite their absences in their children's infancy, they have close, untroubled relationships with their daughters, who show no signs of being or becoming sociopaths. Then we hear from another adoptive mother, one whose daughter is 17; no attachment problems here, she reports, despite her daughter's preadoption history of foster homes, abuse, and neglect. "We've been bonding every day," she says.

The words "attachment" and "bonding" are bandied about without much concern for what they might really mean. Diane Eyer, like a schoolmarm at the center of a three-ring circus, patiently endeavors to explain her thesis and the difference between the two terms. Strictly speaking, in the scientific literature, bonding refers to the moment following birth, when mother, her feet still planted in the stirrups, and infant, fresh from the womb, are united on the delivery table. Attachment is something else altogether: It is the process of establishing a relationship with that child, a process that stretches over many months or even, some would say, years.

Phil Donahue is taking calls from people all over the country. The most disturbing one comes from a new mother. Her husband has been laid off, so she is going back to work. She's afraid her baby, now two and a half months old, won't know who she is. She is certain the child doesn't know who she is yet. She sounds frightened, confused; she's looking for answers.

"I think it's good that she's concerned about her baby," says Eileen Haeney, a social worker who has done extensive work with infants and low-income parents, many of them single mothers—people considered within the psychiatric community to be "at risk" for attachment problems. "It takes time for a mother to get to know a baby and time for a baby to get to know her mother." Attachment formation, Haeney feels, is critical to a child's healthy development.

Given that this caller obviously cares deeply about her baby, and clearly has few choices, Haeney's answer is not particularly helpful. Jane Gordon, another panelist, jumps in: "Everybody can sit and say, 'We must give these children attention; we must give these children love during the first year.' If I have to go back to work, tell me: How I do both? Don't tell me I'm wrong. Don't tell me I should feel guilty. Help me cope."

Gordon's comment brings down the house.

***

No one is suggesting that by going back to work in the early weeks of a child's life, working mothers are doomed to produce a bunch of sociopaths. The studies of maternal employment and attachment, which are reviewed in this chapter, are not about children who fail to form attachments to their parents. All children, except in the most severe cases of neglect and abuse, form strong attachments to their parents. These studies are not concerned with abnormal behavior and pathologies. Rather, they're concerned with subtle differences in the character of the relationships between babies and mothers, and how those relationships may affect a child's development.

The Beginning of the Debate

In the mid-80s, a debate surfaced in the scholarly community over mounting evidence that appeared to suggest infants with mothers working full time were more likely to be insecurely attached to their mothers and therefore at risk for developmental problems. Jay Belsky, a psychologist from Pennsylvania State University, stood at the center of this debate, and his views received a good deal of attention in the mainstream press.

Anytime you see a statement like "A mother who is absent more than 20 hours a week during the first year of the child's life puts her child at risk for future problems," you are seeing the results of the attachment studies as they're commonly distilled, oversimplified, and translated in the mainstream press. That's a pretty frightening statement, given that few employed mothers can manage even a part-time schedule that fits into less than 20 hours.

Certainly, when Jay Belsky raised the specter of the potentially harmful effects of infant day care, the idea that maternal employment might compromise a child's development was not a new one. For decades, popular child-rearing experts, most of whom are believers in attachment theory, have been telling mothers to stay home. Despite the fact that more than half of new mothers now return to work before their babies reach age one, most of these experts still contend that full-time mother care is the best child-rearing option, at least for the first six months—but in some cases for the first three years. The central reason: the process called attachment.

Penelope Leach, whose *Your Baby and Child* has sold millions of copies since it was first published in 1977, has long maintained that mothers of preschool children should stay at home from birth until the kids are in school. What if they can't? In her 1994 book, *Children First*, Leach holds up Swedish leave policies as an ideal alternative: Parents can take a combined total of up to 18 months off during each child's early years and are free to work six-hour days until children reach age eight.

Infant care, argues Leach, raises special issues. "Whoever it is who cares for infants, they need to have permanence, continuity, passion and parent-like commitment that is difficult to find or meet outside the vested interests and social expectations of family roles and cannot be adequately replaced by professionalism," she writes in *Children First.*[1] Good enough infant care, Leach argues, may be an impossibility. "Every baby needs at least one special person to attach herself to."[2]

Nearly two decades ago, in 1977, psychoanalyst Selma Fraiberg, author of an extraordinary book on the inner lives of children called *The Magic Years*, published a lesser-known book called *Every Child's Birthright* that makes a similar case against child care during the first three years of life. Like Leach, she makes a passionate case against child care as we know it. Her book proposes that mothers simply stay home and that laws be enacted to enable them to do precisely that. She writes, "Since babies and toddlers make extraordinary demands upon their own mothers, the requirements for a substitute mother, in the true sense of the word, are also extraordinary."[3] Quality day care, according to Fraiberg, is an impossibility.

Fraiberg and Leach are not alone. Burton White, who as project director of Harvard University's Pre-School Project wrote *The First Three Years of Life*, has advised mothers to stay at home for all of those three years, although he sees the potential for other work/home combinations. He told author Anita Shreve, "My ideal pattern is this. No substitute care for six months, with the exception of an occasional night out; part-time substitute care with parents equally sharing child care the rest of the time." He added, "I am not in the business of making life easier for young couples."[4]

Why? In a word, attachment.

Other child-rearing experts have attempted to adapt traditional attachment theory to a world in which most new mothers have jobs. In his latest book, *Touchpoints*, T. Berry Brazelton encourages parents to spend "at least four months at home"[5] and notes a bit later, "Sometimes parents ask, 'How long would you recommend

I stay at home if I had a real choice?' If this choice appears possible, I suggest one year."[6]

Given the pervasive emphasis on attachment and early mother care in our culture, perhaps the most radical prescription for parental leaves comes from Sandra Scarr, a developmental psychologist from the University of Virginia with impeccable credentials and four children of her own. In her 1984 book, *Mother Care/Other Care*, she seems to have abandoned the attachment model altogether in suggesting that mothers return to work before their babies reach the age of six months. "I recognize that this is radically different advice from the usual expert opinion, which calls on mothers to stay home with their babies for at least the first year," she writes. "But I think that most of that advice is based on obsolete notions of mothers and babies and on erroneous information about the nature of newborns and young infants."[7]

The Attachment Theory: More Questions Than Answers

Attachment means many things to many people. Some developmental psychologists believe that a strong attachment to a loving, nurturing, responsive mother—an attachment born of many months of extensive, near-exclusive maternal care—is the surest route to a compliant, well-socialized, well-adjusted child. They argue that full-time employment, particularly during the first year of a child's life, may be disruptive to the relationship between mother and child. Others, like Scarr, disagree: Babies are resilient creatures, they argue, capable of forming numerous relationships and emerging healthy and happy; there's no reason to assume that an infant's only, or even primary, attachment must be to the mother.

The central questions raised by attachment theory are these: Just how much does a baby need her mother? Just how disturbing is it to a baby if the mother is unavailable? And just how good must child care be to serve as an adequate replacement some of the time? The answer, based on available research, seems to be: It depends. It depends on many factors—not all of them directly related to this thing called attachment. It depends on how a mother feels about leaving her baby, and on the baby's own temperament. Some babies appear to be more resilient than others. It depends on the stresses in the home situation, the stability of the child-care situation, how old the child is when the mother returns to work, and how many hours she works; it depends on the involvement of the father and, perhaps more than any other single factor, the quality of the child care. There is no magic formula, no simple prescription, no easy answer.

If you look beyond our popular child-rearing experts, authors like Leach and Brazelton, and you ask researchers in the field of child development, flat out, "Is it harmful for a baby if his or her mother goes back to work during the first year?," the answer, like as not, will be "We don't know." Why? For any number of reasons, not all of them having to do with attachment. New research tells us that infants are not just blobs who "eat, sleep, and poop," as one new mother described her eight-week-old's day. They are instead remarkably aware of what's going on around them, particularly sensitive to change, and able to distinguish between people even in the early weeks of life. In 1994, for the first time, the Carnegie Corporation released a report compiling the cumulative new evidence on neurological development from the field of molecular biology, which confirmed the idea that the first year of life is a crucial one. During the first 12 months, the baby's brain is, quite literally, still growing, and stimulation, nurturance, and responsiveness are crucial to the development of the neural pathways, the synapses that will enable children to learn in the years ahead. Moreover, the report states that according to a study released in 1992, early stress "can quite probably activate hormones" that disturb the brain's growth and close off the development of these neural pathways forever.[8] All of this, of course, lends new meaning to the idea that babies need consistent, relaxed, responsive care and stimulation. Then, of course, the report goes on to discuss the importance of attachment.

Experts in the day-care field are concerned about the rate at which new mothers are returning to work, not just because of the potential for a disturbance in the mother-child relationship but because of the nature of child care *as we know it*. Good care, as I endeavored to show in chapter two, is hard to come by. And during the first year of life, children may be more vulnerable to the effects of poor, or even mediocre, child care than during any other point in their development.

In truth, there is no conclusive body of research to support any particular theory about when and how much a mother should work during the first year of an infant's life or when and how new babies adapt to child care. There are virtually no studies of the impact of in-home, one-on-one infant care on later development; no studies comparing the development of infants whose mothers returned to work, say, at six weeks versus six months; and no studies that specifically focus on the impact on babies of turnover in the child-care field.

Consequently, when I asked researchers in the field, "What are the effects of a mother's employment on infants? What are the effects of child care on babies? What's the optimal parental leave? What kind of child care is best for babies?," the response was, "We don't know"; then whomever I interviewed would inevitably volunteer, "There's a major national study under way at the National Institutes of Child Health and Human Development . . . ," better known as the NICHD study.

The NICHD Study

The NICHD study on the effects of infant day care is the largest, most comprehensive study of its kind ever undertaken. Funded by tax dollars, it represents an unprecedented collaborative effort by the community of developmental psychologists, who are under extraordinary pressure to come up with answers to these questions. More than 25 researchers—the biggest names in the child-care field—are involved in the project. They will follow 1,364 infants from birth into the first grade at ten sites throughout the country, a process that began in January 1991. They are looking at a variety of factors that they believe may influence how a baby adapts and develops. These include:

- the type of child care
- the quality and stability of the child-care arrangement
- the age at which an infant begins child care
- the mother's work schedule
- stress on the family
- the infant's own temperament
- and, of course, the role of attachment among caregivers and parents

Some preliminary results should begin to surface in 1995, but the study is slated to go through the year 2000, and researchers are not making any promises about when conclusive results will be released.[9]

In the meantime, what answers does the existing research hold? Most people in the field of child development—regardless of their opinions about the effects of day care on infants—seem to agree that attachment is an important, even critical, stepping-stone to healthy emotional development. So it behooves any parent faced with the prospect of returning to work during the first year of a baby's life to linger for a moment in the literature on attachment, if only to get a grasp of what social scientists know and don't know about how infants develop in relation to the people who care for them.

What Is Attachment? What Difference Does It Make?

According to attachment theory, children's sense of the world is determined in infancy, by the relationship with their primary caretaker—most frequently the mother. If mother and child adapt to one another—if the mother is responsive, caring, loving, and nurturing and the baby is not hypersensitive or temperamental, or if the two aren't somehow completely out of step—the child emerges with a strong sense of security and a "secure attachment" to that figure, all of which, generally, happens quite naturally. As a result of this process, an infant knows that her needs will be met and that the world is a safe, reliable place. From the "secure base" represented by the mother, a child begins exploring the world.[10]

Attachment is the process by which a mother, or a primary caregiver, gets to know a baby and how to comfort that baby. Does that cry mean hunger? Thirst? Exhaustion? The mother gains confidence in her ability to do this job called baby-raising, developing a closeness to and understanding of this particular human; thus, together with a healthy dose of what we might call enduring, constant, near-perfect love and what psychologists call attachment, a relationship is born. Within the framework of attachment theory, the baby associates comfort with that mother or mother figure, which becomes the foundation for everything from self-discovery ("That's my mother! I'm a person!") to a sense of mastery ("I can get her to feed me by crying") to a sense of trust ("This is somebody I can count on, no matter what time of day or night"), and ultimately, much later, of course, to compliance ("If you say so").

The process stretches on for months, even years. Theoretically, during the first six months attachments are said to be "forming"; from six months to a year, attachment is said to be "solidifying." There are those who believe this relationship, the attachment, is pretty well established at 12 months; others speculate that the process continues until 18 months or two and a half or three years, depending on what you read. A few skeptics argue that the very idea that a parent-child relationship is somehow formed at any particular age is absurd; like all relationships, they argue, it is really a continuum.

We know for a fact that in the early weeks of life babies begin to distinguish one person from another, but only to the extent that they can tell a mother's milk from water, or a rough object from a soft one. Those who have spent a good bit of time observing babies tell us that by four to five months a baby is able to distinguish familiar from unfamiliar people (stranger recognition);

that by six months babies show a strong preference for their caregivers; and that by eight or nine months they cling and cry when anyone they love leaves their sight (stranger anxiety or separation anxiety). At 15 to 18 months, separation anxiety eases, although it may rear its head off and on throughout the first three years.

Are these "symptoms" of attachment formation—or cognitive leaps? Does a baby cry and cling to his mother at eight months because attachment is peaking or because suddenly he is able to recognize her as a separate entity, is able to recognize strangers, and prefers the familiar to the unfamiliar? Does a two-and-a-half-year-old let go more easily because attachment is formed or because she has, cognitively, achieved the ability to recognize that her mother will be back through the acquisition of something called memory? These are the kinds of questions begged by attachment theory.

Attachment and Healthy Development

Theoretically, when securely attached babies become toddlers, they carry that sense of security, derived from their relationships, around with them wherever they go. Some psychologists believe that these securely attached children generate mental images of their mothers and carry those images around like so many built-in "security blankets." They don't mean that symbolically, either.

Consider this description of a healthy child, found in a book written for working mothers called *The Woman Who Works, The Parent Who Cares:* "In a strong attachment, an infant's or toddler's mental image of his mother—the picture he carries of her in his mind—becomes so palpable and vivid that it acquires lifelike properties. Quite literally, the reason a secure child feels secure no matter where he is and what he is doing is because mother, in the form of this evoked companion, is always there right beside him holding his hand."[11]

A strong attachment, it is argued, helps a child let go more easily once she has passed through various degrees of separation anxiety at various ages. It helps a child more easily form other relationships and other secure attachments, to fathers or caregivers, for example. Psychologists have linked secure attachments in home-reared kids to a laundry list of positive characteristics, including emotional adjustment, the ability to focus on a task, and the ability to get along with others—traits that set the stage for everything from learning to forming friendships to becoming productive members of society. In other words, attachment theory is the catch-all for this basic idea: Nurturing mothers produce better children.

Understanding Attachment: The Maternal-Deprivation Studies

The evolution of attachment theory is well beyond the scope of this book. For anyone who's interested, I recommend Robert Karen's thorough 1994 book on the subject, *Becoming Attached*. Attachment theory is based on the belief that mothers play an extraordinary role in shaping the psyches of their children, from infancy on up. Attachment studies focus, in essence, on how children grow within the context of exclusive mother care. As such, some social scientists have raised questions about their applicability to our understanding of how humans develop in other contexts.

The roots of attachment theory lie in psychoanalytic theory, which stresses the early relationship with Mom as the key to healthy development, and in the results from studies of maternal deprivation, which began in Britain following World War II. British psychologist John Bowlby, the father of attachment theory, conducted research on the effects on British children of being orphaned or separated from their families during the war. He examined the rather serious consequences to infants who were raised in group care under incredibly difficult conditions. The children did not fare well. Deprived of affection, stimulation, and attention, many failed to thrive, experiencing the tragic effects of inept, round-the-clock institutional care.

Thus was born a whole body of literature on the effects of maternal deprivation, all of which provides conclusive evidence that babies will not grow—mentally, physically, or emotionally—unless they are held, stimulated, cooed at, catered to, and loved.

Bowlby took his explorations well beyond the study of maternal deprivation. He looked closely at how infants and toddlers react when they are torn away from or even abandoned by their parents. They become depressed and withdrawn; they mourn the loss; they become anxious or even angry; they look for someone else to "attach" to. And he drew on other research that studied the ways in which babies react to separation from their parents. For example, when researchers discovered that babies placed in the hospital before they were seven months old didn't cry for their mothers and those placed after seven months did, they identified a crucial stage in infant development. According to attachment theory, some time around the age of seven months attachment solidifies and separation or stranger anxiety kicks in.

As one study built upon another, Bowlby developed an elaborate construct called attachment, which is probably the most influential child-rearing theory of our time. It has affected our thinking about the importance of one-on-one caregiving, about how to nurture and respond to babies, about pacifiers and special blankets, about the birth process and breastfeeding, about exclusive mother care, and, naturally, about when and if mothers should work.

In 1953, in a book called *Child Care and the Growth of Love*, Bowlby became the first of many to argue that mothers should not leave their babies' sides for the first three years "without good and sufficient reason,"[12] a position he maintains to this day.

Bowlby's work is compelling stuff. In truth, I think all parents owe a great debt to him, because he refined the notion that children, from a very early age, have intense emotional needs and strong feelings for their parents. But looking at child development through the prism of attachment theory may in fact distort some of the processes at work. When a baby in a detached institutional setting fails to thrive, is *maternal* deprivation the

Bonding Debunked

"There is evidence that prompt presentation of the baby to the mother after birth (on the delivery table) is important for the mental health of the mother. Studies of other mammals indicated a delay interrupts mothering impulses and may bring on rejection. Yet the normal hospital routine is such that mothers are immediately separated from their babies for 12 to 24 hours. . . . This is a travesty!"

—Our Bodies, Ourselves, *second edition, 1976, The Boston Women's Health Book Collective*

"Most babies have the capacity to form a strong attachment to another human being after birth. Yet this process, called 'bonding,' cannot be forced or created just by going through the motions. . . . Some hospitals act as if it's a special glue that can be sprayed on and will take in five minutes. After that they think it's too late . . . if for some reason the first moments after birth don't turn out the way you want, you will have many ways of becoming attached. . . . 'Bonding' in humans is an ongoing process."

—The New Our Bodies, Ourselves, *1984, The Boston Women's Health Book Collective*

In her book *Mother-Infant Bonding: A Scientific Fiction*, released in 1992, Diane Eyer publicly blew the whistle on her fellow social scientists and on the widely accepted idea that mother-infant bonding immediately following birth— that is, in the delivery room—is an essential first step in healthy infant development. Eyer's book is not really about the mother-infant relationship but rather about how science works. Her thesis, admirably proved, is basically that scientific research, particularly in the field of social sciences, is based on the assumptions and beliefs of researchers, which are inevitably influenced by the politics of the time.

The notion of in-hospital bonding was introduced in 1972, as Eyer tells it, when two pediatricians, John Kennell and Marshall Klaus, published a study in the *New England Journal of Medicine* stating that "mothers having sixteen extra hours of contact with their infants right after birth showed better mothering skills and their infants did better on developmental tests than mothers and infants who did not have the extra contact."[13]

Eyer argues that bonding caught on not because of the validity of the research itself but because of politics. Women wanted more control over the birth process. Obstetricians were afraid of losing customers to current home-birthing trends and midwives, who were becoming increasingly popular among the post-60s generation. Nurses wanted to promote more humane birthing processes. Fathers, too, wanted to be more involved. Along with the Lamaze approach to childbirth and a new wave of dedication to breastfeeding came bonding—the defining moment of mother-child reunion.

As Eyer explained it, during an interview, "In fact, many people realized right from the start that this was not very good research and it really didn't stand up under scrutiny. However, they did not speak out because they were in favor of the reforms that the bonding idea was ushering into the hospital."[14]

What does Eyer's book tell us? It tells us to be skeptical. Be skeptical about what you read in child-rearing manuals, because notions about what's appropriate today might be inappropriate tomorrow. Be skeptical, too, about the scientific research—on everything from the effects of day care to attachment—because what you read on these pages today may be disproved tomorrow.

issue? Or, as a molecular biologist might suggest, is *deprivation* the issue? When a baby clings and cries at eight months, are we witnessing a symptom of attachment formation or a symptom of cognitive growth? Is three years of exclusive care by a mother—or either parent—the only route to healthy development, or are there more realistic options?

There's a good deal of disagreement in the field of child development over the answers to those questions—about how to, in effect, adapt attachment theory to reality. These disagreements don't center around the issue of whether attachment is important; most experts agree that a secure attachment in infancy, to at least one adult, is critical to healthy development. The debate over attachment is not over the theory but over methodologies and interpretations and applications.

Measuring Attachment: The Strange Situation

Since John Bowlby devised this construct called "attachment," the mother-child relationship has been subjected to extraordinary scrutiny by researchers. Social scientists, confident that attachment is a very real phenomenon, have concerned themselves not with whether it exists but with subtle differences in the quality of attachment relationships and with measuring degrees of responsiveness and nurturance. They have found a way to quantify the mother-child relationship, to measure the attachment between mother and child, and to determine whether that relationship is happy and secure, or somehow less so—a discovery that, as a mother, I find both fascinating and frightening.

It's one thing to say a warm, sensitive mother helps an infant develop a sense of trust. It's quite another to put that relationship to a test, slap a grade on it, and on that basis attempt to predict the future health and well-being of that child, to the exclusion of other relationships and factors in the child's life. But that is precisely what developmental psychologists have been doing for the past 30 years or so. That is, after all, how they've managed to link a "secure" attachment *to the mother* in infancy with everything from grade school conduct to achievement in early childhood.

The yardstick for measuring attachment was developed in the early 60s by Mary Ainsworth, an American psychologist and a colleague of John Bowlby. It is a lab procedure, lasting less than 30 minutes, called the Strange Situation, and it is strange indeed. Infant and mother enter a room, and after a few minutes a stranger comes in; Mom leaves the baby with the stranger; Mom comes back and the stranger leaves; Mom leaves again and baby is alone; the stranger returns and leaves again; then Mom returns for the final reunion. Each of these "episodes" lasts three minutes.[15] This sequence is videotaped and viewed so that the infant's behavior can be scrutinized by an impartial observer. The observer is looking for signs of anxiety, ambivalence, or disorientation when the mother is reunited with the baby. The central issue: Does the baby seek comfort from the mother in a manner that suggests a secure, trusting relationship? Compared to circumstances in Bowlby's studies, the Strange Situation sounds like a family picnic. But for some infants it can be profoundly distressing.

Yet one of the most disturbing aspects of this whole body of inquiry, as T. Berry Brazelton has pointed out, is the fact that mother-infant pairs emerge from this test with labels. Some are labeled "securely attached"; others, labeled "insecurely attached," display behavior toward their mothers that is classified as either anxious or avoidant. It's important to note here that the Strange Situation was not designed to predict future emotional disturbances in general; rather it is, in theory at least, designed to pinpoint "disturbances" in the mother-child relationship that may lead to later problem behaviors.

As measures go, the Strange Situation enjoys a good deal of respect. When Ainsworth developed the procedure, she began with in-home observations and found a striking correlation between what she observed to be responsive, nurturing behavior on the part of the mother and a secure mother-child attachment in the laboratory.[16] And provided it's conducted on children 18 months old or under, the Strange Situation, bizarre as it is, has held up under repeated tests. When psychologists test middle-class mothers and infants, a predictable number of mother-infant pairs, fairly consistently in the 65 to 70 percent range, emerge securely attached. When they revisit older children who displayed insecure attachments in infancy, they find that these kids tend to have behavior or adjustment problems. In the field of developmental psychology, an insecure attachment in infancy is viewed as a symptom of a problem—a problem in the relationship between mother and child.

The Strange Situation has become the foundation for an extraordinary body of literature, all of which has prompted more than one social scientist to urge caution. Psychologist Uri Bronfenbrenner argued years ago that researchers should abandon lab procedures altogether and study infants in the settings in which they actually operate. He once called the field of child development "the study of the behavior of children in Strange Situations with strange adults for the briefest period of time."[17] And in 1981, psychologist Michael Rutter expressed "concern about drawing conclusions from curious procedures involving mother, caretakers, and strangers not only going in and out of rooms every minute for reasons quite obscure to the child, but also not initiating interactions in the way that they might usually do."[18] Many researchers express similar sentiments today.

Yet despite those concerns, this laboratory procedure has been road tested and found quite useful, particularly in working with what are euphemistically called "high-risk" mother-infant pairs— low-income mothers, teenage mothers, and uneducated mothers coping with the combined stresses of poverty, lack of education, and motherhood. Much of the early research on attachment dealt with these "at-risk populations."[19]

When new mothers started going back to work in droves in the 70s and 80s, psychologists scratched their heads and sounded the alarm: But what about attachment? What's going to happen to all these babies if they can't form secure attachments to their mothers? And so working mothers and their infants became the focus of a new wave of research on attachment, most of it making use of the Strange Situation. All of which brings me back to the work of Jay Belsky and his colleagues.

Enter Belsky: The Attachment Debate

In 1985, as the congressional debate over federal parental-leave legislation kicked in, Belsky, a researcher from Pennsylvania State University, hoisted a big red flag. Mothers who return to work during the first year of their child's life, he proclaimed, may be putting their children at risk for later problems. More precisely, he said infants placed in day care for more than 20 hours a week before age one are at risk for insecure attachment and at risk, in turn, for a variety of future maladjustments—including "heightened aggressiveness, noncompliance, and withdrawal in the preschool and early school years."[20]

This was not a conclusion the researcher came to lightly. In fact, Belsky, long an outspoken defender of infant day care, began to rethink his position in the mid-80s as a result, he says, of the "slow, steady trickle of evidence" that infant day care might be risky.[21] This evidence consisted primarily, but not exclusively, of studies of attachment conducted on mother-infant pairs in a psychologist's laboratory, using the Strange Situation.

Belsky caused quite a stir, despite the fact that he was neither the first nor the only researcher to raise these issues. In fact, for years now, in study after study, researchers of all political stripes have been citing the alarming increases in the employment rates among new mothers—up from 37 percent in 1970 to 54 percent in 1993.[22] In 1986, Edward Zigler and Thomas Gamble, two prominent Yale researchers, raised similar concerns in an article that appeared in an obscure journal called *The American Journal of Orthopsychiatry*. They too had noticed an increased incidence of insecure attachments among infants with full-time working mothers. They demonstrated that most of the early studies suggesting otherwise were methodologically flawed.[23]

Nevertheless, the question of how "attachment security" relates to a mother's employment is a boiling cauldron, frothing with emotional and political overtones. In our society, it's one thing to say that the babies of poor, illiterate teenage mothers are "at risk" for insecure attachments. It's something else altogether to suggest that mothers who work are putting their children at risk.

Belsky became a lightning rod for a tumultuous debate among infant day-care researchers on the effects of infant day care—a debate over methodologies, theoretical assumptions, and, ultimately, ideologies that preoccupied academics during the late 80s.

Given the sensational nature of Belsky's reversal—from defender of child care to skeptic—and his willingness to talk openly with the press, his warnings attracted a good deal of media attention. To this day, Belsky's "findings" appear in print a lot—just about every time there's a story on the dangers of day care. Here's how Belsky's speculations were interpreted in a 1990 *Newsweek* article entitled "The Day Care Generation." None of these statements are direct quotes from Belsky, but all are attributed to him:[24]

> " . . . Belsky says that mothers who aren't with their kids all day long don't get to know their babies as well as mothers who work part time or not at all. Therefore, working mothers may not be as sensitive to a baby's first attempts at communications."
>
> "In general, [Belsky] says, mothers are more attentive to these crucial signals than babysitters. Placing a baby in outside care increases the chance that an infant's needs won't be met."
>
> ". . . [Belsky] also argues that working parents have so much stress in their lives that they have little energy left over for their children."

It's easy to see how such comments might raise the guilt levels—and the hackles—of working mothers, and it's not surprising that the press picked up on this rather sensational story. "Jay Belsky put his finger on the pulse of everyone's worst fears," says Deborah Phillips, a prominent child-care researcher who has expressed strong disagreement with Belsky's conclusions. "In our society, which eulogizes maternal care—exclusive maternal care— and is nervous about child care . . . you could not have raised a more frightening specter than the possibility that by dint of work, you are somehow hurting your child."

Many researchers, even those who agreed with Belsky, quickly became concerned about the potential repercussions of Belsky's outspokenness, recognizing that raising these issues in the popular media might do more harm than good. They were well aware that this whole body of research would have the undesirable effect of fostering anxieties in working mothers and disturbing the very relationships—between mothers and babies—they were studying. Wrote Deborah Phillips in 1987, in an article directed at her fellow social scientists, " . . . parents are reading the articles on infant child care, and their hard-won confidence in their decisions is being shattered."[25]

In 1987, in an attempt at damage control, 16 experts in the field of child development—from both sides of the infant-care debate—gathered in Washington. They issued a public statement and, in effect, agreed to agree that the quality of care, *not* the absence of the mother or the risks of insecure attachment, was the central issue in the debate.[26] After all, the last thing they wanted to do was make working mothers feel guilty.

Due in part to the media attention Belsky attracted, social scientists came under enormous pressure to address the many unanswered questions about the so-called "risks" of infant day care, and not long after that 1987 meeting, researchers at NICHD began the process of putting together the proposal for the study that may ultimately provide some answers.

What the Research Says

The trickle of evidence for the "risks" of infant day care that raised Belsky's concerns in the mid-80s has since mounted; it now consists of at least 16 studies showing that infants with full-time working mothers are more likely to be insecurely attached, based on Strange Situation experiments undertaken between the ages of 12 and 18 months. The more hours a mother works, the greater the likelihood of an insecure attachment. But *all* of these studies on infant attachment have confirmed the finding that *most* infants of working mothers—no matter how many hours Mom works—are *securely* attached, when measured in a psychologist's laboratory.

As an example, here are the results of a study of 149 babies and their mothers, who had various work schedules and child-care arrangements. The study was conducted by Jay Belsky and Michael Rovine of Penn State and was published in 1988:

	Full-time child care (n=38)*	Part-time child care		Mother care
		(n=20)	(n=24)	(n=67)
Hours in care per week:	35 plus	20-35	10-20	5 or less
Securely attached	53	65	79	75
Insecurely attached	47	35	21	25

*n represents the number of mother-infant pairs in the sample. Percentages based on raw numbers that appeared in the original report.[27]

Looking at this table, you see that 53 percent of the infants in full-time child care were rated "secure," in comparison to 65 percent of those in child care 20 to 35 hours a week, 79 percent in child care 10 to 20 hours a week, and 75 percent in near-exclusive care by their mothers. You'll recall that a "rate" of secure attachments in the range of 65 to 70 percent is considered quite normal—in other words, a "population" in that range is not considered "at risk," to use the language of the trade.

Given that, the only "at risk" population in these particular numbers is infants in care more than 35 hours a week. But the trend toward higher rates of insecurity with increased hours of work is pretty clear. When measured in a psychologist's laboratory, more children of full-time working mothers appear to be insecurely attached. That is precisely what this research says—and all that this research says.

The evidence may be mounting, but it is hardly conclusive. Not all Strange Situation studies corroborate these findings. Some have found no differences between working and nonworking mothers and their babies on attachment ratings. Most studies that make use of other methodologies (observations in the home or day-care setting and those that use another attachment measure called the Q-Sort) find no such differences.

Just as important, the Strange Situation studies on the effects of day care have been attacked on a number of fronts by some of the most prominent people in the field of child development, including T. Berry Brazelton, Carollee Howes, Deborah Phillips, Tiffany Field, and Alison Clarke-Stewart. Many claim the methodology is flawed, precisely because it was developed as a vehicle for understanding child development in the context of exclusive mother care. How so?

The test being used isn't valid. Some researchers maintain that the Strange Situation is invalid for infants with experience in child care—that they may be more accustomed to strange places and strange people and thus might react a bit differently to the lab procedure than do home-reared babies.[28] For example, if a baby's mother generally leaves five days a week and doesn't come back for eight or nine hours, but in the laboratory test she leaves, comes back, leaves, and comes back again, the baby is likely to react with particular confusion, as in: What's going on here?

The conclusions are flawed. What Strange Situation studies don't do is follow babies with day-care experience over time, to determine whether they in fact turn out more aggressive or more impulsive or less compliant. Researchers have simply projected that link, based on previous research on home-reared children. Are these infants necessarily "at risk"? Does an insecure attachment to a *working* mother predict later problems? Not necessarily, according to the research.

At least one study, conducted in 1985,[29] did track "insecurely attached" infants with full-time, employed mothers through early childhood and found the insecure attachment "rating" didn't correlate with later behavioral problems. What does that mean? It means the model may not hold up for the children of working mothers.

Putting the emphasis on 20-hour absences as a threshold is arbitrary. What troubles me most about the Belsky controversy is that mothers might read these numbers literally, surmising that a 20-hour work schedule is the optimal work schedule. In fact, no one has established a direct, linear link between work hours and infant attachment. And no one, not even Belsky, presumes to say that a 20-hour schedule is better than, say, a 25-hour schedule. In truth, 20 hours is somewhat arbitrary.

Says Belsky, "Twenty hours was the cutoff you could make in the evidence. Is it 20 versus 22? Is it 15? I can't say. I can say that at some point more hours become more risky. And less hours become less risky."

The focus is too narrow. Most researchers agree that there are many factors involved in determining if an infant is securely attached; boiling it down to whether a mother is employed is hopelessly reductive. "It's too simplistic," says T. Berry Brazelton. "There are many too many variables that Belsky left out." What the mounting evidence fails to take into account is the quality of the child-care arrangements, when these children entered care, and whether they had more than one child-care arrangement. We know nothing about their personalities, their mothers (other than their employment status), their fathers, or their circumstances (other than their social class).

Since 1988, when the Attachment Debate reached its apex and an entire issue of the scholarly journal *The Early Childhood Research Quarterly* was devoted to the subject, the dust has settled. Most researchers have come around to the view, based on several published analyses of numerous studies, that an infant with a full-time working mother is about 6 to 8 percent more likely to be insecurely attached than the infant of a nonworking mother.[30] But the question that lingers is: Why?

What Conclusions Can We Draw?

Why are some infants with working mothers securely attached while others are not? Is it a matter of when a baby begins care? Does it depend on the child care itself? Does it relate to the amount of time the child spends with Mom or in day care? Or with Dad? (In one of Belsky's studies, all seven of the infants in a father's care emerged securely attached to both Mom and Dad.) Or does it depend on a multitude of factors? These, of course, are some of the questions the NICHD study proposes to answer. We'll have to wait for those findings, but here is what the existing research tells us about some of the factors that appear to come into play:

The longer a mother's work hours, the greater the likelihood of an attachment problem. Most attachment studies show little or no difference between attachment ratings when comparing home-reared babies with those in part-time care. But long work hours, particularly beyond 40 hours a week, may pose a problem. That is, in fact, one of the few areas of the research in which there is a near consensus. In a 1988 study, psychologists Margaret Tresch Owen and Martha J. Cox found that mothers who worked long hours—more than 40 a week—during their child's infancy were more anxious than those who worked fewer hours and more likely to have insecurely attached babies.[31] Numerous studies tell us that mothers experience different amounts of stress, anxiety, and guilt about leaving their babies (a subject addressed in the next chapter). And there's general agreement that those who feel less guilt, less anxiety, and less stress are better able to foster secure attachments in their babies.

It appears that infants learn how to adapt to separations by experiencing regular, moderate separations. One 1984 study found that infants have the most difficulty separating from their mothers—evidenced by showing more distress at separation—if they've experienced either *exclusive* mother care or *extensive* separations. This research tells us that "secure attachment and moderate separation experience both contributed independently to the capacity to cope with separation during the second year."[32]

Indeed, much of the research supports the view that the mother-infant relationship can tolerate moderate absences—even up to 35 hours a week. It tells us that even when a mother works more than 35 hours a week, in most cases her baby's going to be securely attached.

Infants who are well taken care of—regardless of who's providing the care—are more likely to be securely attached. One study of low-income mothers and their babies implicates the quality of child care as the critical factor in promoting infant-mother attachment. The study's results were dramatic: 75 percent of the babies with "excellent" child-care histories—babies in stable, high-quality care—were securely attached to their mothers, while only 38 percent of the babies in extremely poor child care—characterized by abuse and neglect—were securely attached.[33]

The child's temperament may be a factor in how easily he forms a secure attachment. Some babies appear to be more resilient than others, more capable of adapting to new people and a variety of child-care arrangements. Psychologists believe that some babies are less open to forming secure attachments, precisely because they're less easily soothed and comforted; they may be particularly sensitive to light, sound, and touch, preconditions that make the job of "nurturing" that much harder.

Some research suggests that boys, who mature at a slower rate than girls, are more prone to insecure attachments and more sensitive to child-care changes. See the box for a review of Rita Benn's studies on boys and working mothers.

Attachment, Boys, and Working Mothers

Are boys with working mothers more prone to insecure attachments? And if so, what makes a difference? In 1986, psychologist Rita Benn published a study in which she explored these issues.[34] She looked to the personalities and what she calls the "underlying emotional states" of 30 highly educated, employed mothers for a clue to the key that unlocks secure attachment. All these mothers returned to work sometime during the first year of their baby's life and worked at least 30 hours a week.

For any mother trying to work and raise baby boys, Benn's findings are interesting. She found that "highly integrated mothers were significantly more likely to have securely attached sons than were poorly integrated mothers, whose sons, in contrast, displayed insecure attachment."

What is a highly integrated mother? One who is relaxed,

warm, and sensitive to the child's needs and handles daily separations with care. One who views the substitute caregiver as an accessory, not as a replacement figure, and has "ongoing communication" with the caregiver. One who views her work life not as defining her self-worth or as critical to her identity but as a way to expand herself. An "integrated" mother, in Benn's view, may experience some ambivalence, some anxieties over separations, and some conflicts over her dual role as mother and worker, but that ambivalence is not so frustrating, so disabling that it impedes her ability to select good care, deal sensitively with her baby, or communicate with the caregivers.

The good news here is that you don't have to be a perfect working mother—just a good enough working mother. Even mothers who were rated "ambivalent" and "frustrated" fell into the securely attached group. It's worth mentioning, too, that a smaller preliminary study by the same author did not find the same correlation between maternal integration and secure attachments in daughters.

The problem with studying the effects of child care on infants is that no one really knows what the threshold for quality is. How do infants fare when the child care is merely adequate? What if they have healthy, secure attachments to both parents but experience mediocre child care? What if the child care is great but there are stresses at home? One thing is clear: The single most important measure of high-quality infant care is the degree to which caregivers, whether in family day care, center care, or in-home care, are able to foster healthy, secure attachments.

Does all this mean one-on-one care—by a sitter or nanny—is the best form of child care? Not necessarily. At least one Strange Situation study, published in 1987, looked exclusively at children cared for by in-home sitters. Researchers in Chicago studied 110 infants and their middle-class mothers, who worked full time, part time, or not at all during their infants' first year. All the infants in child care were with in-home sitters, and although no attempt was made to objectively evaluate the quality of care, most of the mothers "expressed satisfaction with the quality of care." (You'll recall from chapter two that satisfaction is not considered a particularly reliable gauge of quality.) Although more than half (53 percent) of the mothers who worked full time had securely attached infants, there were still significantly more insecure attachments among full-time working moms than among part-time working moms or moms at home.[35]

***

Knowing what we do know about infant day care—and it isn't a lot—is it a risky business? Ultimately, Jay Belsky provides the best answer to that question: "The real risk of early and extensive [day] care as we know it in this country," he says, "is when risks accumulate. We get unstable care, turnover in care givers, poorly paid care givers who are unresponsive and impatient. We get parents who are exhausted at the end of the day who have no wherewithal to care sensitively for their kids. We have employers who have no tolerance for the fact that their employees are parents, too."[36]

In taking the issue beyond attachment, Belsky offers the best summary of the problems facing working parents with babies, all of which are reviewed in the next chapter.

CHAPTER FIVE

Mothers, Infants, and Child Care: The Reality

I t is foolish to imagine that, somehow, we can extricate the subject of a new baby's well-being from the feelings, the actions, and the reactions of his or her mother. For a time, babies and mothers are like one and the same, adrift in the fog, the blur, the limbo between reality and unreality that Louise Erdrich captures so well in a personal journal published in *Harper's*:

> One reason there is not a great deal written about what it is like to be the mother of a new infant is that there is rarely a moment to think of anything else besides that infant's needs. Endless time with a small baby is spent asking *What do you want? What do you want?* The sounds of her unhappiness range from mild yodeling to extended bawls. *What do you want?* Our baby's cries are not monotonous. They seem quite purposeful, though hard to describe. They are a language that changes every week, one that is so primal that the meaning I gather is physical. I do what she "tells" me to do—feed, burp, change, amuse, distract, hold, look at, help to sleep, reassure—without consciously choosing to do it. I take her instructions without translating her meaning into words but simply bypassing straight to action. Until I've satisfied her need, my brain is a white blur. I lose track of what I've been doing, where I've been, who I am.[1]

I interviewed five new mothers during, and following, their maternity leaves and spoke with many more about their past experiences as new mothers. Consider some of their comments: "I had no idea how much separation anxiety I was going to feel when I went back to work," says a mother who took a four-month leave before returning, part time, to her former job. "I cried every day when I left. It took me about a month to get over it," says another, who spent the better part of her disability leave worrying about when and whether to go back to work. "I was kind of like Murphy Brown. I had no idea how I was going to feel until I had this baby. Some days I wonder how anyone else could possibly take care of her when I go back to work; some days I say to myself, 'I gotta get out of here.' I feel incredibly isolated." Says another, who went back to work and left her daughter in the care of her own mother, "I have never been so depressed in my life. The first weeks were absolute hell. I cried all the time." And a second-time mother, with a month left of her leave, a 50-hour-a-week job looming ahead, and the experience of having been through it before under her belt, says, "It's harder this time. Every day I ask myself, How can I do this? How can I leave her?" Every day.

About midway through my research for this book, my friend Olga came to visit from Italy, and with her she brought her four-month-old baby. She was aglow. "This is the most wonderful experience I have ever had in my life," she said. In several months, she said, she would go back to work, but she'd be taking the baby with her. All was right in Olga's world. I couldn't help but feel that Olga, living in a culture that genuinely values motherhood, had an edge over her American sisters, and that gave her baby an edge as well.

We know that if there's one thing babies need, it's relaxed care, free of anxiety and stress. In Europe, where *paid* parental leaves stretch anywhere from four months to a year, attitudes are different. There are no mixed messages; no inherent conflicts (go to work for your own sake; stay at home for the baby's sake). The attitude seems to be: Well, perhaps she'll go back to work, but what's the rush? There is important work going on at home. There is a new citizen among us.

Contrast that attitude with some of the experiences working mothers shared with me: Not long after her return to work, the mother of a seven-month-old and a four-year-old was called into her boss's office. A lawyer employed by the federal government, she was called to the carpet for leaving the office too early—early meaning 6:30 P.M., after a ten-hour day. Her boss advised her to get a nanny and scrap the family day-care provider she'd hired, despite the fact that her first child had been cared for by this provider, with whom she had a long-standing, trusted relationship. Another woman had a boss who had demanded she come back to work after eight weeks, despite the fact that she was eligible for three months off under the Family and Medical Leave Act. Caught between her career and her baby, she was anguishing over whether to quit her job "in a few months" and go back home. Would she ever work again if she stopped now? she wondered. Would the baby be okay if she kept working? She found herself weighing her entire future against her baby's well-being. If she had been permitted by our culture to linger for just a few more months in the limbo of new motherhood, these issues might well have resolved themselves.

Consider the case of a woman I'll call Rebecca, a corporate middle manager who lives in suburban Virginia. She and her husband both work for a major telecommunications company, a company that sends out news releases about its progressive family-friendly policies, a company that I cited in an earlier book as one of the best companies in America for parents. She asked that I not print her name or that of her employer. I interviewed Rebecca four times, during and following her 12-week maternity leave.

When we first spoke, her daughter was only eight weeks old and Rebecca was wrestling with her first child-care decision; she opted for in-home care and was about to interview, long distance from Europe, the au pair who was scheduled to arrive in a few weeks. The baby, she said, was doing fine. But she was torn, conflicted over the decision to go back; she was restless, not used to the isolation that came with new motherhood in her suburban apartment complex. The week she went back to work, her company sent out a letter to all its employees. They were expected to put in not 40 but 50 hours a week. Was she not eligible for all those part-time return options, extended parental-leave programs, and sabbaticals with health benefits that were touted by the company? "That's at headquarters," she told me. "In Virginia it's up to the individual supervisor."

When I spoke with her a third time, the stress was getting to her. Her husband was working a 65-hour week, she was putting in 50 hours, and both were feeling as if this wasn't the best arrangement for the baby. The au pair, however, was working out fine. It was their sheer absence that troubled the couple. By the time her daughter was eight months old, Rebecca had quit her job. The baby, it seems, was not doing well. "The pediatrician says she's not gaining weight fast enough," said Rebecca. "I'm the only one who can get her to eat enough. She's very active. She won't stop to eat." Child care was not the problem. Rebecca was too stressed out, and her baby, for whatever reason, was not adapting well to the situation. Rebecca describes her first eight months of motherhood as "a rollercoaster ride." How much time off does she think mothers should be allowed? A year, she says.

While Rebecca's case may not be typical, it may not be atypical. She had the advantage of a full three months at home—although she spent a good deal of that time tortured over whether to go back to work. But the stresses placed on her by this "family-friendly" company—and, she says, by the conflict between her expectations and reality—undermined her ability to balance her baby's needs against her employer's demands. If she had been able to work part time, she says, she would have done so.

American mothers, I found in more than one case, are set up by their own unrealistic expectations of motherhood and misconceptions about what their families are really going to need—ample time off, some degree of job flexibility, and, following that, child care they can trust. "Before I had my first child, I didn't have any idea what it would mean to have a baby," says the mother of two children, ages six and three, looking back. "Frankly, I thought you have a kid and three weeks later you can put it in a day-care center. This wasn't a philosophical point of view; it's just to say I didn't know. But as soon as I had this baby, I was quickly disabused of that notion."

During the early weeks of a baby's life, child-care decisions are made under enormous pressure. Forget about stability. All the first-time parents I interviewed for this book, with the exception of one couple who split the child care between them, either scrapped their original child-care arrangements (made before the baby's birth) or changed the arrangements during the first year of their child's life. While that's hardly a representative sample, the research confirms the fact that most parents must look and look and look before they find care that's acceptable; and many must make unanticipated changes because of flaws in their original choices. Says one mother, "Parents have no idea how to find child care. It's not in our repertoire. You're just relieved to find *something*."

Parental Leave: How Much Time Is Enough Time?

The sad truth is that for the typical working mother, the prospect of taking six months, four months, or even three months off is hopelessly unrealistic. Most working mothers are ineligible for coverage under the new Family and Medical Leave Act, which allows up to three months' unpaid parental leave for parents whose employers have 50 or more employees. Only 40 to 50 percent of American workers fall into that category, and many of them can't afford to take three months off without pay. Most parents who work for major employers are eligible for a six-week disability leave; some are able to craft a leave of up to three months by combining personal time off, sick days, and vacation days. According to research conducted by the U.S. Small Business

Administration, most mothers who work for small companies are granted time off—but it's generally unpaid and of variable length.[2]

The standard paid leave in the U.S. today for employees covered by disability insurance is six weeks. It's a rare mother who delivers or adopts a baby, then turns around six weeks later perfectly comfortable with the prospect of handing that baby over to someone else for the better part of every working day.

Surveys show that most new mothers aren't physically ready to go back to work for at least three months and aren't emotionally ready for six months.[3] Certainly by the fourth month, if they've gone through labor and delivery, most mothers are physically back on their feet. And after four months they've gotten a good, healthy dose of motherhood; they've had some time to get their baby over the rough spots, the colicky months, the sleepless months. By four months many mothers are ready and willing to share baby care with someone else. But six months, they say, would be even better. Who knows better than mothers—mothers who have been through it—what the optimal maternity leave should be?

At six weeks most babies are still lingering between the half-sleep of the uterus and an awareness of reality. A lot happens between the ages of 6 weeks and, say, 16 weeks. But ask a mother when her baby rolled over, smiled, nodded her head, or grasped an object, and, like as not, she's forgotten, because babies change every day, but so unremittingly slowly and quietly and subtly that many of the most honest people I know label infant care, in a word, tedious. Newborn babies are quite endearing but not terribly charming. That comes with time. At around eight weeks most babies begin to smile, and not long afterward their personalities surface and they begin to connect with people around them.

By four months they are with us: They don't just smile; they coo, gurgle, and chortle, and they smile at *you*. They recognize people around them; they know Mom and Dad; and their own personalities have begun to surface. Their senses are more integrated. Some babies, though not all, are sleeping through the night at four months. Most have fallen into an easy, though not immutable, routine. "Around four months is when, all of a sudden, they come alive," says Amy Voorhes, describing her own four-month-old, her second child. "Until then, you're really hanging in there because of maternal responsibility. But all of a sudden, boom. They start giggling, and they smile. He's really fun."

From a mother's standpoint, four months seems reasonable as a minimal leave. At four months, first-time mothers are just beginning to recover from the shock of recognizing that they are responsible for this new being, from the sleeplessness, and from the process of learning to nurse, to diaper, to comfort, to be there round-the-clock for this incredibly demanding, albeit lovable, little creature.

Six weeks' disability leave is just that: a disability leave. It is set according to medical standards regarding how long it takes a birth mother to recover, physically, from child birth. But it doesn't take the baby into account, or the emotional needs of new parents. The truth of the matter is this: Six weeks is not enough time for new mothers to get in sync with their babies, for babies to get to know their mothers, for both parents to adjust to the changes in their lives. One 1985 study found that even "mothers of four-month-old infants, whether the mothers are employed or not, feel somewhat depressed and overwhelmed."[4] Another study, of mothers with 12-month-olds, found that those who worked were more dissatisfied than those at home—surprising findings, given that working mothers, in general, tend to be more satisfied than nonworking mothers.[5] Perhaps the first year is the most difficult for working moms. After all, this is not an easy process. Becoming a parent is a disorienting experience.

What about fathers? Unfortunately, in America today, parental leave really means maternity leave. Most fathers take virtually no time off—on average five to six personal, sick, or vacation days—to be with their new babies, which sets the stage for a future in which most fathers, according to the research, "assume essentially no responsibility for their child's care and rearing."[6]

In our society, although the media makes much of the new nurturing father, fathers are expected to remain aloof from child-rearing responsibilities. Joseph Pleck of the Center for Research on Women at Wellesley College provides this collection of comments from men, discussing attitudes about parental-leave programs at their companies: "There's something in the corporate culture that says to men, 'Don't do it.'" . . . "There was nothing in the policy that said men could not take the leave, but there was an unwritten rule that men do not do it." . . . "At a number of companies, there's a joke—'Sure, we have parental leave, and the first guy who uses it will have an arrow in his back.'"[7]

Working parents are expected to put jobs first, children second. People at child-care referral services report that parents often aren't allowed time off to visit child-care centers. Parents tell me that even in so-called family-friendly companies, their supervisors frown on employees' taking advantage of work-from-home days or part-time-return options. According to the Families and Work Institute, "at one of the most progressive U.S. companies, 52 percent of employees reported that they believed taking advantage of the company's time and leave programs would jeopardize their jobs and careers."[8] So much for the family-supportive workplace.

Anyone who's followed the parental-leave debate knows that ours is the stingiest parental-leave policy in the industrialized world. "For us to congratulate ourselves on a 12-week unpaid leave is tragic," says Edward Zigler of Yale University. "The way to quit congratulating ourselves is to remember that Haiti has a 12-week paid leave. We are the only industrialized nation who does not have a paid leave [policy]."

Why? The obvious reason is that as a culture we value the needs of business over the needs of babies and their parents, a point well argued by Penelope Leach in her book *Children First*. The biggest argument against paid leave comes from the business community, which maintains it can't afford it. Period. There seems to be a lingering notion that women will grab the money, take the time off, and then quit their jobs. But that's not what's happening. That's not the reality. The reality is that women *are* going back to work. And studies show that women who are given more time off rather than less, women who have understanding employers rather than stingy ones, do go back to work happier and stay in their jobs longer than those employed by less flexible companies.[9] Any business major can tell you that.

During the formulation of the Family and Medical Leave Act, T. Berry Brazelton, an outspoken proponent of enlightened leave policies, backed off from his proposal for a four-month leave, which he felt was the minimal leave necessary to accommodate mother and baby. Brazelton believes that four months gives the baby enough time to form a relationship with his mother; that at four months babies are capable of some degree of autonomy. "We had to water it down to three months," he says, calling a four-month leave "dreamy" for both parents and child. "But the way things go in this country, everybody suffers too much from being a parent." The compromise (a three-month leave), he says, was justified by the fact that this is a *parental* leave—a leave for which both parents are eligible; the idea being that to maximize the benefit, mothers and fathers would each take three months back to back, thus giving new parents a total of six months at home. That's the idea, anyway. Whether the concept will translate into reality remains to be seen.

The caregivers I interviewed felt that while babies adapt well to most child-care settings, many mothers have trouble letting go. And the research on maternal separation anxiety suggests it's harder for some mothers than others; those who feel confident and comfortable with child care are more apt to have securely attached babies. Says Anne Durso, director of a Washington, D.C., day-care program, "On the first day at the [day-care] center, when an older child arrives, that child is going to be crying when the parents leave. But when it's infant care, the parent is going to be crying." If returning to work in the early months of a child's life makes a mother feel anxious, stressed, or depressed, there's ample evidence that babies can pick up on these signals.

I don't want to make mothers feel guilty when they have to go back to work. Nor do I want to suggest that women are somehow incapacitated by giving birth. I took on a 30-hour work schedule when my first child was three months old and a 30-hour work-from-home schedule when my second child was six weeks old. But in both cases I had an extraordinary amount of flexibility; in the latter, going to work meant simply moving from one room in my house to another. Based on the experiences of the mothers I've interviewed over the past five years, a regular full-time, out-of-home schedule after six weeks for both parents borders on the absurd. It is simply too stressful for everyone involved.

Babies need low-stress environments; on that just about everyone from molecular biologists to developmental psychologists agrees. The people I've interviewed whose leaves went most smoothly, who suffered the least stress, seemed to have four things in common:

- They took enough time off—anywhere from four to eight months.
- Their husbands took significant time off; some were home full time, and some took two or three days off a week for up to five months.
- They were not conflicted about going back to work; they felt confident about their decision.
- They could afford—and found—high-quality care.
- Finally, they had easy babies. The easier the baby, the easier the process. And that's something no one can predict or control.

If I could create an ideal workable model for parental leaves, it would be four months' paid leave with the option of a part-time return at least up to the six-month mark. That would enable mothers to ease back into work, and babies to ease into child care.

But we don't live in anything remotely resembling an ideal world. A realistic leave, one at which businesses wouldn't balk, would involve at least three months of paid leave, with the stipulation that whenever possible, both parents would take leave; single parents would be granted up to four months off, with pay and continued benefits coverage. That would enable, as Brazelton suggests, couples to piggyback their leaves. Why? First, to maximize the time babies have with their parents. But just as important, to reduce stress on the mother—because, in truth, it can be hard for new mothers to leave their babies in the hands of a stranger. This not-so-radical approach would enable the child to establish a relationship with each parent, enable the father to become more involved with the child early in the process, and take the stigma of parental leave off the backs of women alone. Keep in mind, too, that many family day-care providers and day-care centers will not take infants under three months old.

In an ideal world, any new parent should have the option of a part-time return to work for the first year, if not for the first three years, of a child's life. It sounds positively radical, but IBM has just such a policy in place, with the guarantee of job seniority upon return; AT&T allows up to 18 months, with benefits and a job guarantee. Yet in a culture where we value our current productivity more than our future productivity, profits more than people, these policies represent the exception rather than the rule.

But What About the Baby?

It may be that "children who are placed in child care at the height of attachment formation (6 to 18 months) may be more disrupted by the placement than are children placed in child care at either an earlier or later point in time," write psychologist Tiffany Field and her colleagues, expressing the closest thing to a consensus in the field of child development on the question of when mothers should—and shouldn't—return to work.[10] That insight is based on theory, not research findings. Given all the variables involved, the research itself has yet to determine the optimal age for a mother's return to work—from a baby's standpoint.

Given everything we think we know about attachment, most child-rearing experts advise mothers to stay home during the first year of a child's life. But in fact, when infants are a year old, they are at the peak of separation anxiety. It may well be the worst time to introduce child care—if "child care" means the sudden introduction of a new and unfamiliar person or place.

As I mentioned in chapter four, in her 1984 book, *Mother Care/Other Care*, Sandra Scarr, a psychologist from the University of Virginia, broke with tradition when she advised new mothers to return to work before their babies reach the age of six months. Recognizing the same stages of development to which her colleagues subscribe, Scarr imposed a healthy dose of common sense and maternal experience on the discussion when she wrote, "One needs to be philosophical about primate separation anxiety unless one wants the baby's company twenty-four hours a day for the half-year from eight to about fifteen months."[11] Her advice, based on attachment theory, empirical evidence, and studies done in the 1970s, is this: Introduce care before a baby reaches the six-month mark, when separation anxiety sets in.

Numerous people I interviewed, including child-care providers and parents, felt that the worst time to introduce care or change child care was during the second half of the first year, when separation becomes an issue. Ironically, the one-year mark, when some child-care centers routinely move children from infant to toddler rooms, may be the most sensitive period of all.

Laura Hubert, a woman with 25 years of child-care experience and head of the infant/toddler room at Broadcasters' Day Care Center, reputed to be one of the finest centers in Washington, D.C., tells me that all infants, no matter when they enter care, still go through separation anxiety at nine or ten months. "Even kids who've been here for three months start getting fussy when they say good-bye at about nine to ten months," she says. "But if a kid comes to the center at nine or ten months, they really explode." Especially, she says, if they've already been in another child-care situation.

Maryanne Lazarchick, a family day-care provider with 22 years of experience whom I introduced in chapter three, suggests that introducing care at or following the six-month mark is asking for trouble. "The most difficult time is somewhere between six months and one year old," she says. "I know all the books say keep a child home until they're six months. But then you're going to get them right during that separation-anxiety time. I had a child who was six and a half months when she started. She cried and cried and cried. It went on for months. Now she's eight years old. She still comes here. Her mother and I laugh about it now. But I'd say children adjust better if they get here before six months."

Dr. Robert Emde, a psychiatrist at the University of Colorado Medical School and president of the World Association for Infant Psychiatry, agrees: "The research supports the view that under ideal circumstances . . . one should not introduce a major change like [child care] between 6 and 18 months."

There's no evidence that returning to work when a child reaches 8 months, a year, or 16 months is harmful—just that it may be more difficult for the child to adapt. Given that, the operative rule for new parents should be: Stay home as long as you can, but be mindful of the fact that introducing care before the six-month mark may make the transition easier for everyone involved.

Getting Beyond the Notion of Exclusive Mother Care

Lest we assume that full-time, exclusive mother care is somehow the natural and perhaps even the only good approach to child rearing, we should consider these cross-cultural studies: One survey of 186 nonindustrial societies found that exclusive, one-on-one child rearing by the mother is "rare." Some other caregiver is present in 40 percent of these societies during infancy and in 80 percent during early childhood.[12]

Consider the Australian aborigines, whose babies are left with babysitters while the mothers go out into the fields each day. Or the Éfe in Zaire, whose child care is shared among a group of mothers who breast-feed a variety of babies. These infants might be passed from hand to hand six to nine times *an hour.* Or the

Polynesian tribe that considers fathers "inept" until an infant learns to walk or crawl, at which point "the father begins child care as a matter of course." After a year, children go to work with their parents—boys with the father, girls with the mother. Then there's the African !Kung tribe, in which mother and child are "virtually inseparable" for the first four years of life. Mothers "carry their children constantly" while they gather food.

There's no evidence that babies are damaged in any way by any of these approaches. According to the psychologists who conducted these studies, all of these approaches work; the babies grow up to be healthy, productive members of their respective societies.[13]

What have we to learn from these tribal cultures? After all, we live in an advanced, enlightened society, one that offers not one but two theoretical child-rearing models (although in actuality there are many more options): If mothers can afford to, they may stay home and raise their babies in near-isolation, watching over them and offering them all manner of stimulating activities—the approach recommended by most baby books. If they can't afford to stay home, they are generally expected to go back to work within weeks of their baby's birth and stay far from home for 40 or more hours a week, thereby spending little time with their babies during the workweek—an approach often, but not always, dictated by the American economy and the American workplace. They are forced to look for child care in a culture that has yet to catch up with their needs. And if mothers look to the father for help, they find that he is under even more pressure than they are to stay away from home.

Certainly these approaches are not optimal for babies or mothers—or fathers, for that matter. I'd imagine that an anthropologist studying our culture might muse over the fact that most parents prefer arrangements that fall between those extremes—a fact reflected in public opinion polls. They might muse as well over the fact that our ideals as a culture—our belief in the importance of exclusive mother care—are hopelessly out of sync with the reality of most American parents. And they might surmise that when it comes to child rearing, ours is a culture in conflict.

When babies are born, they don't know whether they're !Kungs, aborigines, or the children of middle-class Americans with a $150,000 mortgage and two jobs to go back to. Babies should be open, you would think, to just about any child-rearing practice our culture might have to offer. What do we know that might help us develop a working model that's good for them?

Infants and Group Care

We take it as a given that one-on-one care, in the form of mother care, is the optimal arrangement for children from infancy through toddlerhood. But the assumption that babies need isolated, focused attention all day long is just that—an assumption. Many second, third, and fourth children do just fine in the group situation that is their own family. They may even profit from the experience by becoming less self-centered, more empathetic, more independent, and more outgoing. Family day-care providers who care for one infant along with three or four small children say the older children are drawn to the baby and vice versa. Young kids get a quick lesson in sensitivity; the babies, as they become toddlers, learn from the older children. In fact, some of the best centers in the country have experimented quite successfully with mixed-aged groups of kids ranging from seven weeks to 24 months.

Janet Mann, an assistant professor of psychology at Georgetown University who teaches a course on attachment, bemoans our cultural bias toward one-on-one infant care. She calls the idea that mothers should be home all day stimulating their babies "absurd": "We've been extremely myopic as a culture. We focus so much on individual infants. Babies develop a view that the world focuses on themselves and their needs. They're not reared to be as responsive to others as they could be."

Says Tiffany Field of the University of Miami, "Our society is very strange. In most societies children are exposed to an extensive network of children and adults. It's only in the Western cultures that one even thinks of children staying with only the mother all day. There's nothing biologically mandated about having this kind of one-on-one care."

You'll recall Field's studies from chapter three. At her three day-care centers at the University of Miami, Field and her colleagues take pulse rates to search for signs of stress in infants—and have found no such signs. According to Field's studies, the more extensive an infant's day-care experience is, the better; those who enter her centers before the age of six months and stay on full time are enriched rather than disabled by the experience. Field's findings tell us that infants can and do thrive in high-quality day-care centers, particularly if the care arrangement is kept stable over time. In fact, on some measures, her full-timers do better than part-timers. As for attachment, in one study she compared preschoolers who had entered these programs before and after the age of six months—either full time or part time. She found no differences in "attachment behavior and sociability" between preschool children who had started day care earlier versus later.[14]

But the day-care programs at the University of Miami are among the best in America. Generalizing those findings in today's day-care market may be a risky business. Unfortunately, while studies tell us that early, extensive experience in *high-quality center care* can promote healthy development, studies of children with early, extensive experience in more typical day-care settings tell us that it may be problematic: The more years in care, the more hours spent there per day, the earlier an infant enrolls, the greater the likelihood of a problem.

The quality of group care is a major issue. But stability—not over months but over years—may be just as critical a factor. A study conducted in the 1980s by Wendy Goldberg of the University of California at Irvine and M. A. Easterbrooks of Tufts University looked at a mother's work hours, the stability of child care, and the timing of a mother's return to work (during the first or second half of the baby's first year) in relation to how well-adjusted 75 children appeared in toddlerhood and again in kindergarten. They found that toddlers whose mothers returned to work before the age of six months were more likely to have at least one insecure attachment—to mother or father—*unless they had a stable child-care history.*[15] A 1990 study of 835 kindergartners from urban, suburban, and rural schools with a variety of different child-care histories (part-time, full-time, and interrupted or uninterrupted care of various types) found the two groups that were least aggressive in kindergarten were home-reared kids and kids in an uninterrupted, full-time child-care situation from infancy. They also found no significant differences in intellectual or social development between home-reared children and those who entered group care during the first year of life. Continuity, it appears, makes a big difference.[16]

Infants in Center Care

I spent a morning watching 18 infants and toddlers at an extraordinarily well-run program in Washington, D.C. It has all the earmarks of quality day care. Caregivers are obviously well trained, and with a ratio of one adult to every three children there are plenty of them to go around. They are as quick to respond to a baby's cries as they are to "moo" and "coo" in response to a toddler's first stabs at words; they laugh and talk during lunch.

The space was designed for infant and toddler care, with carpeted, interconnected rooms, all visible through carpeted dividers that are no more than a foot high. The toddler "graduates" of the infant room can visit their old friends and old caregivers anytime. Nearby is a changing space with a sink for the mandatory hand-washing after every change. Both rooms connect to a kitchen that leads to a nap room, where babies sleep uninterrupted.

The systems work. An intercom in the nap room alerts caregivers to a waking baby. I witnessed the changing of the guard, as new caregivers came in for the afternoon shift; it was smooth, with a nice long overlap of staffers. During one of my visits, a baby had an asthma attack (he later turned out to be allergic to the rubber in the roll-around mats that line the floor). Calmly and quickly, the head caregiver got the program director, who called the baby's parents and emergency help. The ambulance was there within five minutes. On another occasion a caregiver noticed that a fussy baby had a rash on her stomach; within 15 minutes the baby's mother was there to confer with the staff and call the doctor.

I saw toddlers—over 12 months but under 18 months old—hugging one another, rolling about, watching each other. They were absorbed in the moment, reading a book in a caregiver's arms, tinkering with a toy telephone, playing peek-a-boo. They gathered for a group sing-along, although those who wished to play and wander did so—rolling around in the empty plastic swimming pool, climbing up and down the stack of rubber mats, tossing scores of bright blue foam rubber balls that fill the room.

As the toddlers made merry, the infants—children under a year old—were in another world. I watched a six-month-old who spent a good 30 minutes entertaining himself: lying on his back on a big, cushy blue mat and playing with a rattle toy; squealing with delight; turning on his tummy to gaze into the big mirror on one wall—entertainment in itself. This kid was having a great time. "A good day," said a caregiver. Yesterday, she reported, he was fussy all day long, but today he had a "nice quiet bottle" and a long nap in the morning, "and he's been happy all day." The babies at the center are alternately fed, sung to, engaged, hugged, pacified, and held. Some are alert, watching all that's going on around them; others are less so.

The dynamics of the place change by the minute—because at any given moment these adults are reacting to the babies. The dialogue among caregivers goes something like this: "Would you change her?" "Grab her, she's about to fall." "Simon, if you want a toy, you have to wait your turn. Let's find something else to play with." "Would you get him out of that seat? He needs some attention." "Somebody's waking up!" "He's really cranky today. I think he's coming down with something." "Jim's having a great day—look at him, just playing by himself." "I think she's teething." "Will you get her pacifier?"

This is individualized care in a group setting, and it's sometimes soothing, sometimes chaotic, but an extraordinarily demanding job for the six caregivers. Quiet time came after a walk in the park and after lunch, when most of the toddlers settled down for naps. The lights went down and soft music went on. Those who couldn't fall asleep in bed just rested or fell asleep in a caregiver's arms.

I watched the babies, the little ones, with interest. One four-month-old captured my attention. He spent much of the morning sitting in an infant seat, watching the world. "That's what he likes best," said Mary, in whose care he spent most of the morning. Mary, a substitute, would probably spend only a few weeks at the center. That seems problematic—if, indeed, this thing called attachment is such a crucial issue. The baby was expressionless, observant, still. At one point late in the morning, another caregiver picked him up and laid him across her legs. She tickled his tummy and spoke to him in a high, soft voice. The child lit up. He smiled, he looked at her, and he seemed to come alive, as if waking from a long stupor.

Some people in the field of child development believe that infants under 12 months in group care are somehow diminished. T. Berry Brazelton shares disturbing observations of infants in group care in his book *Touchpoints:* "[Babies] seem to cut down on the intensity of their interactions during the day. They play, but not as vigorously as they would with their parents. They nap but don't sleep as deeply. They store up their powerful reactions for the reunion at the end of the day. When the parent looms into sight, the baby often pointedly turns away, as if to master the intensity of her feelings at the waited-for reunion with this all-important person."[17]

For years, Amy Dombro, now an author and researcher with the Families and Work Institute, headed up the infant room at the Bank Street College day-care program, reputedly one of the best in the country and the training ground for some of the top people in the child-care field. What's her read on infant care? "I've seen babies who just kind of thrived," she says. "And I've seen babies who, when you see them at day care and see them at home, they're two very different people. . . . If you looked at them in day care, you'd say they're doing fine. But they are kind of dampened. Their energy level and enthusiasm are much higher at home. At the end of the day, when their parents arrive, it's like the baby's emotional temperature goes up a couple of degrees." Dombro believes such behavior depends on the baby. Brazelton appears to feel otherwise, saying, "I think it shows how vulnerable the infant is. They have to work very hard to protect themselves in a situation they're not quite sure of."

When I asked two prominent researchers—Tiffany Field of the University of Miami and Carollee Howes of U.C.L.A.—about Brazelton's observations, they came back with the same reply: "I think it's Brazelton's bias coming through. He does not do research on infants in group care," said Howes. "There is no research to support that view," said Field.

It may be that Dombro is right: that some babies are better suited to group care than others and some babies adapt more easily than others. If, indeed, that is the case, it makes sense for parents to stay home as long as possible—at least four months—to allow their babies' personalities to begin to emerge, to get to know their babies well enough to best judge how they may react to group care.

Is One-on-One Home Care Best for Infants?

Is in-home care by a nanny, sitter, or au pair, then, a better option than group care? That may be a moot point, given that the price puts it out of reach of most American parents. The research on quality suggests that in-home care—particularly by a friend, neighbor, or relative—is no better than other forms of child care. Yet there are few studies of in-home care; and no one has really explored the impact on an infant of losing a trusted caregiver. For those who believe attachment to a primary caregiver is crucial, one-on-one care, by a sitter, au pair, or qualified nanny, offers obvious advantages. "It may be that the needs of infants are different from the needs of toddlers and preschoolers in terms of ratios," says Deborah Vandell, a psychologist at the University of Wisconsin. Vandell believes that the 12-month mark is a kind of watershed and that the research is insufficient to draw simple conclusions.

The caveats for in-home care are these: The turnover rates offer little guarantee of stability, and most in-home caregivers tend to come from the ranks of the less educated. The Chicago Study, cited in chapter two, pointed out the need, early on, for some kind of preschool program in combination with in-home care; otherwise it appears that children as young as two do not get the cognitive and language stimulation they need. Vandell points out that by "two and a half or three, centers are probably, as a rule, providing more interesting places for children to be."

Child-care researchers need to use caregivers too. What do they do? Vandell, for one, chose the following for her own daughter: one-on-one care up to the age of 12 months (during which time Vandell, a university professor, had a fairly flexible schedule), followed by a shared-care arrangement with another child (one sitter, two children), ultimately combined with a morning pre-school program (starting at about age two).

What about Robert Karen, clinical psychologist, believer in attachment and author of the 1994 book *Becoming Attached*? In his book he describes the arrangements he and his wife, Thaleia, used for their first child: Thaleia, an architect, stayed home full time for the first year; she had the help of a part-time sitter who, reportedly, "took [their son] out of the house for several hours each day" as well as "frequent help from me," writes Karen. Following that, "Thaleia was more than eager to resume work, although she was prepared to adjust her hours, depending on the baby's reaction. When she started working about twenty-five hours a week at the beginning of the second year, we increased the hours of the sitter, who had become a valued person to the baby, not to mention us."[18] Karen adds that the couple "probably will not consider group care until sometime in the third year."

What's the Best Child Care for Infants?

Who's right? Robert Karen, who thinks mothers should spend the better part of a baby's first year at home? Tiffany Field, whose research tells her babies can and do thrive in group care? Deborah Vandell, who finds the research on infants and group care inconclusive and opts for one-on-one care during the first year? T. Berry Brazelton, who says a parent should stay home at least four months—a year if possible? Sandra Scarr, who says go back to work before the six-month mark? The best approach depends on what you believe about infants, mothers, and child care based on your interpretation of the research summarized here and on what you can realistically do. Given that, I have to agree with the working mother who advised, simply, "Stay home as long as you can and then find the best child care you can."

Behavioral psychologists used to warn parents not to "give in" and respond every time a baby cried; the crying would worsen, they argued, because infants would "learn" that crying was the best way to get attention. The behavioral approach has fallen out of favor and has been replaced by a recognition that responding to a baby's cries is the best way to raise a healthy baby. In the old days, "spare the rod and spoil the child" was the operative principle. But recent research belies the wisdom of such an approach; routine physical punishment, we now know, breeds anger and resentment in our children.

I half suspect that as our understanding of infant development grows, our love affair with attachment theory—and, by inference, the necessity of near-exclusive mother care for the first three years of life—will come to an end. We will undoubtedly muse at our limited knowledge about the issues at hand. But I strongly suspect, too, that we will look back 50 years from now in shock at employment policies that allowed infants, mothers, and fathers virtually no time off to spend with one another and policies that bowed only superficially to the need for parental involvement in child rearing.

***

Parents clearly care more deeply about their children than does even the most extraordinary caregiver. Caregivers are not parent substitutes. Supplemental care—be it family day care, in-home care, relative care, or center care—is just that: a complement, a support, an extension of the family. Viewed in that light, it stands to reason that parents must give this relationship room and time to grow, from infancy on.

Make no mistake about it: Raising children requires a good deal of on-the-job training, an enormous emotional investment, and time—which must be carved out somehow, some way, by working parents. Of all the variables that determine whether our kids are all right, the single most important one is the parents—regardless of how much or what form of child care they use. That is the subject to which the next chapter is devoted.

CHAPTER SIX

How Our Work Lives Affect Our Kids

hild care is woven into the fabric of our children's lives. My four-year-old is as likely to visit a friend's house with a sitter present as with a mother present; he has as many friends from his after-school day-care program as from our neighborhood; and when we make plans to get him together with friends, as often as not we're talking with a father or a babysitter. A walk around our block at 5:30 in the afternoon yields images that illustrate the degree to which our family lives have changed over the past 20 years.

Groups of babysitters linger on front stoops, snuggling infants and watching preschoolers, awaiting parents' arrival home at the end of the day. At one corner three fathers watch their three toddler sons in a front yard, waiting for three young mothers to come home from work. Snakelike, a chain of children holding on to a long rope makes its way down the block, from the neighborhood park to the nearby day-care center. I pass a nine-year-old, just home from his after-school program, with his older brother, who cares for himself every day after school. I am one of his neighborhood checkpoints. And, of course, I pass homes where mothers have been home much of the day caring for their young kids. None of these arrangements stands out as the exception or the rule. Diversity, the buzzword of our times, is the order of the day.

Child care is so much a part of our lives that raising the question, Should mothers of young children work? seems patently absurd. Yet to address the central question posed by this book—are our kids all right?—I feel compelled to raise the question that lies behind the day-care debate and the attachment controversy: By working, does a mother somehow hurt her children? Not surprisingly, that question has not gone unexplored in the field of social science research.

The Mother Studies

Forget everything you've read about the impact of bad day care on children or the importance of attachment to child development. Forget what Penelope Leach or Burton White has to say about when and how much a mother should work. Then consider this statement made in the summary chapter of *Maternal Employment and Children's Development: Longitudinal Research*, a scholarly book published in 1988 and devoted exclusively to analyzing what impact a mother's employment has on children's intellectual, emotional, and social development. "Across studies, the overwhelming finding obtained was that maternal employment status *per se* was not significantly related to children's development . . . [An] impressive array of findings across a broad spectrum of developmental domains and at ages ranging from infancy through adolescence shows that there are no detrimental effects associated with maternal employment *per se*."[1]

What does this *per se* mean, hanging there so equivocally and with such obvious deliberateness? It means that children can do fine without exclusive mother care. Working creates problems for the kids only if and when it creates problems for the family.

The research to date (1988 is considered quite up-to-date in the world of academia) has uncovered no earth-shattering negative effects—or positive effects, for that matter—on kids growing up in families with a mother who works. A mother's employment status doesn't make her kids more or less secure, more or less emotionally stable. It doesn't make them more or less liberated, more or less sociable, or more or less rebellious.

The Role of Home Influences

Generally, researchers have found that in families in which mothers work, *home* influences are as important as, if not more important than, child-care influences; and in such families, a mother's influence is far less pervasive than it is among home-reared kids. What matters is how a number of factors interact, including:

- income and education level of the parents
- the character of the home environment, particularly as reflected in the child-rearing styles of the parents
- the extent to which parents are present and involved, regardless of their employment status
- when (meaning how early in her child's life), how much (meaning how many hours), and why a mother works, including the mother's attitude about working and the extent to which she communicates anxiety or confidence, distress or satisfaction to her children
- the extent to which the parents' awareness and concern are reflected in their child-care decisions
- the quality of child care, particularly as reflected in the sensitivity and professionalism of the caregiver
- the child's age, temperament, even sex—a subject discussed in chapter three
- last but not least: the extent to which the father is supportive and involved

Given all that, the research has raised a couple of red flags:

The case for reasonable work hours. Not surprisingly, workaholism does not appear to be compatible with parenthood. According to a comprehensive review of the research by Lois Hoffman of the University of Michigan, working long hours—meaning more than 40 hours a week—seems to be associated with lower achievement in kindergarten—although employment itself is "not related."[2] And studies have linked extensive work hours to adjustment measures among school-age kids.[3] These findings are particularly troubling in a culture that still measures job commitment by a time clock, and one in which the workweek is growing.

Numerous parents I interviewed felt pressured to stay at work after six o'clock or to attend early-morning meetings. Says one working mother, a graphic designer who lives in Boston, "People who aren't parents really don't understand when you can't make it to a meeting until 9 A.M." Reformers have called for "core business hours" that mirror the typical school day, giving working parents—who make up 38 percent of the American labor force—more flexibility. In *The Best Jobs in America for Parents*, Lynn Hayes and I recommend that schools routinely open 30 minutes before area businesses, a practice that is remarkably uncommon and could go a long way toward easing the stress on working families.

The case for long leaves and part-time returns in infancy. The attachment studies, of course, provide a fairly strong case for reduced work schedules during infancy. One study of working mothers, conducted by Margaret Tresch Owen and Martha J. Cox and described in chapter four, is of particular interest because it suggests a link between a mother's anxiety, long hours, and insecure attachments. It begs the conclusion that insecure attachments don't result from the *baby's* inability to adjust but the *mother's* inability to adjust—a subtle but important distinction. For all the reasons outlined in the preceding chapters, establishing reasonable leave policies is the crucial first step in accommodating the needs of working families.

It's fair to suspect, then, that long work hours—more than 40 hours a week—may be incompatible with parenthood and that full-time work can get in the way of baby raising, at least during the early months of life. But beyond that, the links between a mother's employment status and child development are fairly insubstantial. This flies in the face of conventional wisdom; it flies in the face of everything we believe, as a culture, about how children should be raised. It seems to contradict much of the research on children and child care and on attachment. Or does it?

The maternal employment studies reviewed in this chapter are not studies of young children and child care; they are studies of children and mothers, studies that attempt to measure the meaning of a mother's absences and the full weight of her presence. They are not attachment studies, which attempt predictions about how children will turn out; they are, in many cases, long-range studies that measure how children *do* turn out when their mothers work during infancy, the preschool years, or the school years.

What these studies tell us is that many working parents are able to carve out time for their kids, and many parents do manage to find child care that accommodates their children's needs; and for many mothers, working is the best option for any number of reasons—including financial reasons. For some, the stresses of being home full time would be greater than the stress of balancing two roles. And for many families, a second income is not merely nice but necessary. It may enhance the lives of their children.

Researchers from California State University and the University of California who followed a group of 130 children from infancy up to age seven found no significant differences in cognitive, social, academic, and behavioral development among children whose mothers did or didn't work during any stage of the children's growth, including infancy. They concluded that the quality of the home environment was a far more important determinant of how children turned out than whether the mother worked.[4]

At least three studies published in 1988 found no significant differences in the cognitive, language, and intellectual development of children from preschool through the early school years based on whether their mothers were employed.[5]

When comparing children with working mothers and mothers at home, other studies have found no differences in school motivation, academic performance in the early school years, problem solving in toddlerhood, emotional expressiveness in kindergarten, behavioral adjustment at ages four through seven, or attachment in infancy, kindergarten, or the preschool years.[6]

The longitudinal studies have not found any significant "sleeper effects"—effects of a mother's employment early in a child's life that show up later in the child's development.

How Working Parents Compensate

One reason such differences don't show up, I think, is that most working parents compensate for their absences in many ways, as much evidence indicates. The truth is, most American parents are well aware that infants and young children need special care. Even in an era when most mothers with preschool-age kids work, most such kids in two-parent families are cared for primarily by their parents.

Consider these numbers: According to U.S. Census data, among married couples with preschoolers, 57 percent are families with both parents in the labor force. But in only about one-third (36 percent) of those cases are both parents working a full-time day job. In most cases at least one parent is working a nonday shift, part-time hours, or a seasonal job, or working from home full time, part time, or during odd hours, which allows that parent to be with the kids. *Among more than half of these couples (53 percent), either the father, the mother, or both work a nonday shift.*[7] That fact alone suggests to me that parents are making every effort to accommodate their family's needs—both financial and emotional.

It's clear that working parents compensate for their absence in numerous other ways as well:

- When they're not at work, working mothers make time with their children a high priority. Obviously, working mothers spend less time with their young children than do those who stay home. They spend about half as much focused time with their children as nonemployed mothers, but still spend twice as much as fathers (employed or not).[8] Numerous studies indicate that working mothers try to make up for the time gap by "setting aside time to be with their children and by planning activities for them."[9] Working mothers, particularly those who are highly educated, compensate by creating more focused time with their kids and cutting back on other activities—such as leisure time and sleep, according to one report.[10]

- Parents are having fewer children and spacing them further apart. In fact, children today get more attention from their parents than they did two decades ago, due simply to the fact that there are fewer of them.[11] Given that, for an increasing number of families group child care has become a child's social world, replacing the neighborhood and other siblings; it's the place where kids get to be with other kids.

- Father care is on the rise. Increasingly, men are taking a more active role in child rearing, filling in when mothers are at work. The biggest change in child-care arrangements recorded in the 1991 U.S. Census reports was "a substantial increase in the fathers caring for kids." Says Martin O'Connell, chief of the Fertility Statistics Branch of the U.S. Census Bureau, "There's a shifting of child-care arrangements for preschoolers out of family day care and into care at home, principally by the father." The numbers show an increase in the number of preschoolers in "father care," from about 15 percent in 1988 to 20 percent in 1991. That's no blip. Nor is it a trend driven entirely by economics. "It cuts across all types of employment status," says O'Connell.[12]

Are Working Parents Neglectful?

Are working parents a bunch of "yuppies" using kiddie kennels, as Amitai Etzioni suggests in his book *The Spirit of Community: Rights, Responsibilities and the Communitarian Agenda*? That's not what I found. I found families pushing the envelope to make ends meet, grappling with a child-care system that has yet to catch up with their needs, and juggling their schedules to accommodate their children's needs.

Consider a handful of middle-class families I encountered in a single subdivision in suburban Virginia. They included a couple who split shifts—she worked days, he worked nights, both operating in a state of perpetual exhaustion; a family day-care provider who would prefer part-time work but could not get it and so devoted her days, reluctantly, to caring for several other children along with her own; a woman who worked nights, out of an in-home office, so she could spend her days taking care of her kids—a setup she described as stressful; another family day-care provider who quit her office job because her daughter was beaten in child care; and the young woman I call Rebecca (introduced in chapter five), who quit her job when her daughter was eight months old because her employer expected not 40 but 50 hours of her time each week.

All these parents felt strongly that their children needed them at home, at least part of the time. All were disappointed with the child care they'd encountered or child care as they imagined it. All of these mothers wanted part-time or flexible job opportunities outside the home but could not get them. And all these families needed a second income.

These mothers were disturbed by the options available to them and to their children. They seemed somehow caught in limbo between the 1950s and the 1990s. The inadequacy of our child-care system reinforced their belief that they needed to be home, putting pressure on them to work and raise their children simultaneously.

Given all this, it's not surprising that parents at all income levels are scrambling for ways to combine work and home, scrambling for ways to compensate. Consider these examples:

- Between 1989 and 1993, the number of adults working from home increased from 26.8 million to 41.1 million. According to Link Resources, a New York–based consulting firm, most U.S. telecommuters—people who work from home but are on a company payroll—are people in two-income families, and roughly half have children living at home.[13]

- The number of U.S. businesses owned by women "soared" between 1977 and 1987. As of 1987, according to one report, women owned 30 percent of all businesses in this country. Ninety percent were sole proprietorships with few or no employees, and nearly four out of ten had total receipts of less than $5,000.[14] I think it's safe to assume that a good number of these women are carving out a niche for themselves while trying to raise their kids.

- At least in the corporate world, job flexibility is on the rise, although it's still relatively uncommon. In 1993, Catalyst, the New York–based nonprofit research and consulting firm specializing in women's issues, found that flexible arrangements, a relatively new phenomenon in 1989, lasted an average of five years. Of the 70 companies surveyed, more than one-third noted increased interest in and use of flexible arrangements and had 100 or more employees using such arrangements—including job sharing, part-time work, and working from home. Although women still dominate the flexible workplace, 61 percent of the companies reported men using flexible schedules.[15]

Flexibility seems to relieve the stress that comes with working parenthood. And for working families, stress is no small issue. When the Families and Work Institute asked kids what changes they'd like to see in their parents' work lives, they didn't say they wanted "more time" with their parents. They said they wanted their parents to be less stressed when they came home.[16] The National Study of the Changing Workforce, a survey of 3,400 working people conducted by the Families and Work Institute, reported that "families tend to bear the brunt of work-family conflicts" and that there was "more than three times as much 'job to home' spillover as 'home to job' spillover." In other words, working parents bring more work-related stress home than vice versa.[17]

Money Matters

An argument I heard again and again while researching this book was this: As a culture, our priorities are askew. Our values are bankrupt. We should stop worrying about making money and start worrying about our kids. Yet the research tells us that income creates opportunities for children and that most working mothers (about two-thirds) work out of financial need. If a mother's income enables her to feed and clothe her family, who can argue with that? What if it allows a family to purchase a home, save for college tuition, take a vacation, pay for private school, afford a great summer camp, or buy a sailboat? At what point does income become an indulgence? It's clear that in many cases a mother's employment enhances rather than diminishes the lives of her children.

Long-term studies of the children of working mothers that take into account many factors, such as the mother's education, income, and attitudes, indicate that whether a mother works outside the home is not the primary or even the most significant factor in how well-adjusted a child turns out to be. The truth is, children whose parents make more money, are better educated, and create a healthy, happy, supportive home environment seem to outperform other children on measures of intellectual, social, and emotional development *regardless of whether the mother is employed*. Nevertheless, many American mothers feel ambivalent, even guilty, about the fact that they work.

Ambivalence and Working Mothers

"When my first daughter was born, I took a ten-week leave," said a woman I interviewed whom I'll call Nancy Lundgren. "When I went back to work, I was sort of depressed. I missed her. I worried about her." That was in 1977. Lundgren was something of a pioneer, a woman who, if she had become a mother ten years earlier, would have stayed home.

Lundgren practiced law for nine years after her daughter's birth. Then, when her third child was three, she elected to stay home. Looking back, she muses at the difficulties she faced while she was working. She was the first female lawyer at her New York law firm to take a maternity leave: "No one at the office ever asked about the baby; no one sent me flowers at the hospital; no one even asked whether I'd had a boy or a girl."

She was astonished, she says, to find that her husband didn't share her concerns about the baby, her conflicted feelings. "I was calling home two or three times a day," says Lundgren. "One day I asked my husband, 'Why don't you ever call home?' He said, 'Because I know she's well taken care of.' The truth is, he never had these feelings. He left in the morning, and he never thought about that child again until he came home at night." But she had "these feelings"—worry and guilt—in spades. "A working woman feels guilty when she's away from her baby," she says. "A working man feels guilty when he's away from his work."

Guilt. Ambivalence. Angst, worry, conflict. These are feelings that plague many working mothers. They couldn't be more real. Is it that we buy into what we've been taught—that we are needed at home, that we are the center of our children's universe, that they will suffer without us? Or are these feelings just part of what it means to be a mother?

At a recent conference on children and learning disabilities, a kindergarten teacher told me about a little girl who she suspected had a learning disability: "I had a conference with her parents last week. Before we could even address the issue at hand, I had to spend 15 minutes trying to convince the mother that this wasn't because of something she had done wrong." Every mother knows that feeling. We blame ourselves for imperfections in our children because we live in a culture that assumes that how a mother handles any given situation will determine how a child responds—an attitude driven home by most child-rearing books.

Where these feelings come from and how to cope with them are not the subjects of this book. These concerns have been amply explored in a vast body of literature on working mothers, on feminism, and on motherhood in America, including the classic *For Her Own Good: 150 Years of Experts' Advice to Women*, by Barbara Ehrenreich and Deirdre English (1978), *Juggling*, by Fay Crosby (1991), *The Crisis of the Working Mother*, by Barbara Berg (1986), *Remaking Motherhood*, by Anita Shreve (1987), *Inventing Motherhood: The Consequences of an Ideal*, by Ann Dally (1982), *A Lesser Life*, by Sylvia Ann Hewlett (1986), and, more recently, Melinda Marshall's *Good Enough Mothers* (1993).

But it's impossible for me to write a book about working parents and their children without addressing the subject of Motherhood, as an ideal and a reality, and how a working mother's attitudes, as they reflect the conflicts between our beliefs and reality, can and do affect her children.

Despite the fact that women are working in record numbers, we haven't come very far in addressing our own ambivalence about it. "To be utterly torn between mothering and working . . . is the *norm* for the current generation of women," writes Melinda Marshall in *Good Enough Mothers*. Born in 1961, Marshall was a teenager when Nancy Lundgren gave birth to her first child and rushed back to work. And so the torch is passed from one generation to the next, evidence that this conflict between work and home, between motherhood and livelihood, is still very much with us.

We know full well where the roots of all this ambivalence lie. On the one hand, mothers must and do work; on the other hand, many mothers suspect they are doing a disservice to their children. Unfortunately, our experiences with mediocre child care only serve to reinforce those feelings.

The Press: Feeding Our Ambivalence

We don't read front-page articles about happy working mothers and their happy kids. We don't see stories about great child-care programs. Rather, we read about cases of abuse and neglect. The average person never sees all the research that indicates there's no difference between the children of working mothers and the children of nonworking mothers, because studies like those don't make for particularly exciting reading—a point amplified and exhaustively documented by Susan Faludi in her landmark book, *Backlash*. As Faludi points out, Jay Belsky's research suggesting that the infants of working mothers are "at risk" got plenty of press play; but his detractors and the studies that contradict that view got next to none.

Researcher Tiffany Field of the University of Miami recounts the tale of a conference on infants and day care held in Washington, D.C., around the same time as the Belsky brouhaha. Almost every speaker at the symposium presented positive findings on the effects of day care on infants. "But the next day in the *Washington Post* the headline said something about how infants may be harmed by day care," says Field. "I think the media contribute enormously to the problem."

Mothers, of course, are not immune to the impact of this bad press. And few women are immune to the mixed messages of our culture, the catch-22 of modern motherhood: Interesting women work; working mothers hurt their kids. Over the past five years, in the course of researching this book and another, I have interviewed scores of working mothers. I know that this conflict between work and home is the central issue of many women's lives. It seems to me—from what I've seen, from my research, and from what I read—that some degree of ambivalence infects most mothers. That ambivalence runs the gamut from concern, which seems healthy, to deep conflict, which is certainly unhealthy.

And attitudes are infectious. They affect our kids; they affect our relationship with other parents; and they affect our perceptions of other people's children. Work, for American women, has become the measure of our self-esteem. But even so, mothers who work full time, nonstop, are often viewed with a kind of disdain, as if they are neglecting their responsibility to their children, as if they are inflicting harm.

Kathleen McCartney and Deborah Phillips, two noted researchers in the field of child development, write, "Most mothers are not familiar with the scientific evidence [that contradicts the necessity of exclusive mother care]. . . . Rather they are familiar

147

with the advice from friends, family, and 'experts,' all of which reflects beliefs of the larger culture and most of which promotes conflict between working outside the home and motherhood. . . . Ironically, in contemporary American society, women feel pressure both to stay at home and raise their children *and* to enter the labor force." Employed mothers, maintain the authors, are split into two selves: "One self believes that a happy mother who works outside the home is better than a resentful mother who stays home. A second self believes or at least fears that one's work somehow hurts one's child."[18]

Imagine the burden that would be lifted from the shoulders of working mothers if our society made a genuine effort to improve child care, if we acknowledged a mother's right to work by investing in the systems that will support that right.

Exclusive Mother Care: What's Wrong With It?

I always clip stories from the newspaper on Mother's Day. It's the one day when the press steps back and considers what Motherhood—in its latest incarnation—means to us now. On May 8, 1994, I clipped a piece from the editorial page of the *New York Times* entitled "Do You Work? Are You Guilty?," by Susanna Rodell. She argues that in her case working was better for her four kids than staying home. Put on the defensive by a fresh round of apparent "attacks" on working parents in the spring of 1994—the publication of Penelope Leach's stay-at-home tract, *Children First*, the Carnegie Corporation report on the negative effects of infant day care, and the Families and Work Institute's "startling" findings on the poor quality of family day care in America—she writes:

> Indeed, the most damage I did to any of my kids was during a period, shortly after graduating from college, when I was briefly swayed by the Leach Theory and stayed at home for some months with my first daughter. She was (of course) a bright child; she

became my Project. I bombarded her with flashcards, organized activities for her, and was generally so obnoxious that, after learning to read at 3, she subsequently refused to read for nearly five years. (She's 18 now; she still can't spell.)[19]

What's wrong with the home-rearing model? What's wrong with exclusive mother care? Nothing, provided that's where Mom is and wants to be, provided she's good at the job of child rearing. But if she's not, exclusive mother care isn't going to be good for her or for her child. In America today, a full-time stay-at-home Mom is likely to have near-exclusive control over the rearing of her child, a point raised by Ann Dally in *Inventing Motherhood: The Consequences of an Ideal.* Entire days may pass when not only does she not see another adult but her child may not see another adult. As a mother I have always felt that it's unhealthy and unnatural for a single individual to have so much influence over another's development—particularly within the isolating context of American life. Full-time mothering *is* a big job; it should be reserved for people who are particularly well suited to child rearing. Some mothers are; some aren't.

The research, by and large, has confirmed what common sense tells us: Mothers who prefer working should work. But surveys also tell us that most working mothers (about two-thirds) are not working for self-fulfillment or because of personal preference; they *have* to work. Many would prefer to be home.

How a Mother's Feelings About Working Affect Her Children

Back in 1981, when I was working as a speechwriter, my first and at that time only child was three and enrolled in a top-notch day-care program. (Any parents who have found good center care will tell you that aside from their child's college years, the period from age three to five was the easiest of their working lives.) I was earning more money than I had ever earned in my life, I was happy with the work, and although I've never been immune to guilt, I would undoubtedly have scored pretty low on an ambivalence scale. Everything was going fine.

At a desk outside my office sat a woman I'll call Pam. Just about every morning she came into work depressed and upset, often recounting some tale about dropping off her kids at day care. The mother of three, she'd recently returned to work because her husband, an air traffic controller, was on strike. Although she didn't know it at the time, he was about to be laid off by the Reagan administration. Before the strike, she'd been a full-time mom; now she was the sole supporter of her family. But she knew exactly where she wanted to be: at home. I can remember her decrying the horrors of day care. As I recall, she didn't mince words. "My children need me at home," she said. "That's where we belong."

Our situations and our perceptions of our situations couldn't have been more different. Pam had several kids, and she felt strongly that they needed her at home. I had one, and I felt just as strongly that my working was the right thing for me and for him. Not long ago, researchers began to recognize that lumping us together as working mothers in order to compare the differences between our children and those of at-home moms made no sense. In her heart, in her attitudes, Pam was really a stay-at-home mom. Not only did she want to be home but she felt it was important for her children that she be home. I, on the other hand, preferred working and felt my son was perfectly fine in his day-care program.

It wasn't until researchers began making that distinction between a woman's work preferences and work status that some genuine insights into the impact of maternal employment on kids began to emerge.

One of the first such studies, published in 1980 by Anita Farel, looked at kindergartners and their mothers, exploring the impact on a child's development not of a mother's work status but of her work preferences. Children with working mothers, whether or not the mother preferred to be home, didn't appear to suffer any ill effects. Indeed, only one group of children appeared to suffer:

those whose mothers stayed home but wanted to work. Farel found that "children of mothers who are at home but wish they were working score significantly lower on certain measures of competence and adjustment than children of mothers who work but wish they were at home."[20]

These were important findings because, in effect, they gave ambitious, high-achieving mothers—mothers who might be frustrated or, as Susanna Rodell suggests, a bit overbearing at home—society's permission to go to work and offered reassurance to mothers who must work that everything would be all right. Farel's findings have appeared again and again, often in books that address the subject of a working mother's guilt.

Since then, numerous researchers have explored the idea of how and whether a working mother's attitudes affect her children: the impact of a working mother's anxiety, guilt, ambivalence, and something called role strain—the stress of trying to be both mother and employee. Some studies suggest that ambivalence has no negative impact on kids; in fact, it may make working mothers compensate admirably—even overcompensate—for their absences. Others suggest that a mother's attitudes, negative or positive, have far more impact on kids if she's home with them full time. A dissatisfied at-home mom may be far more dangerous than a dissatisfied working mom. Those studies that look exclusively at working parents have found, not surprisingly, that the most poorly adjusted children are those with dissatisfied working mothers and the best-adjusted children are those with satisfied *working* moms—parents who have positive attitudes about their work and their children.[21]

Here are the results of a few of the most recent studies:

Role satisfaction. In a longitudinal study conducted at California State University and the University of California that followed a group of children from infancy through age seven, researchers found that mothers who were less stressed and more satisfied with their dual roles reported fewer behavior problems among their kids in kindergarten and grade school; their kids had more interest in school, more motivation, and higher levels of academic achievement. Satisfied working mothers are likely to be more involved with their kids and, interestingly, are likely to have more kids than their dissatisfied counterparts.

One caveat here: Any study that relates role satisfaction to a child's temperament seems to raise a chicken-and-egg question. In a review of the research, Lois Hoffman of the University of Michigan reminds us that it's hard to tell whether a mother is satisfied with her role(s) because the children are doing fine or the children are doing fine because the mother is satisfied with her role(s).[22]

Role strain. Researchers have also found that role strain, here defined as the overload of doing two jobs, was unrelated to how kids turned out. But women who had more supports, such as household help and good child care; fewer preschoolers in the family; or job flexibility or part-time jobs are more likely to feel less conflicted and less stressed.

Depression. In a mother, depression is unquestionably hazardous to young children. A depressed mom who's at home is going to be more detrimental to a child's development than a stressed-out or depressed working mom. The at-home mother, after all, has almost sole control over her children's day; whereas ideally the children of a working mother would spend the better part of their day in the care of someone who genuinely enjoys caring for children.

Studies tell us that infants with depressed mothers are less animated and tend not to develop particularly well. Studies of toddlers with depressed moms show that these children are less able to sit down and focus on a task because their mothers are less able to do so.[23] Researchers continue to find that at-home mothers who would prefer to be employed are more prone to stress and depression than other mothers. According to a review of the research by Lois Hoffman of the University of Michigan, at least one study of mothers with infants confirmed that finding and, curiously, found that "employed mothers who preferred nonemployment obtained the lowest depression scores."[24]

Ambivalence About Child Care Makes It Tough for Young Kids

People in the field of child care maintain that the single most important determinant of how well a child adjusts to high-quality child care is the parent's attitudes about child care itself. Says Gail Solit, a day-care director who's been in the business for 20 years, "Aside from exceptional cases, like a special needs child, the most likely reason why kids don't do well in child care is because the parents are ambivalent about it or someone—one parent or a grandparent—doesn't want the child to be in child care. If the parent has a lot of guilt, it comes through to the child. The child doesn't trust the place because the parent doesn't trust the place. That's assuming that we're talking about good child-care programs."

"Ambivalence—I can pick it up on a tour of the center," says Neesy DeCherney, owner/operator of Little Folks Too in Wilmington, Delaware. "[Ambivalent parents] ask a lot of negative questions. You can see immediately that they have no faith in the operation." DeCherney runs a unique operation. Located downtown and catering to lawyers and other professionals, the center keeps its doors open all day long. Nursing mothers wander in and out. Parents often join their children for lunch. DeCherney's basic philosophy is that her center is designed for children *and* parents. "These people are very involved with their kids," she says.

But she has little patience with parents who are outwardly ambivalent, because "they're going to pass that attitude right on to the kid. They're going to be draped over the kid, weeping, when they say good-bye. They're going to make an issue out of everything: 'He has a bump on him. Do you know where he got that scratch? He didn't finish the bottle—was he distracted? Was something wrong?'" DeCherney tells such parents, up front, that group care may not be the situation for them; she asks them to go home and think about it. "These women really didn't expect to have to work. I tell them to wake up or take their anger someplace else."

Working Mothers as Role Models

Does having a working mother make daughters more ambitious, sons less traditional in their views of women? Does it promote changing views of men and women? Contrary to popular belief, having a working mother does not necessarily make a daughter more career-oriented or a son more egalitarian.

Kyle Pruett of the Yale Child Study Center has done longitudinal studies of children in homes in which the father is the primary caregiver. Curiously, says Pruett, when these young children were asked to draw pictures of their families, they drew "Dad with a briefcase going off to work, when often he did not even own one, or Mother cooking dinner, when she had not done so for years." Why? Because all the messages these children receive from the outside world are, according to Pruett, "so powerful as to eclipse the portrayal of the real details of these children's lives."[25] Working parents can't change the world; the world has to do the changing.

Given that, what does the research tell us about a mother's work and shifting attitudes about sex roles in kids?

- For girls, ambition and achievement tend to be related to a mother's education, not her employment status. In other words, educated mothers tend to raise ambitious, achievement-oriented daughters, whether or not the mother works.[26]
- When mothers work long, hard hours, daughters are less likely to plan to work or want to work.[27] One study found that the more hours a mother worked during the preschool years, the less likely it was that her daughter would want to work when she grew up.[28]
- Mothers who prefer to work, who would work even if they didn't need the money, are more likely to have daughters who plan to work.[29]
- Many psychologists now believe that children's attitudes about sex roles may have more to do with their father's attitudes and behavior than their mother's. One study found that the more nontraditional a mother's attitudes about work-

ing, the more likely it was that her daughter would expect to work and that she would expect to have fewer children. The impact of a father's attitudes were far more interesting: Daughters with nontraditional fathers not only expected to work but expected to have more children, meaning they were more optimistic about the possibility of balancing home and work.[30]

- The research suggests that parents have little influence over a boy's attitudes about sex roles; boys tend to be more influenced by society as a whole.[31]

- Some studies, however, do confirm the assumption that boys and girls raised by working mothers have "less sex-stereotyped expectations and attitudes."[32] Whether or not their personal goals reflect their parents' work choices, they are more fluid in their attitudes about men and women.

Maybe having a working mother, in and of itself, doesn't determine a child's attitudes or aspirations. As with everything else related to a child's attitudes about goals and roles, many factors are involved. One of those factors will, naturally, be whether having a working mother is a positive or negative experience for the child.

Take the case of a 40-year-old woman I'll call Ellen. Her mother was a teacher, and in the 1950s Ellen was in a large family day-care home in California from the age of 18 months until she entered kindergarten. "I hated it," she says. She remembers having to take a nap in the provider's upstairs bedroom every day, although she could never sleep. "It was a huge double bed," she says. "I can remember just lying there perfectly still—she wouldn't let me move. She was very strict. If I moved, I knew I would be punished." Ellen thinks there were about 20 other kids in care, and there was only one adult—a situation that would be illegal today. "We were pretty much on our own," she recalls. She maintains that the experience made her more independent but less secure. "Basically, all my life I have always felt I was alone."

Where's Ellen now? Although she has a law degree, for now she's home with her preschool-age children. "I want to be home with them, and I think my experience in child care is one of the reasons," she says.

Are Working Parents Indulgent?

Parenting styles do matter. And psychologists have come up with a fairly consistent working model for what makes a parent effective and able to raise a healthy, well-adjusted child. Basically, the model centers around how a parent establishes and maintains authority. Successful parents, be they men or women, are affectionate and firm; they set clear limits and maintain them without being rejecting or overly punitive (i.e., authoritarian). The prevailing view is that permissive parents, who are unable to consistently set limits, or authoritarian parents, who rule with an iron hand and may be almost hypercritical, overcontrolling, and rejecting, breed children who range from unmanageable to downright hostile.

A number of people I interviewed for this book, including caregivers, mental health professionals, and researchers in the field, suggested that too often working parents may err on the side of permissiveness. That stands to reason. It may be difficult to set limits when you're hell-bent on having happy, "quality" time with your kids. Better to give in, a parent might think, than create a fuss.

At least one study suggests that working parents are less likely to be effective and affectionate than are parents in families in which one spouse is at home. A study that looked at the impact of maternal employment on a group of Michigan children, first in toddlerhood and then in kindergarten, found that employed mothers were "less likely than nonemployed mothers to hold child-rearing attitudes that emphasized warmth and firm control" and that the fathers with employed wives were "more likely to feel annoyed and concerned about their children and display less behavioral sensitivity" during a lab test.[33]

Working has an impact on children if it interferes with a

parent's ability to be loving and firm—a subject that's discussed in more detail in Part II of this book.

Mom Time vs. Dad Time

Employed mothers may feel guilty about their absences; when surveyed, most say they want more time with their kids. Are children feeling this time gap? Consider these results from the 1991 National Survey of Children and Parents, conducted by the bipartisan National Commission on Children:[34]

- Among children of working mothers, overall, fewer than one-fifth wanted more time with their mothers (20 percent of those whose mothers worked 35 to 40 hours a week and 17 percent of those whose mothers worked 41 or more hours a week, compared to 15 percent of those whose mothers were not employed). Very few children (5 to 8 percent) felt their mothers missed important events "a lot."

- In contrast, children's feelings about their fathers' absences are striking, suggesting that the father time gap is a much bigger problem than the mother time gap. Almost one out of every three children (30 percent) would like more time with their father.

- Fathers were more likely to miss special events, more likely to be absent longer, less likely to have attended a PTA meeting or helped out with a field trip or special project, and, most important, less likely to be living with their own children.

- One out of every two fathers surveyed, compared to one out of every eight mothers, reported that they "routinely work more than 40 hours a week."

A Father's Involvement: What Difference Does It Make?

The biggest difference between the studies on fathers and those on mothers is that there are significantly fewer of the former. In the opening to *The Father's Role: Applied Perspectives*, written less than a decade ago, Michael Lamb bemoans the lack of research on the role of fathers in child development, noting that it's a field in which "rhetoric continues to outpace serious analysis."[35]

We all know what the rhetoric says. The new father is more involved with child rearing, more nurturing, more conflicted over commitments at work and home. Yet the research tells us that whether or not the mother is employed, it is she who takes primary responsibility for the children; she who spends not just more time but *significantly* more time tending to home and hearth. Despite polls that suggest that men want to cut back on work hours and take on flexible schedules, most men can't and don't. Whatever changes employed women have wrought, men still see their role primarily as breadwinner; women still see their role primarily as, well, worker and mom.

This is nothing new. Across cultures, even those in which mothers do not take exclusive care of their children, it's rare for men to be actively involved in child rearing. According to one major survey of world cultures, in only 4 percent of the societies "was a 'regular close relationship' apparent between fathers and infants, and in only 9 percent between fathers and young children."[36]

It's been argued, most notably in Arlie Hochschild's *The Second Shift*, that men in two-income households do not do enough—enough child care or enough housework. That indisputable fact was driven home in the Families and Work Institute's 1993 National Study of the Changing Workforce. Even in families in which women contribute 50 percent or more of the family income, women still do most of the cooking, cleaning, and shopping. Oddly, 43 percent of men reported taking on an equal share of the household responsibilities but only 19 percent of women believed that to be the case. As for child rearing, 71 percent of the women surveyed "reported taking the major responsibility for their children as compared to five percent of men."

If fathers aren't doing the child rearing, it's not because they aren't capable. In fact, the studies on father care are far less confusing and complex than those focusing on mothers or on child care. They are almost universally positive. They tell us:

Children raised in nontraditional families, where the father is the primary caregiver, not only do well but do terrifically well. In fact, the authors of these overwhelmingly positive studies seem to have to restrain themselves from saying that these kids do better than kids raised exclusively in the care of their mother. It stands to reason that these kids are better off. Fathers are just as capable as mothers, and kids in father care are almost guaranteed to get attention from *both* parents since the mothers usually stay involved. In contrast, children who are cared for primarily by their mothers often lose out on attention from that second parent.[37]

It appears that men's instinct for raising babies is about the same as women's. Men are just as competent at responding to infants' needs, reading their signals, and caring for and comforting them. Yet researchers estimate that American fathers spend as little as "less than a minute per day" to "slightly more than an hour per day" in "direct contact" with their babies.[38] While in general fathers in two-income families spend more time with their children, fathers of infants appear to be less involved. Some psychologists speculate that fathers are squeezed out during nonwork hours by mothers who are trying to squeeze in quality time.

In general, there appear to be some consistent differences between "male" and "female" child-rearing styles. Men are generally more playful, more physical, more outward in their approach. Kids tend to have more fun with their fathers than with their mothers, but that may simply be a reflection of cultural roles. Child rearing is a mother's work, a father's play—even, it appears, in nontraditional families.

Men appear to be more aware of gender differences. A whole series of studies suggest that men are more devoted to their sons than to their daughters, warier than women of "feminine" behavior in their boys, and more likely to treat boys and girls differently. However, much of this information is outdated, and attitudes may well be changing.

The inescapable conclusion reached by most people who study the differences between mother care and father care is that fathers are just as capable as mothers; that "parenting," if you will, is an acquired skill. The more time a mother spends with her kids, the better she gets at it. The same holds true for Dad. As a result, in American culture the gap between a mother's ability to mother— her understanding of her children and how to deal with them— and a father's ability to father widens as the years go by because Mom puts in that much more time and effort. The only question that really haunts the discussion is this: Why can't—or don't— more fathers become more involved?

To me, the obvious answer is: Why should they? If mothers willingly take on these responsibilities, if no one has ever taught men that child rearing is part of their role, if no one has ever suggested to them that they, too, need to "bond" with their babies, what's the incentive? I'd wager that if you asked a room full of typical American adults how they would most like to spend their day, very few would say they'd like to spend it in the company of small children. As has been amply documented, the job of child rearing is held in low esteem by our culture. It's also a taxing task. Consider some of the words I heard involved fathers use to describe life with children: "Tedious," said one. "Difficult," said another. "Frustrating," said a third. These are men who are caring for their kids *part time*.

What men raised in our society don't possess is the guilt and ambivalence about being away from their children, the compulsion to be involved, that has been bred into American mothers. Nor is our society at large browbeating American fathers to become more involved—although that particular battle is probably waged in countless households around the country.

Father Studies: The Results in a Nutshell

Fathers' attitudes about mothers' employment, if negative, can have a negative effect on children's development. One recent study found that a mother's role strain did not have a negative influence on a child's development, but a father's feelings about his mate's employment did have an impact. Another study of dual-earner parents with toddlers found that these fathers had fewer positive attitudes about their children than did fathers whose partner stayed home. The fathers found their toddlers more difficult and more annoying. Theoretically, negative feelings about one's children infect those relationships; rather like self-fulfilling prophecies, they may affect a child's behavior and self-esteem.[39]

But when a father does feel comfortable about fathering and enjoys his children, there's ample evidence that his involvement has a positive influence on child development. Here are a few of the numerous studies that support this fact:

- The more time boys spend with their fathers, the better they do on academic achievement tests. These findings hold up for both school-age kids and preschoolers, but they are strongest for boys.
- One 1985 study found that preschoolers with involved fathers did better in a variety of playroom tasks. When fathers worked long hours, boys still did okay because their mother tended to compensate for the father's absence. But when mothers worked long hours, the daughters did less well because their father did not compensate by spending more time with them.[40]
- Children with more involved and nurturing fathers have higher I.Q.s.[41]
- Fathers who are more satisfied with their work are more sensitive and responsive to their kids.[42]
- Fathers who are more involved with their kids have a better sense of where their children are developmentally and consequently are more sensitive to their needs.[43]

- The strongest predictor of empathy in children is the amount of time they spend with their father in early childhood.[44]
- A child's perceptions regarding sex roles is determined more by the father than the mother.[45]

There's plenty of evidence, then, that working fathers are as critical to their child's development as working mothers, that fathers have as much to offer their children as mothers do, and that by clinging to the notion that mothers must be the central figure in their children's lives, we are fostering all kinds of feelings—anxiety, ambivalence, and guilt—that work against us and against the best interests of our children.

***

In the opening chapter of this book I quoted from *The Politics of Parenthood*, by Mary Francis Berry, who writes: "All experts agree that the most important ingredient for a child's healthy psychological development is nonabusive and consistent care, whether from a parent, a nanny or a child-care worker in a center." I propose a different definition of what children need, one with which I believe most experts would agree: Children need at least one concerned, involved, loving parent who's capable of creating a supportive home environment and choosing quality child care for them.

It falls upon parents, faced with an inadequate child-care system, to discover not what children in general need but what *their* children need at various ages and to determine how those needs can be met. That's what the second part of this book is about. It's designed to address issues related to child rearing that are rarely covered in standard child-rearing books—books that, even today, frequently skirt the subject of child care.

PART II

Growing Children: A Practical Guide

CHAPTER SEVEN

Raising Baby

Oh! hush thee, my baby, the night is
    behind us,
And black are the waters that sparkled
    so green.
The moon, o'er the combers, looks downward
    to find us
At rest in the hollows that rustle between.
Where billow meets billow, then soft be
    thy pillow
Ah, weary wee flipperling, curl at thy ease!
The storm shall not wake thee, nor shark
    overtake thee,
Asleep in the arms of the slow-swinging seas.

—"The White Seal," by Rudyard Kipling

What babies need during the early months of life is ample, unfettered time with their parents, and following that they need high-quality child care. What the research, much of it presented in Part I, tells us is this:

- In America today, child care in infancy can be a risky business: It's unstable, as evidenced by high turnover rates in every kind of child care, and it's not good enough. Studies of typical American child care, conducted outside the generally superior university-based settings, suggest that the earlier children enter care and the more hours they spend in care from infancy, the greater the chance of problems in social, emotional, and intellectual development.

- The attachment research suggests that working long hours, particularly more than 40 hours a week during the first year, can put so much stress on a mother that it may compromise the establishment of a healthy relationship between her and her baby.

This attachment research is not just about babies, who appear to be perfectly capable of adapting to good group care, forming multiple attachments, and thriving in a variety of settings; it's also about mothers, many of whom feel guilt, anxiety, and ambivalence about leaving their babies in someone else's care because they live in a culture that promotes precisely such negative feelings.

Until we have reasonable parental-leave policies, until we have high-quality care, these are the issues with which working parents must grapple. From a practical perspective, for working parents who are expecting or adopting a new baby, the two biggest questions are these: How much time should you spend with your baby before returning to work? and How do you find high-quality care to cover the hours when neither parent will be available?

No matter how much time you plan to take off, your ability to go back to work—and be productive at work—will depend on finding good child care, child care you can really trust. That is no small task in today's environment. Before the baby is born you'll want to negotiate as much leave time as you can and also explore all the child-care options available to you.

Given that, this chapter looks at four subjects:

- parental leave: How much time is enough?

- child-development issues that relate specifically to work and child-care decisions

- choosing child care for infants in particular (choosing care in general is examined in more depth in the next chapter)

- how parents, both with jobs, can best meet their baby's needs

On Parental Leave: Advice From Parents

Negotiate as much leave time as you possibly can. Try for at least three months, but up to six months if you can. If you can't get more than six weeks of paid leave, look into your company's unpaid-leave policies and negotiate more time on the front end; nothing's more difficult than negotiating a leave when your boss expects you back next week. If you are eligible for coverage under the Family and Medical Leave Act and want more time at home, consider taking the full 12 weeks and swallowing the loss of income.

Take leave time back to back with your spouse. This way you can maximize the time your baby has with you. If you think you can't afford a few extra months off, put a calculator to it; then take into account the value of spending a few extra months with your new baby.

During your leave, relax and try to enjoy being home. Savor this time with your baby. A number of women told me they were afraid that if they didn't get right back to work they might never go back. Others confessed to feeling isolated; being home alone with their baby all day was driving them crazy. People seem to lose perspective, to forget that infancy is a brief moment in a baby's lifetime and a speck of time if measured against their entire work life.

Consider a part-time return option or work-from-home arrangement for the first 12 months. This will minimize the stress on both parents and reduce the number of hours your child will spend in care. Why? For all the reasons discussed in Part I of this book—all the evidence that extensive time (more than 30 hours a week) in low-quality child care during infancy is damaging

Time Off for New Fathers

According to a report on paternity leaves by Joseph Pleck of the Center for Research on Women at Wellesley College, most American fathers (between 75 and 87 percent, depending on the study) take some time off during their child's infancy; but it generally averages out to less than a week, and it's rarely a formal parental leave. Contrast that with Sweden, where liberal leave laws encourage paternity leaves; 44 percent of Swedish fathers take paternity leave, and the average time off is 43 days. Generally, Swedish parents take sequential leaves to optimize their time with their child.

Sadly, while many U.S. companies now give lip service to the idea of paternity leaves, few men take advantage of it, and most people, employers and employees alike, view the inclusion of men in such policies as a "polite fiction," as Pleck points out. In an era when most new mothers return to work, often within the early months of a child's life, there are compelling reasons for men to take advantage of leave.

Studies point to a direct relationship between the amount of time a father takes off in his child's infancy and his later involvement in child rearing.[1] And fathers' involvement in infancy appears to be good for babies. Research conducted in Europe, Australia, and the U.S. has demonstrated that direct contact between fathers and babies has numerous positive effects.[2] And it would seem that if attachment is a real phenomenon, fathers should jump right in while the door's still open (theoretically, between birth and six months) so that both parents can build a secure relationship with their children and each parent can, in effect, substitute for the other.

to healthy social development. And there is ample evidence that much of the available infant care, in your home or out of it, just isn't good enough. Changing a full-time child-care arrangement in infancy—at least during the first year of life—may be more detrimental than changing child care at any other stage of a child's development. Moreover, the stresses on working parents may be greater during those early months than at any other time.

Recognize that if you go back to work before the six-month mark, you may feel torn. But if you give the baby time to adjust to a new caregiver or situation and take the time to find high-quality care, child care won't be problematic for baby or parents.

Developmental Issues
That Affect Child-Care Needs

"When I was a baby," my four-year-old announced not long ago, "I didn't know the difference between an elephant and a potato." And it was as true a statement as I have ever heard. Now, at four, he can write with a pencil, cut and paste, climb, dress himself, clear the table, get up in the middle of the night to go to the bathroom and get right back into bed, enjoy the funny papers, feed the cat (if he feels like it), and be utterly defiant and utterly charming. He can say good-bye and walk himself into school in the morning without batting an eye—in itself a remarkable development.

He knows the buzzwords and byways of his own culture: "Am I a litterbug?" he asks. "But I like commercial TV," he insists. He sings "The Star-Spangled Banner," the lyrics from "Guys and Dolls," and any song that Barney's ever sung.

I consider all these achievements phenomenal, yet his repertoire is as average and as distinctive as every other child's. Like them, he was born with a personality and predispositions, and since that day, bringing that baggage along with him, he has traveled an extraordinary distance. Consider a new baby about to embark on this highly individual yet genetically prescribed journey. During the first five years of life, children learn more about the world and develop more rapidly than they will in any subsequent stage. And the first few months are only the beginning.

When looking at the child-care options for an infant, it's important to remember that your child will be changing quite rapidly during the years ahead. You're looking for a stable arrangement that will grow with the child as his needs change. You need child care for a ten-month-old who may be crawling all over the place; and then a toddler who will not only be walking but running—and into everything. A three-month-old doesn't need playmates; when he turns two, he will. A caregiver for a three-month-old won't need much energy; someone who's caring for your one-year-old will need plenty.

It makes sense for parents exploring the child-care options in infancy to adopt a long-term perspective, but that's not always easy under pressure. I'd advise any parent looking for infant care to read not only this chapter and chapter eight, Choosing Child Care, but also chapter nine, The Young Child, because before you know it that's what your infant will be.

Infant development is not the subject of this book. I invite you to read any good child-rearing book—and there are many—to track the predictable developmental course your baby will take. But don't get too caught up in it. Says Barry Spodak, a psychotherapist and father, "If a kid seems okay, they're okay. If they seem happy, they're happy. You don't need a book to confirm it. The books are largely crazy-making after the first six months. In the first six months, you're crazy anyway, so it doesn't really matter."

The developmental issues that are relevant to parental-leave decisions and child-care choices are these:

- separation-related issues
- attachment
- the baby's personality
- the role of sensory integration and self-regulation in infant development

Separation-Related Issues

During the first six months of life, babies are open to forming new relationships. They're getting to know the people around them. Once babies pass the six-month mark, they have developed strong feelings for the people they know best, feelings often referred to as attachment. Somewhere between four and six months, babies begin to distinguish strangers (stranger recognition). Shortly thereafter, many infants grow increasingly wary of strangers (stranger anxiety)—people with whom they don't have regular contact. You can see it when they pull away or even cry when Grandma arrives from out of town. By eight or nine months, separation anxiety sets in. Babies become clingy. They'll wail when you leave their sight because they exist only in the here and now, and if you're out of sight, you're gone. They'll wail when you go to work. They may even wail when their caregiver leaves for the day (a tough experience for any parent).

The babies of working parents go through these same stages, regardless of what kind of care they're in. Day-care workers tell me that even infants who've been in center care for many months will cling and cry at drop-off when they hit separation anxiety, at eight, nine, or ten months—a stage that can last six to eight months and rear its head, off and on, throughout a young child's life.

Be assured, this will not last forever. Somewhere between 18 months and two and a half years—there's some disagreement over when the magic moment occurs—children are able to separate more easily, because their brains have developed sufficiently to enable them to *(a)* understand that if you leave, you will return, and *(b)* hold on, theoretically, to the idea of you, the fact that you are there for them, even if you're not physically there. In other words, they possess this thing called memory.

From a practical perspective, what all this tells us is that it may be better to introduce child care before the age of six months rather than later in the first year, and it's best not to make a major change in the care situation when children seem to be at a stage in which they are sensitive to separation.

Unfortunately, how all this translates into practice is a different matter. What parents can tailor their leaves to mesh precisely with the various stages of attachment? What parents can ensure that they don't have to change care arrangements at the peak of separation anxiety, at eight, nine, or ten months? What parents can predict exactly when their baby will reach these stages? Not many parents can, which is precisely why so many child-rearing experts steer clear of the issue and simply advise parents to stay home.

There is a very clear line of demarcation in infant development, and it occurs around the midyear mark. In one study, two groups of infants, one under seven months old and the other over seven months old, were put in the hospital. The younger babies were found to adapt well; the older babies appeared to suffer significantly more. What did they do? They cried. Putting a child in a new care situation at seven months won't do irreparable harm, but they will cry—and they may cry a lot. That's what caregivers tell me, anyway. As a result, it's going to be harder for the baby to adapt to child care, and it's going to be harder for the mother, who in all likelihood is herself having difficulty saying good-bye, to leave. New parents may become more anxious, setting off a vicious cycle of worry and concern. Knowing what to expect is the first step toward fending off these feelings.

Attachment

To a newborn baby, adults are the world. There is near-universal agreement that a baby's take on the world is determined by the responsiveness of the people who take care of that baby—be they mother, father, caregiver, or caregivers. Relationships are the means through which infants develop. If they can't do anything for themselves, then how well adults respond to their needs determines whether they see the world as a happy or unhappy place; whether they see themselves as having some measure of control of their environment. (Hooray! I can get food, water, attention when I want it!)

Getting Off to a Good Start: Before Six Months

To make your transition back to work easier on a baby, mothers advise:

- Even if you're breastfeeding, introduce a daily bottle as early as possible. Fill it with breast milk or formula and give it to baby even during the first month. Many mothers are trapped into forced weaning, a difficult process for baby and mother, because at three, four, or five months, their babies will not take a bottle from anyone while they're still nursing.

- Let there be noise. Certainly no one wants to wake a sleeping baby. But try not to fall into the habit of whispering and walking on eggs every time your baby falls asleep, despite the natural desire for peace and quiet. If you keep the noise level normal, most babies will adapt and sleep through noise.

- Encourage a father's involvement from day one. Studies show that fathers who are present in the delivery room, who participate in feedings, who get to know their babies early, are more involved throughout childhood. Mothers should resist the impulse to establish their own primacy.

- Let other people care for and spend time with your baby from the beginning. Studies show that babies who are exclusively cared for by one person have more difficulty adapting to others. Moderation is the key here. Infants learn to separate more easily from the parents through regular, moderate separations. Both extremes—extensive separations from parents and exclusive care by one parent—make it harder for the infant to adjust.[3] Our obsession with the idea of bonding and attachment is like a self-fulfilling prophecy. Even in the first month of life, babies can distinguish familiar people from unfamiliar people. If the only arms your baby knows are yours, everyone else will feel like a stranger.

The word *responsive* appears in the literature on infant care again and again. Does it just mean having someone around who knows when to get a bottle, change a diaper, pick a baby up, or put a baby down? In a word, no. It means having a provider at a center or a family day-care home or an in-home sitter who has the training and commitment to invest energy in getting to know your baby, to establish a relationship that's comforting and supportive enough to make the baby feel secure. That is a pretty tall order, and that's why the quality of child care is such a big issue.

The research on attachment tells us:

Babies can and do form attachments to caregivers. It's more likely in settings with fewer children per caregiver and trained caregivers who know how to respond appropriately to babies.

Babies are capable of forming multiple attachments. This is true as long as they have time to get to know the people who are caring for them. The big issue isn't whether a baby can form the attachment; it's whether the caregiver is able to foster an attachment, by providing sensitive care.

Children's primary and strongest attachments are to their parents. They know the difference between parents and caregivers. There is no room for jealousy between mother and caregiver, although it happens all the time. I've heard of parents who abandon trusted caregivers because the mother can't handle the fact that her child or children love this other woman. No matter when you introduce child care, make every effort to resolve these issues within yourself and, if necessary, with your caregiver.

If jealousy rears its head, talk about it. A simple comment like "Sometimes it's hard for me to watch Jessica with you. She seems so close to you. But I hope you know how much I appreciate it" can help break the tension that can develop.

Your job, as a parent, is to help foster the relationship between caregiver(s) and child. You can do this by *(a)* arming the caregiver with information about what makes your child happy, *(b)* maintaining an ongoing dialogue with the caregiver, and *(c)* hiring someone, or finding a center, you trust, so that the trust is communicated to the child.

174

Losing a cherished full-time caregiver is upsetting to young children. Parents who use au pairs, who are available for only a year, report that children are upset when these temporary nannies leave: They regress or have trouble sleeping; they experience loss. Sensitivity would seem the best approach to helping infants and young children cope; parents should try to be soothing and available and, depending on the child's age, prepared to talk it through before and afterward. I don't mean to suggest here that children cannot sustain a change in child-care arrangements. But babies, for the first 18 months, may be most vulnerable to such changes. Some babies seem to adapt easily to new situations and new people. Others are less flexible. That's where knowing your own baby comes in.

Both working parents should be actively involved with their child and his needs. The baby becomes attached to both parents, and one parent can substitute for the other when necessary.

Your Baby's Personality

I recall a birthday dinner for my husband during which my son, seven months old, awoke with a shriek. I held him; he fell asleep almost immediately; I put him down and went back to my chicken; and five minutes later he was shrieking again. I tried again, and again he awoke the minute I put him down. I knew something was terribly wrong because his behavior was so out of character. So I stayed in his room with him, soothing and rocking him, and returned to the table with him, asleep in my arms. "Just put him down," urged one of my dinner guests, a parent himself. "He probably just needs to be left alone." "Don't you ever just let him cry himself to sleep?" asked another. "What do you think it could be?" I asked the one woman who hadn't said a word, who had raised four children of her own. "I don't know," she said. "He's your baby."

As I said, I knew something was wrong because this wasn't like him; but a precise diagnosis was out of my reach. The next day the doctor found a rip-roaring infection in his left ear. Knowing your

175

child doesn't always make it easy to find out what's going on, but it does make it easier for you to be sensitive to what your own child needs. In this case, I knew my son needed to be held. As numerous experts I interviewed pointed out, parents are really the experts when it comes to their own children.

All children are different; over the past 20 years, an extraordinary body of literature on infant temperament has confirmed that fact. Baby A is calm but alert. Baby B is anxious and timid. Baby C is unresponsive and withdrawn. Baby D is excitable, sensitive to sound and light, and hard to comfort. Difficulties may arise, according to numerous child-rearing specialists (most notably T. Berry Brazelton), when the infant's personality is dramatically different from a parent's.

Imagine, for example, a lethargic baby with an active parent or a slow-to-warm baby with an enthusiastic, affectionate parent. Such relationships take a fair amount of adjustment, and the responsibility for adjusting falls to the parents and caregivers. Some babies are outgoing, active, and alert. They may be better candidates for group care than those who seem timid and lethargic. Some babies require constant attention and must be held, soothed, and rocked for endless hours—a joy to an adult who loves to snuggle infants, a headache for one who doesn't.

You'll want to spend as much stress-free time with your baby as possible during the early months of her life, getting to know her particular needs and style. And you'll want a child-care arrangement that will enable the caregivers to get to know your baby as well.

Difficult or easy? If you've got an easy baby, one who sleeps well, is easily comforted, sits happily watching the world, is engaged by objects, tolerates transitions well, and is just plain good-natured, the child-care world is open to you. Such babies will probably adapt well to any high-quality child-care arrangement, and caregivers will adapt easily to them.

But according to Stanley Turecki, author of *The Difficult Child*, maybe 15 percent of newborns are born "difficult." Difficult babies are hard work, for parents and caregivers alike. It takes a good deal of second-guessing, creativity, and concern to make them happy. But it's important to keep in mind that it's really the infant that's having a hard time; the parent's or caregiver's job is to help them find ways to soothe themselves. Some babies have colic—a catchall term for a fussiness that comes maybe once or twice a day, when some babies seem inconsolable; colic generally disappears at around three months. Some babies need to be held all the time; that's what they need, so that's what you've got to do. Some babies prefer not to be handled as much. It's just a matter of temperament.

For parents with difficult babies, I offer the following advice: ***During your parental leave, take a break.*** Get a babysitter and go to the movies. Hire a doula—a baby nurse who is available, even part time, in most cities to help new mothers. Take your baby and go stay with your mother. Call a friend or neighbor and ask for help if you need it. The dual stress of isolation and dealing with a difficult baby can strain even the perfect parent to the breaking point. It may push you back to work, your confidence eroded; it will certainly make you anxious; and ultimately, neither response—although both are perfectly natural—will be good for the child.

When you're looking into child care, tell the caregiver about any difficulties you're having with your baby. Don't sugarcoat reality. You will need to work together to help this child adapt to the world. Don't feel awkward about telling a caregiver what you've learned about how to comfort your baby.

Sensory Integration

In recent years, developmental psychologists have begun to pay increasing attention to how babies develop during the first year of life. During the first four to five months, sensory integration is taking place; the child is, quite literally, adjusting to the outside world: adapting his or her own vision, hearing, and sense of touch to the sights, sounds, and feelings he or she experiences and learning how to screen out and process stimuli.

What About Breastfeeding?

The evidence in favor of breastfeeding is fairly compelling. In fact, there's near-universal agreement that mother's milk is better for babies than commercial formulas. It builds up immunities that babies, particularly babies in group care, need. However, whether to breast-feed is an extremely personal issue. What many women don't realize before they give birth is that nursing is not an easy and natural process for all mothers and all babies. In fact, many mothers find it extremely difficult; but those who struggle through will tell you it's worth it.

For some mothers, the ability to breast-feed becomes a measure of their self-worth; one more thing to feel guilty about. "I couldn't nurse my first child. I stopped after a few weeks, because it was so hard," says one mom. "The day I gave it up, I cried all day long. I thought I was a total failure." With her second child, she enlisted the help of LaLeche League, a nationwide organization that promotes breastfeeding and helps new mothers by offering support groups and training. If you feel strongly about breastfeeding and need help, contact the group at 800-525-3243.

Working mothers are more likely to nurse than nonworking mothers but less likely to keep nursing for many months.[4] Some seem to feel it's their way of connecting and reconnecting at the end of the day. "Because I'm gone all day," says one nursing mom, "it's my special time. It's really for me. I hold on to it emotionally." Some mothers feel it's the one thing that distinguishes them from everybody else, so they continue to nurse as long as they possibly can. Others feel it promotes attachment.

If you choose to nurse, there are obvious advantages to introducing a bottle—even one filled with breast milk—early in your child's life. First, it encourages a father's involvement by enabling him to participate in feeding. Second, it enables you to go back to work more easily. But most important, it's going to make the transition easier for your baby. Some babies who've been nursed from birth will not take a bottle, no matter what's in it. I heard tales of working mothers who went through traumatic weanings in the days before they returned to work because they'd never introduced a bottle. "I had to go away for an entire day," says one mother of the weaning process she undertook before she went back to work. Her son was 11 weeks old. "He just wouldn't take a bottle, and I couldn't bear to be there and listen to him crying. So I went to my mother's, and my husband stayed home with him. He refused the bottle for 11 hours."

Nursing at work involves a breast pump (available at any drugstore), an understanding supervisor (not as easy to come by), and ten-minute breaks maybe two or three times a day—depending on how often you nurse, the baby's age, and your milk supply—to expel breast milk. Some companies are supportive of nursing mothers; others are not. Not long ago, a Detroit assembly-line worker sued the Chrysler Corporation because the automaker refused to allow her time to nurse. The settlement is not public, but she's still working and they've accommodated her needs with a "breastfeeding plan."[5] In recent years, some businesses have even introduced nursing support groups and special nursing rooms.

Nursing and working are not mutually exclusive. Don't be shy about it. "People used to bang on my door at work when I was pumping," says Roberta McInerney, a lawyer in Washington, D.C. "I'd try to be polite and say, 'Just give me a few more minutes.' If they kept banging, I'd just say, 'Look, I'm pumping my breasts.' That would always get rid of them."

For most babies, this process is a natural one. They are trying to get in step with the world. Frequent or abrupt changes in child-care settings are not going to facilitate that process.

Some babies have an unusually hard time integrating their five senses, and psychologists now believe that the adults who care for these babies may need training. Some babies are particularly sensitive to light, sound, or touch. They may wail, arching their back, no matter what you do; react to the sound of your voice as if it were a fingernail on a chalkboard; startle at slight environmental changes; or be easily irritated by fabric or by being touched.

Such babies will have particular difficulty with transitions— from one place to another, from one person's arms to another— because, in the words of one psychologist, it's painful for them. They are ill-suited to group care. Babies who seem hypersensitive may need more than even the most committed and sensitive parent can deliver. Professionals in the mental health field can teach parents and caregivers how to care for and handle overly sensitive babies. If you're concerned, you may want to consult an expert.[6]

Self-Regulation

There is strong consensus that you cannot spoil a baby during the first year of life. An adult's job is pure indulgence: helping the baby stay comfortable, quenching her need for food, water, sleep, mild stimulation. Ultimately, babies discover how to soothe themselves—e.g., fall asleep or play quietly and delay gratification for a time. Babies recognize that they will be fed and learn to wait for an ever-increasing number of minutes until food appears; to adapt to environmental changes; to respond to comfort. This process is called self-regulation.

Babies achieve self-regulation in a consistent, responsive, comforting, and not-too-chaotic setting. That means babies should be fed when they're hungry, soothed when they cry, quenched when they're thirsty, changed when they're wet, played with when they feel playful, and left alone when it seems appropriate. According to the prevailing view of baby raising in our culture, adults who spend time with a baby and are sensitive to that baby are able to pick up on various cues and signals that enable them to fall into that baby's rhythm.

The schedule into which a baby falls is set by the baby but recognized by the adult, so that ultimately a rhythm emerges that fits the baby's natural patterns. That's the ballet that's going on in the early weeks and months of a child's life.

If you introduce child care during your baby's first year, the program should be flexible enough to adapt to your baby's natural rhythms—not vice versa. Nap and feeding times should be established according to the baby's needs. Some babies nap for short intervals throughout the day. Some hardly sleep at all. Others take long, deep naps. Be wary of any program that requires your baby to fit its schedule, just as providers are wary of parents who establish a fixed regimen for infants. Be wary of a family day-care program in which five, six, or seven other preschoolers and toddlers are vying for the caregiver's attention. Under such circumstances, it's hard to imagine how even the most sensitive adult can be responsive to your baby's needs. "I have to put the older children in front of television so I can feed the baby," one family day-care provider told me, making it quite clear that babies do not fit easily into some of these programs.

Recognize, too, that schedules will change weekly, even daily, during the early months of a child's life, and parents and caregivers will need to communicate schedule information to each other. Make sure there's a mechanism for communicating, verbally or on paper. Some centers use diaries and chalkboards to record information about when and how much a baby slept, played, ate, and needed changing.

Quit Worrying

All parents, first-time parents in particular, worry about whether their babies are okay. Because they spend less time with their baby, worry about child care, and may be prone to guilt, working parents may overreact to normal baby behavior. What's normal? Here are a few guidelines.

Probably not problems:	Possibly signs of psychological disturbance:
Birth to 1 month	
Preference for eating every two hours Prickly heat rash "Not satisfied" with feeding Wanting to be held "all the time" Grunting and red face with bowel movements Sucking finger or thumb	Failure to gain weight Excessive spitting up Absence of eye contact Failure to hold head up Failure to show anticipatory behavior at feeding Failure to hold on with hands Ticlike movements of face and hands
2 to 3 months	
Irritable crying Colic Constipation Not sleeping through the night	Failure to thrive Indifference to human face, voice, and play overtures Persistent hyperactivity Persistent sleep disturbance Vomiting and diarrhea without physical illness Hyperresponsiveness or hyporesponsiveness
4 to 6 months	
Demands for attention Preference for being propped up "Spoiled" Teething or biting problems	Wheezing without infection Failure to enjoy upright position Indifference toward feeding Excessive rocking, except at night or when alone Rumination (swallowing regurgitated food)

Probably not problems:	Possibly signs of psychological disturbance:
7 to 9 months	
Dropping things Messy feeding Disrupted sleep associated with teething, move to new home, or illness "Temper"	Unpatterned sleeping and eating Eating problems like refusing to use hands or to hold glass, or a very limited diet Failure to imitate simple sounds and gestures Lack of distress with strangers Failure to show and respond to recognizable signals like joy, surprise, or fear Self-destructive behavior Withholding of bowel movements Apathy
10 to 16 months	
Getting into things; climbing Declining appetite Problems with self-feeding and being fed Screaming Mild tantrums Attachment to "security blanket"	Absence of words Withdrawn behavior Excessive rocking and posturing Absence of distress at separation Night wandering Excessive distractibility

Adapted from Justin D. Call, M.D., in V. K. Kelley, Practice of Pediatrics *(Harper & Row, 1984). Reprinted by permission of the* New York Times *and* Harper & Row.

Choosing With Care

Guidelines for finding, evaluating, and choosing child care in general appear in the next chapter. Choosing infant care involves special considerations, and they are explored in this section.

Parents should plan to take time off, if possible, *before* the baby is born to look into the child-care options in their community. I use the term *parents* advisedly; this should be a joint effort, involving both mother and father. Working mothers need all the help they can get, every step of the way. The impulse for many first-time mothers is to take on all the responsibility for finding child care themselves. Don't do it; it sets the stage for future problems. Make every effort to involve the father in this decision. One caveat: For some parents, the search for child care is so confusing, almost frightening, that they really don't want to have to deal with it. Such parents sometimes settle for substandard care because they grasp almost desperately at the first situation that comes along.

Start by hooking into the child-care network. Explore all the options available in your community. (See Finding Quality Care in chapter eight.) Ask friends, but don't stop there. Most of the people I interviewed made a choice based on a friend's recommendation; but in many instances that choice was not the best and did not last.

Recognize that your desires and expectations regarding child care may change dramatically after your child is born. You're not out to hire anyone or commit to a care situation at this point, unless you find an outstanding caregiver or center. What you're after is a sense of the best care options in your community. Most important, you'll want to avoid the trap into which countless working parents fall: the need to change arrangements during the first year of a child's life.

Be clear about what you're looking for. You're looking for the best child care in your area—be it a day-care center, family day-care home, relative, neighbor, or in-home caregiver. The beauty of going through this process before your child is born is that you'll have an understanding of the community and all the options, and you'll be well informed once you have to make the final decision about child care.

Adopt a long-range perspective. Ideally, you're looking for a child-care situation that has the potential to last for the next five years or, at the very least, until the age of two and a half or three. That means child care that will grow with your child and remain in place for many years. Numerous studies have found that school-age kids who began child care in infancy seem to do better if the child-care situation has remained stable for most of their young lives. For guidance on how to gauge the stability of the care arrangement, see Looking for Stability and Consistency in chapter eight.

Be open-minded. As I said in Part I, there's no evidence that group care is inherently harmful to babies or that isolated one-on-one care is essential in infancy. The search for child care, at any age, begins with challenging your own assumptions; and the need for one-on-one infant care is one of the most entrenched assumptions in our culture. In the long run, a stable group-care situation may be better than hiring an in-home sitter who may leave at any time. If, as a first-time parent, you spend time observing group care, be open-minded. Remember that life with large numbers of children is an unpredictable experience. Don't judge the setting or the caregiver too harshly. For guidelines on signs of good care, see chapter eight.

Don't be afraid to sign up. If you find a good care situation, you may want to do so immediately. The waiting lists at top-quality centers are long; they care for few infants, and it might take six months to a year to get in. The same holds true for family day care.

In November 1993 I visited one of the best providers in Montgomery County, Maryland. She takes one infant at a time, along with five toddlers and preschoolers. Most of her babies stay with her until they begin school; some stay through their early school years, in after-school care. She has 20 years' experience and ample space stocked with an extraordinary supply of puzzles, games, toys, and play equipment. She also has an outstanding reputation. Three rooms of her home are devoted to family day care, including a special kitchen for the kids.

Not long ago the mother of one of her charges asked her when she would be able to take on another infant. Said the mother, "If you'll agree to take my next child, I'll plan my pregnancy around your next opening." In November 1993, this provider knew she'd have an opening for an infant in September 1994. "If someone came in today and wanted to reserve that slot, I'd sign them right up," she said. The interview process, during which she screens prospective families as they screen her, involves a telephone interview, a visit, drop-ins if the parent wants to get a sense of the

Splitting Shifts: Full-Time Parent Care

A number of couples I interviewed split the care of their children with their spouse, thereby sidestepping the need for outside child care. Census figures tell us this approach is increasingly common: Father care is the second most common form of child care for children under three with working mothers, right behind family day care. The most serious problem with splitting shifts during infancy is that it can be exhausting for parents, sapping the strength they need to adapt to the lows, and appreciate the highs, of taking care of a baby.

A New Jersey couple I'll call the Martins tried to make it through the early months of their child's life with no outside help. Karen Martin went back to work part time, nights, when her son was eight weeks old. She'd get home at 11 P.M.; the baby would wake up at 2 A.M. and again at 4 A.M. Her husband, who was in graduate school, would take the night shift with the baby, and Karen would take the day shift. During the day their son, Christopher, now two, would sleep in ten-minute stretches. "There were times when he would just cry for hours. I remember feeling so helpless, so frustrated, and so alone. I'd sit on the floor and cry as he was crying in my arms," remembers Karen. "At least if I hadn't gone back to work so soon, I might have gotten some sleep." People like the Martins need one thing or another: time off from work or school, or child care.

program, and, finally, a contract signing. She's a pro. If you find a pro like her, sign up with her early.

Is One-on-One Care Essential?

One-on-one care, at your home or someone else's, offers obvious advantages. But in-home care has some drawbacks, including high turnover rates, low levels of caregiver training and commitment, and, most obvious, high costs, all of which are discussed in other sections of this book. In many cities, in-home caregivers are drawn from the ranks of recent immigrants, who often don't speak English well. While parents may imagine the advantages of raising a bilingual child, the process appears to slow language development by about six months. In addition, there are reports indicating that children raised with in-home caregivers may have poorer verbal skills. But the main point to keep in mind is this: There's no evidence that children in the care of a relative, a friend, or a neighbor fare better than those in the hands of skilled caregivers—in either one-on-one or group settings.

For most people, center care and family day care are the most accessible options; given that, the amount of attention your baby will receive is an important consideration, and the number of caregivers and children in the program become critical issues.

Ratios for Center Care

You want an environment that promotes direct one-on-one interaction between baby and caregiver—a ratio of 1:2 or 1:3 (one caregiver for every two or three babies). Many states allow a ratio of 1:4. That's not good enough.

For an article published in *The Progressive,* Dorothy Coniff, a woman with 20 years' experience in the day-care field, calculated how much time each day a caregiver responsible for four infants would spend on physical maintenance alone: feeding, changing, hand washing. For an eight-hour day, she figured a total of 16 diaper changes and 12 feedings, plus two and a half minutes for hand washing after each diaper change—a critical step to prevent illness in group care. "That makes seven hours and 20 minutes of the day spent just on physical care—if you're lucky and the infants stay conveniently on schedule," she writes. That leaves 40 minutes for playing with those babies. She adds, "So, if there's to be any stimulation at all for the child, the caregiver had better chat and play up a storm when she's feeding and changing."[7]

Many centers assign a "primary caregiver" to each infant. This is a good policy for parents because it gives you one contact person in the program. But a 1980 study showed that even in centers with primary caregivers, the babies are cared for by many people.[8] Don't assume a "primary caregiver" means one-on-one care—or that a "primary caregiver" is necessary.

Ratios for Family Day Care

A good ratio means no more than one other infant and a limited number of additional children, depending on their ages (see Ratios and Group Sizes in chapter eight). When looking at family day care, the provider's license will tell you precisely how many kids she's allowed to care for. Ask to see it. Make your judgment based not on the number of children currently in care but on how many could potentially, legally, be in care. Many licensed family day-care providers take on more children than they can handle, because the law allows it and their budgets require it. So use your judgment. If someone's caring for three preschoolers and two infants and has three other children coming over after school— which would be perfectly possible in most states—ask yourself, Is my child going to get enough attention?

Group Size Matters

The number of children in the group—or children per room, in the case of center care—should be kept small. Research tells us that particularly for infants, overall group size may be just as important as the caregiver-child ratio. In a day-care center, two caregivers in a room with 6 infants is better than four caregivers in a room with 16. Fewer kids mean the babies are getting care from fewer people overall, caregivers have fewer distractions, and the environment is less chaotic. Given that a ratio of 1:3 is probably the best you can expect from center care, the overall group size should be no more than nine infants. Six is even better. But keep in mind the research, which tells us family day-care providers who care for two or fewer children tend to be among the least committed, least nurturing, and least well-trained providers.

In-Home Care: Viewing Caregivers as Professionals

If you're looking for one-on-one, in-home care—at your house or someone else's—remember that you are hiring someone to do a job that requires certain skills. Most parents will tell you they hire on instinct. Instinct should play a role in the decision, but if we expect our caregivers to be professionals, as well we should, we have to raise our expectations about their abilities. That process begins with the job interview. We all want loving, nurturing caregivers who get along with our children, and research tells us that trained people with a knowledge of child development are better at it, are more nurturing, than those who are untrained. They understand the stage a child is in, so their behavior and expectations are realistic.

Hiring a person to care for your infant may seem to be the easiest child-care choice you'll ever make. But don't assume, as many parents do, that all you need is a loving person who's raised babies.

Consider what happened to Andrea Zintz. A vice president with Ortho-Biotech in Princeton, New Jersey, Zintz knows how to prepare. Before her pregnancy was even detectable to the casual observer, she had started reading up on child rearing. And before the baby was born she'd chosen a caregiver, based on her image of the ideal babysitter—"a mature woman, kind of a grandmotherly type, who'd take my baby and, basically, grandmother her."

Keep in mind that Zintz is in the human resources department of a subsidiary of Johnson & Johnson, which has gone great guns in recent years in introducing work-family initiatives. So she has access to on-site child care and corporate child-care referral. "I was given lots of literature by a consultant on choosing child care. And I read some of it, but most of it didn't seem to apply to me because here this woman landed in my lap who looked grandmotherly. So," says Zintz, miming the casualness with which she tossed all this advice in the trash, "I said, I don't need this."

Zintz had met her ideal grandmother in the company cafeteria. "She was this very warm, maternal type. She'd raised three children and had two grandchildren. She'd never done any child-care providing, but as a mother and a grandmother I figured she knew what she was doing."

The results, according to Zintz, were disastrous. Five and a half months into her six-month leave, she began the process of introducing her daughter, Allie, to her new surrogate grand-mother, Catherine. She began by telling Catherine everything she could about Allie—that she liked to roll around on a blow-up barrel, that she was intrigued with mirrors, when she slept, how she ate. When she took Allie to the sitter's house, she brought a box of Allie's favorite things; when she returned several hours later, she found the box untouched. How had Allie spent her day? She was in the playpen while Catherine folded the laundry. Then she sat in her infant seat while Catherine cooked a meal. Then she sat some more while Catherine did the floors. Says Zintz, "What I got a picture of here was like advanced babysitting, all-day babysitting, not child-care providing in the sense that I had envisioned it."

When she picked Allie up the next day, Andrea sat down immediately to nurse her. She'd been gone this time for eight hours. Catherine brushed by them and muttered "spoiled" under her breath. Catherine's grandchildren were there. "I watched her with her grandchildren, and two things I noticed: her constant use of the words "good girl" and "bad girl" and "good boy" and "bad boy"—it seemed like she was using those words not when they were misbehaving but when she wasn't in the mood for them to be acting like children. And her husband, who was not home a lot, was there. He kept saying, "No, no. Don't touch that. You're going to make a mess." Or "sit down over there with your hands in your lap." Finally the husband said, "Go pick up what you left in that room or I'll smack you. I'll get my belt."

That was it—the end of Allie's life with the perfect grand-mother. Was this episode avoidable? Yes. The problems, in this case, are pretty straightforward. Catherine came with no recom-mendation, no experience, and no background in child care. Having raised children in no way qualifies someone to care for your own. Child care is a profession. To look at it otherwise is to make a big mistake.

Interviewing Caregivers and Family Day-Care Providers: What to Ask

Here are some questions to ask that will help you demand a certain level of professionalism when interviewing prospective family day-care and in-home providers to care for your baby:

- How would you calm a crying baby? The answer should be some variation on the following themes: First, figure out why they're crying (hunger, thirst, need to play, dirty diaper, need to be held, need to be put down). But all babies are different; some are comforted by rocking, some by singing, some by being held. Babies fuss, too, when they're tired and they just want to be put down. Look for answers such as "I'd need to get to know your child better" or "What does your baby like?"
- How can you tell when a baby's overstimulated? The answer: Babies tend to turn away, clench their fists, or cry when they want to stop playing.
- When should a child be potty trained? The answer: any variation on the theme of "When the child is ready" and "They usually start at about two or three" or "Girls start earlier than boys."
- When do you think I should introduce solid foods or finger foods? Check the answer against your pediatrician's advice and use the subject to test how you and the caregiver might resolve your differences.
- What do you like to do during the day? Every babysitter in the world answers, "Take walks and go to the park." You're looking for "Read stories, get down on the floor and play, sing songs."
- What would you do if my child hit another child? You're looking for thoughtful responses here, responses that will tell you whether this caregiver can take your child past infancy.

191

Babies quickly become toddlers, and suddenly limit-setting, discipline, and teaching "social skills" become issues.

Consider the case of a child I'll call Mark Herbert, whose caregiver—I'll call her Patricia—loved, and understood, babies. But when Mark passed age two, something changed. His father, who worked at home, noticed that Patricia was having a good bit of trouble keeping Mark in line; whenever she said no, he'd balk, like any two-year-old. Says Dad, "Her strategy, I began to notice, was that she'd chase him or tickle him whenever she wanted to set limits. It was her way of distracting him, I guess." While Dad worked upstairs, he'd hear Mark and his sitter running around hysterically downstairs, Mark screaming, tearfully, "Please don't tickle me. Please. Please."

Did he speak with her about it? "I'd have to go intercede, which means I'd talk with him or calm him down or find some constructive way to distract him," says the father. "The problem seemed so fundamental that I couldn't imagine what to tell her. She obviously was unable to handle him at this age; I think he'd just outgrown her abilities."

For additional interview questions for evaluating child care in general, see The Selection Process: How It Works in chapter eight.

In-Home Care for Infants and Toddlers

The beauty of in-home care in your own home is that a baby doesn't have to go out (e.g., be rushed out in a fall rainstorm or a winter snow; be exposed to the illness that sweeps through group-care situations; be exposed to the overstimulation inherent in large groups). But a toddler needs to get out. If you're considering in-home care, recognize that your infant or toddler and her caregiver will need the following:

A social world. Help your caregiver connect with other caregivers in your neighborhood for walks and trips to the park. Start a neighborhood play group for caregivers and infants, or see that your child is included in a play group with at-home moms and their infants. A weekly play group can start at any age.

Daily outings. Make sure your caregiver has a way to get to the nearest library and local community center, the grocery store and drugstore. The smallest outing can be a major event for a toddler, and such activities can become the focus for the day. Many public libraries keep materials on hand for caregiver education. Some community centers open up their gyms to toddlers and sponsor tumbling programs or music programs. Keep abreast of programs for toddlers.

Play space. Make sure your house is baby-safe and that ample space is available for climbing, crawling, and rolling about—all important developmental tasks for babies.

It's important, too, to discuss the following issues with an in-home caregiver:

How much housework is the caregiver expected to do? The most important rule for any caregiver is: Baby comes before housework. A caregiver's responsibility for housework should be clearly outlined before you hire, but be realistic. Caring for an infant or toddler is a demanding job; don't expect someone to be a full-time housekeeper if you also expect them to provide full-time baby care. Baby will surely suffer, because the results of time spent on housekeeping are measurable but the results of time spent on good baby care are not so obvious.

How much television is allowed? And when? And what sorts of shows? Some parents allow their sitters to watch a favorite soap opera. Others allow the television to be on all day. Still others restrict viewing times. I spoke with an in-home caregiver who believed it was wise to teach infants to watch television by putting them in front of *Sesame Street* for lengthening stretches of time. Yet there is no evidence that television, even public television, is good for young children, much less babies. Studies show that children with in-home caregivers watch more television than any other group of children. You decide how much television your child should watch and set the rules accordingly.

Center Care for Infants: What to Look For

When you visit a good day-care center, you're going to want to see kids who are happy and engaged and caregivers who are enthusiastic and involved. But the caveats when choosing center care for infants are fairly substantial. Look into the following:

Health and Safety First

Safety is every parent's chief concern. When using an in-home caregiver, you should take the following minimal precautions:

- Provide emergency numbers.
- Require a class in CPR for anyone who cares for your baby and offer to pay for it.
- Have your in-home caregiver keep a key around her neck or hide one outside. You'd be amazed at how often caregivers lock themselves out of houses, usually by taking out the garbage while baby's napping (if you're lucky).
- Provide the name of at least one contact neighbor— anyone who can help out in an emergency.
- Require a TB test. Most states require it for center and family day care. I know a child who contracted tuberculosis from an in-home caregiver. Pay for the test and ask to see the certificate.
- Request frequent hand washing. Studies show that regular hand washing retards the spread of illness in group care. In-home caregivers should be instructed to wash their hands after each diaper change and frequently throughout the day.

Adult-to-child ratios. Be sure caregiver-child ratios are 1:3 or better.

Turnover. Look for centers where staff stay for many, many years. An annual turnover rate higher than 20 to 30 percent may be cause for concern.

Illness. Infants in center care get sick with some frequency. Be sure to check the hand-washing procedure. Regular washing, at least after each diaper change, will reduce the spread of colds and other infections. Studies of infants in group care show that they are more prone to illness, but it appears they build up immunities and are less prone to minor illnesses as preschoolers. If you have an infant in center care, you'll need backup care or an understanding boss. Family day-care providers, according to studies, are more willing to accept mildly ill children.

Transition policies. Find out at what age centers move infants to the toddler room. Some centers shift children at age one, which can be a particularly difficult time for a change. Others connect the infant and toddler areas to allow for a free flow from one to the other and provide a sense of continuity for the child in transition.

Group size. This is particularly important for infants. Big groups can be distracting and chaotic to sensitive infants. The total number of infants in one room or area should be no more than nine, with three caregivers. A group size of six is preferable. As I noted earlier, at least one study found that group size is a more significant indicator of quality than ratios when it comes to infant care.

You should spend as much time as you can observing the center, ideally with your infant in tow, so you can get used to the setting. Ask questions. Be sure to observe a mealtime and changing shifts. (See Observe and Learn in chapter eight.)

Starting Group Care

How do infants react to group care? In a word, differently. "We can't deliver one-on-one care, and some children need one-on-one care. Some can get along with the group. You see it in the personality of the child in infancy," says Anne Durso, director of

Broadcasters' Child Development Center (BCDC) in Washington, D.C. "All of them adapt, but for some it's harder."

How do infants who aren't adapting appear? "They get dazed or they cry a lot," says Laura Hubert, who runs the infant/toddler rooms at BCDC. "They're simply overwhelmed." Hubert tells of a child who arrived around the age of six months and cried daily,

---

Signs of Good Group Care for Infants

From the National Association for the Education of Young Children come these guidelines for what to look for in a good infant-care program:

- Babies are not kept for long periods in cribs, playpens, or restricted spaces.
- Caregivers respond to babies' cries.
- Caregivers speak in soft, soothing voices and move relatively slowly.
- Infants are held frequently.
- Caregivers talk to, read to, and play with infants.
- Caregivers respond to an infant's sounds to promote language development.
- Caregivers play games such as peek-a-boo.
- The setting includes mirrors, soft climbing pillows, and toys that are safe, too large to swallow, washable, and responsive to a child's actions (such as bells, busy boxes, or snap beads).
- Staff appear warm, relaxed, and congenial, not rushed or overburdened by the need to care for too many infants.

Reprinted by permission of the National Association for the Education of Young Children. For a complete pamphlet entitled Developmentally Appropriate Practice in Early Childhood Programs Serving Infants, *contact the National Association for the Education of Young Children at 800-424-2460. Copies are available for 50 cents each, 100 for $10.*

---

all day, for months. She tells of another, a 12-week-old, who simply slept all day, every day, for weeks, then went home and slept some more at night. "He didn't do it at home on the weekend, just here," she says. "That was his way of adapting." Both of these children are still at the center, now preschool age and reportedly "doing fine." But the transition was tough. Then there are the infants who do fine from the beginning. They are by nature more adaptable or more outgoing or less sensitive to what can be a stimulating environment.

Easing Babies Into Care

Let the baby get used to a new child-care arrangement before you go back to work. Ideally, you should introduce care gradually, for lengthening periods of time over a period of weeks, before you go back to work. At Little Folks Too in Wilmington, Delaware, which caters to parents who work nearby, director Neesy De-Cherney encourages parents to visit frequently throughout the day. Nursing moms come and go. It's the center's policy to invite new mothers and their babies to drop by early and often, and at no charge, before they go back to work. That enables baby and mother to feel comfortable and get to know the staff, which in turn facilitates an easy exchange of information.

That policy should be, I think, in place at all centers and family day-care homes. If possible, people who can afford in-home care should start it well before they return to work—the sooner the better—paying for full-time care and having the sitter come by for increasing stretches of time over the course of many weeks. It's a worthwhile investment, not only because it will enable the baby to get to know the caregiver and the parents to observe the caregiver with the baby but because it also enables you, the parent, to start a relationship with the caregiver, this new person who is about to become an integral part of your life and an intimate part of your child's life.

Not all centers promote the policy of easing into care; according to the providers I interviewed, few family day-care providers do. Even the best family day-care providers seem to cherish their privacy and their routine. Once you're signed up, most will tell you to bring your child and leave—period—to let the child adjust to the new routine. Says one, "Easing the child into care is for the

Adapting to Care in an Ideal Child-Care World

After the age of six months, separation will be an issue. How do you work it out? Consider the case of David, described by Annette Axtmann in a journal article on the Center for Infants and Parents at Teachers College, the education school within Columbia University.[9] David's parents, both graduate students, enrolled him in the center when he was seven months old for seven hours a day, two days a week. After several preliminary visits to the center with his parents, David's transition began. The staff agreed "to try these hours during their adjustment period," but David refused food and cried inconsolably when his father departed. So his parents rearranged their work hours so David's mother could bring him to the center. She stayed for seven hours for several days, nursing him, watching him with his primary caregiver, asking questions. Still, if his mother left, even for a short time, David panicked.

What next? The staff brought in a clinical consultant to observe and assist. The consultant suggested a shift to a different schedule: four hours a day, four days a week. Still David's behavior didn't change.

Then they tried a new tack. David's mother would wait until she got to the center to nurse him. It worked. When she left, he didn't cry. He began to whimper around four hours later, when it was about time for his mother to come back. Finally, David adapted.

Consider all the elements that made this child-care situation work: the parents' job flexibility, the staff's concern about parent and child, and everyone's willingness to adapt to the child's needs, and invest time and energy in the process. David's case provides an example of the rather phenomenal level of care and support that can be available in a university setting. The center functions as a training and research facility and works with parents to help them understand their children. The primary goal of the program, as articulated by Annette Axtmann, is this: "... we place the highest priority on the support and strengthening of relationships between infants and parents." Why? Because of "our understanding of the parent-child relationship as the crucial context for human growth and development in the earliest years." The ratio—three caregivers to eight babies—is extraordinary. Each family is assigned a primary caregiver to work with them. The schedule for care is determined not just by the parents' hours but by how well the child is adapting.

In an ideal world, that would be the standard against which all infant care is measured. But even in the real world, you can come close. Some programs allow, even encourage, parents and babies to visit frequently before they begin care. Says Neesy DeCherney of Little Folks Too, "I always tell my moms, 'Come in and sit down with us, hang out with us, on the house. You have to get to know us before you go back to work or you're going to be a wreck.'" That's the kind of care all families need.

If you're considering a day-care center for your infant, be sure it's a good one. Spend time in the toddler and preschool-age rooms. The chief advantage of center care is that it will be a stable environment in which your child can spend the next five years. The characteristics of high-quality centers in general are covered in chapter two and chapter nine. Choose with care. I'd go with my gut on this one. If you feel you need time to get used to a new setting, if you feel your child needs time, ask for it—because your feelings will affect the ease with which your child adapts.

parents. It's not for the children. Most of them stop crying immediately when the parent leaves." Says another, "Easing them into care just confuses them, no matter what the age. If you're going to be away for nine hours every day, they need to adjust to that. It's easier for them if you don't start with three hours and increase to nine hours."

Getting Through the Rough Spots

The toughest times of day for any working parent are pick-up and drop-off. Transitions are examined in some detail elsewhere in this chapter and in chapter eight. But special consideration must be given to new parents and new babies. If you return to work in the early months of a child's life, recognize that the separation will be much harder on you than it is on the baby. If you return to work in the latter part of the first year, brace yourself. At some point your baby is going to cry when you leave, like every baby before him. Give a gentle hug, hand him over, and turn and leave. It will be easier for everybody involved. Always say good-bye, no matter what your child's age—unless, of course, he's sleeping.

Coming back to baby at the end of the day is an exciting business. But before you reconnect, take a deep breath, slow down, and lower your expectations. Whether your baby is in group care or home care, hope that she is engaged and involved. Recognize that not all reunions will be perfect. And then get ready, because you can be sure that your baby will unload her feelings on you.

Sharing Parenting With Dad

Mothers are raised to believe that they are central to their children's lives. And that's as it should be. But working mothers must be willing to share that role. That's easier said than done. Some mothers bristle when offered advice on how to handle their babies. Others are less confident and eager for assistance. It's a delicate balance. The question of how much to defer to a caregiver and how much control to retain is a tough one; developing a relationship with a caregiver is discussed in more detail in chapter eight. But for working couples, one of the most important questions during a child's infancy is how to integrate fathers into their role as fathers—recognizing that what happens in these early months counts, big time, in setting the stage for the future. Father involvement is good for babies and good for children; this is one of the few areas of consensus in child-care research.

How to Get Dad Involved

Some men are really scared of babies. Others are just plain not interested. Then there are those who seem born for the role. But most fathers seem to imagine that women have an instinctive ability to change a diaper or soothe a child. Tell them it ain't so. One stay-at-home dad told me, "I think women are better prepared for this. My parents never talked to me about raising kids. None of my guy friends and I, until we had kids, ever talked about kids." Somehow, this man imagined that a woman's parents teach her how to be a mother; that women talk about child rearing before they have children; that we are trained.

The sad truth is, most women are just as poorly equipped as men to handle and care for an infant. In our culture, most adults have no prior experience when it comes to infants. Women, like men, learn as they go. How can a mother facilitate the process for Dad?

For starters, tell him the truth: that you know as little about baby raising as he does. Recognize that men are perfectly capable of what author M. E. Lamb, in his book *Father's Role: Applied Perspectives*, refers to as "the kind of nurturance and child-centered concern" for which women are known. In fact, research suggests that these are acquired skills and that even with newborns, mothers and fathers "do about the same" as far as skills, competence, and abilities.[10] Don't let your assumptions fool you.

Whatever you do, do not correct what he does. Don't position yourself as the expert. Don't lean over his shoulder and say, "The diaper's on backwards" or "That sock is on the wrong foot." Let it pass. Criticism is the surest route to discouraging a father's

---

Special Delivery

If your infant is in a group-care situation, here are some tips from *Nothing But the Best: Making Day Care Work for You and Your Child* on how to make the morning drop-off easier:

- *Lump of Home:* Sit down with your baby and be still. Don't talk, hand [out] toys, or point things out; just be there. Let your baby case the joint and make contact with people and things, in his or her own time and fashion. When your baby has made some contacts, give the teacher the news quietly, tell your baby good-bye, kiss, and go.

- *Tour Guide:* Sit holding your baby, pointing out favorite people and things: "Look! Here's Esther, and Michael, here's the soft bear and the red train. . . . " Actively but gently remind your infant of familiar pleasures at day care. Then pull back and wait a bit, or hand your baby to a teacher, kiss, and go.

- *Delivery Service* (for speed-emergency days and for easy phases): Stop at the door and take a deep breath. Go into motion for just a few minutes. Hold your child while you unpack and give the teacher the news, then hand your baby to your teacher, kiss, and go. Your teacher's arms should be full of warm touch and smell memories strong enough to evoke quickly the sense of a safe, familiar place. As long as you hand your child over in slow motion and leave looking confident, fast good-byes with familiar people can work fine.

Reprinted by permission from Diane Lusk and Bruce McPherson from Nothing But the Best: Making Day Care Work for You and Your Child, *Quill/ William Morrow, New York, 1992.*

---

involvement that I know of. For one thing, it provides him with an excuse: "But every time I try to help, you tell me I'm doing something wrong."

Share responsibility. If your husband says, "Let's go out," say, "Great. See if you can get a sitter." If he says, "I mean let's all go out," say, "Great. Why don't you pack the diaper bag?" Advises one counselor who works with new parents, "If a woman can get her husband to do just those two things—call a babysitter and pack a diaper bag—she's making giant leaps." Otherwise, now hear this: You'll be calling the babysitters for much of the rest of your adult life.

Defer. Recognize that your husband is a partner in this. Ask his advice. Get him to look things up in the baby books. Get him to call his mother and ask what she thinks (swallow your pride). Make sure he takes the baby to the doctor sometimes. And don't choose a child-care arrangement without his active involvement and approval. One 1979 study showed that 40 percent of fathers want to be more involved with their children, but many women (60 to 80 percent) are unwilling to share. Those same findings held up ten years later.[11]

Establish priorities early. Most parents, when they have to make work-related sacrifices because the baby's sick or the sitter doesn't show, get into this battle: My work's more important than yours. Women always lose, unless they earn the most money. Turn that argument on its head before it becomes a pattern. The issue is: What makes you think I'm more important to the baby than you are? Both parents need to learn that the priority is the baby.

Encourage your husband to take a leave, a real parental leave. It is the first step toward integrating him into the process. And it will be an education for his supervisor and his employer. Bundle your leaves—Mom's first, Dad's second. Why? For the baby's good: If Mom takes six weeks and Dad takes six weeks, your baby will have three months of solid parent attention. Better still, if each parent takes three months off—one following the other— their baby gets six months of full-time parents. No one can argue with the benefits of such an approach. (See the box Time Off for New Fathers on page 168.)

Give Dad time alone with the baby. What better way to integrate Dad into parenting than to have him spend uninterrupted time with his child? The fathers I spoke to who've taken time off or who've been forced into full-time fatherhood by unemployment learned a triple lesson. They learned to enjoy the rewards of being with a child and getting to know that child; they gained confidence in their own skills; and, just as important, they came to appreciate the difficulties of caregiving. Caring for a child is not an easy job.

Our attitudes as a society will only change if each of us, within our own families, promotes change. And the most disabling attitude confronting women in business and politics today is the feeling that, somehow, child-rearing issues, work-family programs, and parental-leave policies are women's issues. Indeed, at the peak of the parental-leave debate in Congress, I asked a couple of reporters why the discussion was getting so little play in the press. "It's a women's issue," they agreed, dismissing the subject offhandedly. That despite the fact that both of them were women. Editors don't give major coverage to something they believe is a women's issue—unless it is Mother's Day or Father's Day or Hillary Rodham Clinton is making a speech about it or someone's been shot at an abortion clinic. For most American men, subjects like child care and parental leave still rank with diaper rash and baby anecdotes as hot topics. But if men were to get into the picture, imagine the possibilities.

***

What to Remember

- *Be sensitive about introducing your child to new people.* After they are about four months old, babies recognize strangers. After six months, they will find strangers particularly, even profoundly, disturbing—some babies more than others. It is not unheard of for a baby to cry all day long when left suddenly in a new situation. Certainly, the harm won't be irreparable. But sensitivity is in order. Provide opportunities for your baby to experience separation and build relationships with others. If possible, introduce care, even part time, before a baby reaches the age of six months.
- *Ease into care.* It may be confusing to the baby, at any age, if one parent is around all the time, round-the-clock, for six weeks, three months, or four months, then suddenly disappears five

days a week, ten hours a day. Allow your baby time to get used to your absences and time to adjust to a new care situation.

- *Involve your partner in baby care whenever possible.* It gives you more flexibility when, for example, a caregiver's sick or the baby's sick and can't go to group care, or when one parent is away on business. Father can stand in for Mother; Mother can stand in for Father.

CHAPTER EIGHT

Choosing Child Care

"Child care is not just a service for working parents; it is a setting that constitutes a significant portion of the total environment in which our nation's children are developing physically, intellectually, and socially."

—*Edward F. Zigler and Mary E. Lang,* Child Care Choices, *1991*

When? Where? And how much? Those are the three big child-care questions. From the perspective of parents—and books on choosing child care—those questions often mean: When will I have to get back to work? Where is the most convenient place to put my child? And how much will it cost?

But look at these questions from the perspective of a developing child and you might rephrase them this way: When is the best age for what forms of care? Where is the best place for this particular child? And how much time should a child spend in alternative care? Given that, here are the choices:

- care at home—by a family member, paid sitter, or certified nanny
- care outside the home—by a relative, neighbor, unlicensed family day-care provider, licensed family day-care provider, or nonprofit or for-profit center
- shared care—in your home or someone else's, with a neighbor, friend, or acquaintance

- combined arrangements—for example, three days in family day care, two days with Dad; preschool plus in-home care; split shifts between parents; part-time mother care combined with family day care—the combinations are endless

The consensus among people in the field is that no child under age three needs group care, although kids of all ages can and do thrive in day-care centers and homes, and it can be a very healthy experience. New research tells us that babies learn from other babies, and being integrated into a group can have all sorts of positive results, from lasting friendships to a more outward focus and outgoing nature. But group care is not going to change your child's personality or make her smarter. Until about the age of 18 months or even two years, children don't necessarily need to be with other children. Until then, their play is parallel play. Any parent knows that watching a group of toddlers interact more nearly resembles crowd control than a social experience.

In a perfect child-care world—in which cost was not a factor, quality was not an issue, and practical considerations like transportation were of no concern—the safest bets for child care would be pretty simple: in-home, one-on-one care until the age of two and a half or three; then in-home care combined with a preschool or nursery school program for two or three hours a day; then a six-hour-a-day program at ages four and five. That's how the 1950s home-rearing model translates into a child-care model for the 90s, and it's the approach most experts would probably recommend. Parents, when asked to imagine a best-case scenario, choose care by a relative or parent until the age of four, when center care emerges as the most popular option.[1]

Most people I interviewed favored an in-home caregiver for infants and toddlers or, if that's not feasible, family day care—with its homelike appeal—until at least age three; most saw no problem with center care for threes, fours, and fives.

But in the present day-care environment, my recommending any particular form of child care over another is like my suggesting that your family buy a particular used car—without knowing the make and model, what you can afford, who's going to be driving it, and who's selling it. The only reasonable approach to choosing child care in America today involves some serious shopping and a fair amount of road testing. Most of what you'll see will be poor care; and unless parents start demanding more from child care, and from the people who can change it, I see no hope that it will change.

Where to begin. Start with a bit of self-examination. You've got to challenge your own assumptions about child care, whatever they may be. If you believe in your heart that child care is going to harm your child or that you, as a parent, are really the only person who can do this job of child rearing, then you have two options: you can reexamine your finances and, possibly, stop working for a time or you can attack your assumptions head-on. Experts in the field tell me that the quickest way to undermine your child's adjustment to a good day-care situation is by communicating your own distrust of it. The surest route to banishing your own ambivalence is by making a thorough and careful child-care choice.

Recognize that good child care exists. It's just a matter of finding it. Some parents assume that all child care is inadequate. Their expectations are so low that they settle for mediocrity or worse. "I've got this child; she's wonderful. Her mother is wonderful. She's a good parent," says one family day-care provider. "Before she came to me, she was in a horrible [family day care] home. I couldn't understand it. When I asked her mother why, she said, 'I thought that was all there was.'" Better to start with high expectations and work down.

Save your instincts for later. Most parents will tell you they went with their instincts when choosing child care; then they'll tell you about all their child-care nightmares. Research comes first, instincts second. Remember: You're not looking for a temporary arrangement. You're looking for a child-care situation that could last until your child enters school.

Challenge your own assumptions. That family day-care provider across town who's raising her own two children along with three others may be a better choice than Aunt Bertha's former housekeeper, who loves children and has raised four of her own. She may be better than that slick chain-operated center down the street. The church-sponsored day-care center near your office may be a better place for your child than the arms of that nanny from Utah, who sounds so nurturing and homespun but may not like the city—or worse still, your child—once she gets here. Don't assume anything until you've experienced it firsthand.

Forget money for the moment. Money should become an issue only after you've seen what's out there. Good care is not always more expensive than bad care. Like instincts, money should weigh in as the final consideration: when choosing one situation over another, for example. The cost of child care ranges from $60 to more than $300 a week. Most group care falls in the range of $100 a week. Infant care is the most costly of all. (See page 40.)

Take your time. Set aside at least a month to find child care; studies show that it takes parents, on average, five weeks to settle on child care. This is a process you hope to go through only once. (Most parents who find good child care use it not just for their first child but for the next, and the next.)

Finding Quality Care

For starters, you're looking for leads from anyone and everyone you know. Your objective is to find the best care available in your area, so don't stop until you have a good sense of what's out there. Are there any parent support groups in your area? In some places, formal networks have been established to help parents connect and share in-home care. Talk to other parents in your neighborhood and workplace. Find out what arrangements they've been happy with. But use that as a guide, a reference point—not an end point. Explore every resource: the yellow pages, area bulletin boards, local parent groups.

Get hooked into the local child-care community. Call your area Family Day Care Association; in most communities, the association will hold regular meetings, sponsor training sessions, and host support groups for providers. Find out if you can sit in on such a meeting and make contact with these people. They are intimately involved in the child-care community. They can steer you toward the best providers in your area. Many family day-care providers will have recommendations or may know someone with an opening. Just as important, they'll steer you away from the bad providers.

Contact area referral services. Check the phone book or contact Child Care Aware at 800-424-2246 to locate the referral agency nearest you. It will give you a list of providers to visit. (Keep in mind that these agencies do not screen providers.) Keep going back until you find someone you like. The squeaky wheel gets the best care. I talked with one mother, a former family day-care provider herself, who kept going back again and again to the referral agency, dissatisfied with the providers it had recommended. Finally, after several months, the referral agency called her: A spot had opened up with one of the most popular and reputable providers in the county. She got the opening out of sheer persistence; and she stuck with the provider for years.

Check with your employer. Some offer child-care information and referral services. If yours does, check them out; read the information they provide.

Visit some area day-care centers. Talk to people you know about what's in your area. Which centers have the best reputations? The best training programs? The lowest turnover? Which directors have been in the business for a long time? Find out if there's an association of day-care directors in your area and call them. You'll be amazed at how much you can discover just by talking to the professionals.

Screen in-home care candidates. Even if you're using employment agencies to help you find a nanny, don't assume they'll do a proper screening for you. Contact them to find out the cost of care, the fee for placements, and the guarantees, but be prepared to do a fair amount of screening on your own, including hiring a detective to do a background check. Screening an in-home provider means checking for a criminal history to ensure your child's safety.

You probably think all this sounds like a lot of work, even a lot of unnecessary work. But if you own a house, consider the amount of time you spent looking at real estate, calculating the costs, sitting down with agents and bankers and lawyers. If you've ever bought a car, you know how much time and research can go into that decision. Yet referral agencies tell me parents don't make that effort for child care. They assume that someone else has done the research for them; they assume that, say, a license means quality or a recommendation from a friend is good enough. They wait until the situation is desperate, forcing themselves into a corner. It's not because parents don't care; I think it's because they care too much. They don't want to make such an important decision until they really have to.

Factors to consider in choosing care:

- your child's age and personality
- the long-term reliability, stability, and consistency of the arrangement—in a center, that means low turnover; in family day care, evidence of a long-term commitment
- the caregiver's attitudes and personality
- the environment, including health and safety issues, equipment, and supplies
- the caregiver's ability to communicate with parents
- the caregiver's training
- group size (the number of children in a room or grouping) and optimal staff-child ratios (the number of adults for every child)

Licensed, Registered, Accredited: What Does It All Mean?

I have seen advertisements for day-care centers with the words "fully licensed" emblazoned across the ad, a case of misrepresentation to be sure. The truth is, all states require that day-care centers be licensed (although in several states it's referred to as accreditation or registration). And any center that is licensed is fully licensed.

Ratios and Group Sizes

Here are the recommendations from the National Association for the Education of Young Children for center care:

- for infants, a 1:2 or 1:3 staff-child ratio; maximum group size: nine children (six is better)
- for toddlers (up to age two and a half to three), a 1:6 ratio; maximum group size: 12
- for young preschoolers (three and four), a 1:7 ratio; "optimum" group size: 14
- for five-year-olds, a 1:15 ratio is acceptable for a kindergarten program[2]
- for family day care, when one adult is present, no more than five children age five or under (including the caregiver's own children under age ten); no more than two children under 30 months old; no more than two additional school-age kids[3]

Licensed. A licensed center or family day-care home meets a set of minimal requirements established by state law, which vary dramatically from one state to another. Most states regulate health and safety standards (fire safety, staff immunization and health checks, CPR training and first aid) and set minimal, measurable quality standards (staff-child ratios, group sizes, director and teacher training requirements). In recent years, some states have banned smoking in child-care facilities and required AIDS testing and criminal screenings for child abuse.

But regulations and enforcement levels vary dramatically from state to state. Different regulations apply to day-care centers, family day-care homes, and group family day-care homes, which keep large numbers of children. In some states, certain centers (for example, those that do not receive public subsidies or those affiliated with religious institutions) are exempt from licensing.

Licensing is a formal process; it means that regular inspections, license renewals, and compliance are, technically, required. Many states have formal mechanisms for filing and responding to complaints. But a license is not a stamp of approval or a guarantee of high quality. It simply means the provider or center has met certain minimal standards.

Self-certified or registered. In order to minimize the requirements for family day-care providers, some states simply require that providers fill out and send in a form certifying their compliance with various standards. The requirements for self-certification or registration may be the same as licensing requirements—e.g., maintaining appropriate ratios and health and safety standards. But with self-certification or registration, providers inspect their own facility. In some states, registration means nothing more than putting your name on a list. In either case, no one visits these homes to assure compliance, but you can register a complaint with authorities. And that means, in turn, that parents can check a provider's record.

Some small family day-care homes are not required to have a license. Some states allow family day-care providers with a certain number of children—for example, two or fewer unrelated children—to operate without a license. These regulations can be quite specific; for example, in Utah unlicensed providers may care for up to three children, including the provider's own children if they are not yet in first grade. Before assuming that a provider is operating illegally, find out whether your state requires that she have a license.

A license doesn't mean a provider is good. But a license is your assurance that the program is on record and being watched and that complaints can be filed. Consider the case of one four-month-old boy I met while researching this book. One day while he was sleeping, his licensed family day-care provider decided to slip away to the post office—leaving the child alone. Who discovered this? The licensing agent, who came by for a random site visit. While a license doesn't mean someone will be checking on your child daily, it does mean someone is keeping tabs—and records—on the provider.

Accredited by the National Association for the Education of Young Children (NAEYC). A day-care center that's accredited by NAEYC has been through a rigorous on-site evaluation, based on high standards. This does not mean it's an academically oriented program; it means that caregivers have been trained in how to deal effectively with children of different ages and schooled in activities that promote positive, *age-appropriate* experiences—not reading, writing, and arithmetic. The program is less than ten years old, and only 2,500 centers nationwide have achieved NAEYC accreditation. It is also voluntary; lack of accreditation does not mean a center is substandard. But NAEYC accreditation is the closest you'll come to finding a guarantee in the child-care business.

Accredited by the National Association for Family Child Care. Such accreditation is a rare thing indeed. Only 708 providers—out of more than a million—are certified nationwide. The program, under the auspices of the National Association for Family Child Care, is just getting under way. So again, failure to possess accreditation is meaningless. A license indicates that a family day-care provider is legitimate; in about half of the 50 states, ongoing training (ten hours of course work a year is recommended) is required to keep a license. Membership in the local family day-care association is probably your best indicator that a family day-care provider is serious, committed, and hooked in to the services provided on a local level. Family day-care associations offer support groups and educational programs; that means your provider is not operating in a vacuum.

Credentials for in-home caregivers. Look for one of the following:

- a degree from an accredited nanny school—there are 14 in the U.S. today
- a Child Development Associate credential (the CDA program is offered by the Council for Early Childhood Professional Recognition in Washington, D.C., and was originally developed for training Headstart teachers)
- courses in child development from a college or university

• credit hours of training through local referral agencies and associations (like the family day-care association)

At the very least, candidates should have completed a class in CPR or first aid (these are offered in most cities on an ongoing basis and generally involve a commitment of a few hours). But don't expect many, if any, candidates to possess formal training. Generally, good references, experience, and, most important, a stable job history are the only guides you'll have.

Au Pairs

The au pair program is monitored by the U.S. Information Agency through eight organizations around the country. Au pairs come to the U.S. on a J-Visa, which is a cultural and educational exchange visa, *not* a work visa. They are allowed to work as mother's helpers for up to 45 hours a week and stay for 13 months. For information on the au pair program and a list of these eight organizations, write the U.S. Information Agency, Office of Exchange, Visitor Program Services, 500 C St. SW, Rm. 200, Washington, DC 20547 or call U.S.I.A. at 202-619-4355.

Evaluating Child Care: What Are You Looking For?

Two children, probably around age two, are playing near an outdoor slide. Jacob has a paintbrush, which he is methodically rubbing in the sand and brushing on the sliding board. Andrew goes for the brush, trying to grab it out of Jacob's hand. Jacob, of course, resists. Teacher Mary Brenan walks over before the situation escalates and bends down to their level.

Brenan: Jacob has the paintbrush and Andrew wants it. Andrew, can you tell him that?

216

Andrew: I just want that.

Brenan: You just want that. You want that brush. Well, he's using it now. Would you like it when he's finished or would you like to choose another one? (Cut to Mary Brenan and Andrew in a corner of the play yard. She's leading; he's following.)

Brenan: We keep them in the basket so you can choose which one you'd like to play with. (Andrew selects a handful of brushes, smiling. Cut to slide. Fade as Andrew begins painting the slide.)

This scene is from a videotape called *Safe & Sound: Choosing Quality Child Care,*[4] developed to educate parents about how to recognize high-quality care. This is a real-life sequence at a real day-care program, not a scene scripted and performed by actors. That is what high-quality child care looks like: Children are engaged by the activities provided. Teachers are available and are trained in teaching children skills like negotiating, problem solving, and cooperation. Those are the lessons of early childhood.

What you're looking for in a good day-care program—be it a family day-care program or a day-care center—are good caregivers and some assurance that they will be around for more than a few weeks or months. That means people with the training to know how to teach social skills; people who are treated well—paid decent salaries and benefits; people who are genuinely interested in and enthusiastic about working with children. Most parents, when surveyed, will tell you training is irrelevant. They're looking for someone loving and nurturing and warm. But studies show that people with training are better at dealing with children; they are better at nurturing self-esteem; they are less punitive; and they are more attentive to a child's needs because they know what to expect from children.

Interactions Between Child and Caregiver

Studies show that the single most important determinant of how a child emerges from child care is the quality and degree of interaction between the caregivers and the children.[5] Even in programs of poor quality—with insufficient material and supplies or with poor health and safety procedures—the children with

217

Looking for Stability and Consistency

Stability and consistency are considered two of the most important elements of good early child-care programs. Given that, here are the questions to ask:

- Center care: What is your staff turnover? How long have the caregivers been in their jobs? What's their experience? What's their training? If possible, ask the teachers (not just the director) about turnover in the center.

- Family day care: How long have you been in business? What's your training? Do you have a license? Are you a member of the family day-care association? Have you had siblings come through the program? How long do most children stay? Get references from parents currently and previously in the program.

- In-home care: Get an employment history. Anyone with an unstable history should be immediately disqualified. (Parents with experience tell me that live-in help tends to be less stable than live-out, "because these people have lives.") Ask: Do you have children? What are their child-care arrangements? Are they in school? How long have you lived at your current address? Why did you leave your last job? Check all references and check them with care. Parents have been known to drive by the homes of references to check whether the addresses are real, or even to stop by for a personal visit.

responsive caregivers turned out more well-adjusted than those without responsive caregivers. The only way to gauge the quality of interactions between children and caregivers is by watching. Look for warmth and affection. Look for indications that a teacher is helping the children deal with one another.

Deborah Phillips, one of the top researchers in the field, explains the concept of quality care to me by describing two hypothetical centers at lunchtime:

"In the first," says Phillips, "the children are told to sit down at the table. The food is put in front of them without any words being exchanged. The teacher doesn't necessarily sit with the children. She may be off in a corner eating her own lunch. To the extent that the teacher does engage, it's only when the children start fighting over the food. If children want seconds, there's not enough food to give them seconds. And at the end of the meal, the time is up, the plates are taken away, and the children are shuttled on to the next activity."

She continues, "Compare that with a center where the children help serve themselves. They're encouraged to get their plates and carry them to the table. They're encouraged to help set the table. The teacher sits with the children and talks to the children about what color the peas are and what color the carrots are. They're encouraged to talk to each other. There's a conversation going on over lunch. Children are certainly given seconds. They're allowed to leave the table if they are done, as long as they leave quietly and politely. And they have to carry their plates to the garbage or whatever. And then they all wash their hands after lunch, and that's the end of the meal."

Where would you rather have your child: in a place where lunch is simply a meal—or a place where it is a social and educational experience as well? In a place where, when Andrew grabs Jacob's paintbrush, he is either ignored or shuffled off to time-out—or a place where the caregiver takes the time to work it out? What's the difference between one center and the other? "One breaks your heart," says Phillips. "The other warms your heart."

Observe and Learn

In her book *Mother Care/Other Care*, Sandra Scarr maintains that it takes about an hour of observation to tell whether a center is good enough. Not true, says Phillips, who's made a career out of observing and evaluating day-care programs. It takes much more than an hour; it takes several visits. It means sitting down and watching. And it means, of course, knowing what to look for. The biggest question to ask yourself when observing a child-care program is this: Are the children being treated with respect?

Looking at Child Care From a Child's Perspective

Educator Lilian Katz of the University of Illinois suggests looking at child care from a fresh perspective: that of a child. Instead of counting heads and calculating group sizes, evaluating the equipment and asking about the turnover, sit down and observe the program. Put yourself in the shoes of the children and ask yourself these questions:

- Do I feel welcome rather than captured?
- Do I feel that I belong, or am I just one of the crowd?
- Do I usually feel accepted, understood, and protected by the adults rather than scolded or neglected?
- Am I usually accepted rather than isolated or rejected by the majority of my peers?
- Am I usually addressed seriously and respectfully rather than as someone who is "precious" or "cute"?
- Do I find most of the activities engaging, absorbing, and challenging rather than just entertaining or exciting?
- Do I find most of the experiences meaningful rather than frivolous or boring?
- Do I find most of the experiences satisfying rather than frustrating or confusing?
- Am I usually glad to be here rather than eager to leave?

From "Multiple Perspectives on the Quality of Early Childhood Programs," by Lilian G. Katz in Childhood Education, *Winter 1992, pp. 66-71 (Eric Clearinghouse on Elementary and Early Childhood Education, ERIC Digest EDO-PS-93-2).*

Don't Confuse Child Care With School

You're not looking for a school but an environment that promotes *learning through play*—one that provides the kinds of activities that are appropriate to the preschool ages. Because play, it has been well documented, is the work of early childhood. The tools? Sandboxes and water bins, climbing equipment (soft for indoors and hard for outdoors), costumes, clay, paints and crayons, books, and toys—not just bright, shiny, new vehicles and plastic people but blocks, balls, bicycles, and games. A child of three can have as much fun, and learn as much, pasting jelly beans and Cheerios onto a piece of cardboard as she will have playing with the most expensive child-size computer money can buy. A child of four will learn as much about math, and have more fun, by baking cookies—measuring out the flour and sugar, counting how many cups—as he will by looking at numbers or trying to write them down.

In *Miseducation: Preschoolers at Risk,* psychologist David Elkind bemoans the emphasis on teaching young children inappropriate subjects like math, reading, or foreign languages, or how to play musical instruments. He blames a number of factors, including overachieving and competitive parents, the research on day care as a successful intervention for disadvantaged children, working parents' guilt-inspired desire to believe that day care is necessary for their child's cognitive growth, and research that tells us young children are like sponges. Sure they're like sponges—but that doesn't mean they're ready for formal schooling as we know it. "A lot of parents are looking for miniature schools when they look for child care," says Sandra Hackley, director of LOCATE: Child Care in Baltimore City, Maryland. That sentiment is echoed by numerous people in the referral field. Why not? After all, that's the only real group learning situation most parents have ever seen.

For whatever reason, many parents imagine that child care should be like school and that school readiness means doing schoolwork at age three, four, or five. Elkind argues that children who learn to read early gain little in the long run and may in fact lose out; and children who are forced to grapple with academic material too early "turn off" before they reach school, because most are not cognitively able to grasp concepts like addition and subtraction and thus are primed for failure and, as a result, low self-esteem.

Elkind cites the Danish and French systems in support of his view. In Denmark children begin formal reading instruction in the *second grade*. "Before that," he writes, "children have a rich exploratory and manipulative language experience; they are read to and talked to, encouraged to dictate their own stories. . . . Denmark has almost 100 percent literacy," Elkind notes. In contrast, in France, where children begin formal reading programs in kindergarten, "some 30 percent of children" have "reading problems." Why? Elkind speculates that they are expected to learn to read long before they're ready.[5]

Until they reach about age five, children learn by touching, seeing, feeling, talking, and doing; by manipulating objects and ideas. It's not until they reach school age that children are really ready, argues Elkind, for more symbolic learning—learning that involves numbers and letters. Montessori programs are so successful because they were designed for the way children learn: by manipulating materials, by using their senses. But a strict, full-day Montessori program lacks elements crucial to the learning process, like pure play.

Given that, when choosing child care for toddlers and preschoolers, look for the following:

A child-structured place. The environment should be designed around the needs of a child, with child-size stuff and organized spaces (a reading corner, a rest area, a block area, a climbing space, a dress-up corner, a child-size kitchen); there should be plenty of time and room outdoors.

Built-in flexibility. The schedule should include some group time but allow plenty of time for children to choose what they want to do. Look for play and projects that don't require adult direction and involvement. For example, the artwork should look like a child's art—not something precut by the teacher and pasted together according to directions. You're looking for a routine without rigidity. If a schedule is too inflexible, providers simply don't have time to do much child rearing.

Says Phylis Benner, a provider with 35 years' experience in the child-care field who now teaches parenting workshops, "What sometimes happens in center care is that somebody in an administrative position decides on the daily schedule, and caregivers are locked in. It takes time to talk things out with children, to get down on your knees when someone's hurt and say, 'Look at her face—she really looks unhappy. She didn't like it when you bit her.' There's a lot going on. You need to teach the 'victim' how to say 'stop.' People don't understand that it's a legitimate learning activity to take time for toddlers to begin to feed themselves with finger food. It's a legitimate learning activity for children to learn how to put their coats on by themselves."

Appropriate group size and staff-child ratios—small enough to give caregivers plenty of opportunities to talk with the children; to respond to their questions; to mend their hurts; to intercede when necessary. That kind of interaction happens not just when there are enough caregivers around but when group sizes are kept small enough.

A sense of order. If children are wandering around glassy-eyed, then they are not engaged. What you don't want to see is a chaotic, crowded place where teachers are overburdened and spending their time managing the confusion and the misbehavior. Children need routines to mark the day. They need a sense of where things go. They need rules to follow.

All of these elements add up to programs that, in the child-care field, are labeled "developmentally appropriate."

The Selection Process: How It Works

If you're considering group care—either family day care or a center—once you've narrowed the field, you'll start calling providers. Tell them the age of your child; ask about openings; ask about the program. Of course, you'll want to know about the cost,

What's Developmentally Appropriate?

When I asked an upscale, well-read, college-educated mother with a high-powered job if she felt she was capable of evaluating whether her daughter's day-care program was developmentally appropriate, she answered, simply, "No." "I just don't know that much about it," she said. Indeed, she seemed to bristle at the term—as if it implied some kind of knowledge that was inaccessible to her. "I'm very seat-of-the-pants on these things," she said. "I don't ask, Do I have the right toys? I ask, Are my kids happy? Do they seem well-adjusted? Are they interested?"

In truth, during the course of our conversation it became obvious that she had a keen sense of what was developmentally appropriate for various ages. She and her husband, a member of their day-care center's board, became concerned about their daughter's program following a change in toddler teachers. At drop-off, the mother noticed two children crying, and no one was responding to them. Another child was wandering around the room, looking bored. A fourth approached a teacher and asked to read a book; the teacher didn't respond. Sure signs of a "developmentally inappropriate" program. "That day, I called [my husband], hysterical, and said, 'We've got to have a meeting because I'm not leaving her there another day.'"

In the language of the trade, a "developmentally appropriate" program—whether it's center care, family day care, or in-home care—is one that suits the age of the child, with caregivers who know what to expect from and how to treat children at various ages.

The National Association for the Education of Young Children (NAEYC), in addition to serving as an accreditation agency, is a clearinghouse for information on early-childhood programs. NAEYC has published three pamphlets

224

detailing the appropriate practices for infants, toddlers, and preschoolers. Available for 50 cents through NAEYC, these brochures are priceless—the best guidelines I've seen for evaluating child-care programs:

- *Developmentally Appropriate Practice in Early Childhood Programs Serving Infants* (from birth until walking): order NAEYC #547
- *Developmentally Appropriate Practice in Early Childhood Programs Serving Toddlers* (from onset of walking until about age two and a half): order NAEYC #508
- *Developmentally Appropriate Practice in Early Childhood Programs Serving Younger Preschoolers* (from age two and a half to four): order NAEYC #516

Send 50 cents along with your order to: National Association for the Education of Young Children, 1509 16th St. NW, Washington, DC 20036-1426.

but save that question for later. Some providers are put off by it. "If someone calls and their first question is 'What does it cost?,' I just tell them I don't have any openings," says Virginia Spitler, head of the Montgomery County family day-care association. If the phone call goes well, you'll want to take it from there, which means interviews, observations, drop-ins, and, ultimately, visiting with your child. Many of the same issues will come up when you're looking at family day care and center care. (Specifics on evaluating family day care appear later in this chapter.) During the initial visit, you'll get a sense of the place and sit down for an interview with the family day-care provider or the center director. They'll explain:

- their philosophy—try to learn whether they give children choices, focus on communicating rather than punishment, treat kids with respect, believe in learning through play

- schedules—group times, nap times, outdoor times, meal-times
- how they communicate with parents—via newsletter, bulletin boards, phone calls at nap time, nighttime calls, diaries
- practical concerns—rules regarding sick kids, procedures for payment, drop-off and pick-up, expectations regarding parental involvement

Listen for evidence that caregivers have been around a long time, that siblings have come through the program, and that there is an emphasis on caregiver training.

Then it's time for your questions. Regarding staff, ask:

- What are your criteria for hiring staff? Or: Tell me about your staff. Listen for a commitment to keeping staff.
- What's your staff turnover? Listen for a low percentage, say around 20 percent or lower. If it's high, ask for the reasons.
- What are your staff training requirements? Listen for a Child Development Associate credential (CDA) or a degree in child development or education for lead teachers; ten credit hours of training a year for family day-care providers or center teachers; ongoing training and staff training days.
- What are your policies regarding benefits, vacations, and salaries for staff and teachers? Again, you're looking for evidence of a commitment to keeping staff.

For feelers, ask:

- How do you handle difficult children? (Ask even if your child isn't difficult.)
- What would you do if my child hit another child?
- How do you promote sharing?
- Do you use time-out?

Check the responses against Strategies for Dealing With Young Children in chapter nine. Listen for thoughtful responses. Here's what some caregivers advise:

Says Denise Merkel, who runs an after-school program for preschoolers in Washington, D.C., "What do you do when a child hits another child? One answer you're *not* looking for is 'We give them a time-out' or 'We make them sit in a bad boy chair.' We talk with the children about taking turns and then not hitting. We used to go around saying, 'We don't hit here.' After I said that about ten times, I realized, we *are* hitting. We *do* hit. Now I say, 'I'm not going to allow you to hit here.' And when a child hits, we don't just say, 'Tell him you're sorry.' We say, 'Tell him you're sorry and that you won't do it again.' "

Early child development consultant Phylis Benner says, "I have a problem with time-out being used inappropriately. When a child is in time-out, that child is not sitting there being sorry. That child is sitting there planning revenge. And as soon as you let them up, he or she generally goes right back into the situation. You know time-out's not working if you have to keep putting a child back in the chair again and again; particularly if the child is doing the acting out behavior for attention. That means he gets that attention every time you put him back in the chair. It's also very demeaning. Everyone knows what that chair is; it's like putting a dunce cap on a kid."

Ellen Galinsky of the Families and Work Institute suggests asking a teacher to describe another child. "What's Susie like?" or "Tell me about John." "Then listen to the words," says Galinsky. "Are they words of appreciation? Are they words of joy? Or are they words of judgment and censure?"[6] If you hang around a little bit, you should get a sense of whether caregivers are overstressed or at ease; even whether they find this to be a good place to work.

Other things to find out about:

Nap time. Ask whether all children are required to sleep at nap time (if it's not covered in the presentation). This is a tough one. Providers are required by law to provide nap space and nap time. All providers depend on nap time for a break. But not all children sleep. A good center allows for flexible scheduling for infants and toddlers; and a good center allows children to read or play quietly or move out of the nap room if they do not sleep. What could be more awful for a child than spending two hours in a darkened room on a cot and being unable to sleep? Yet some day-care centers require children to stay in bed.

Food. If a center is eligible for a federally funded hot lunch program, check it out. Center directors tell me the day-care catering services aren't exactly party planners. "We had to try six services before we found food that we could actually eat," says one day-care director. You don't want your child complaining about day care every morning just because the food doesn't taste good.

Making changes/moving kids up. If your child is starting care at 23 months and is slated to move into a new room at 24 months or even 26 months, work it out on the front end. Certainly, you don't want Billy or Sarah to have to make a change after he or she has just adjusted to a new program.

Policies regarding helping your child adjust. (See page 263 on Easing Into Care.)

Choosing Child Care for Difficult Kids: A Different Ball of Wax

"It's genetic," says Virginia Spitler, who's been a family day-care provider for more than 20 years. "I have a child who has an awful temper. His father has an awful temper. As far as I'm concerned, that's all there is to it."

Says another provider, "I have this child who pitches a fit every time his mother comes to pick him up. One time she looked at me almost pleading and said, 'Why does he do this?' She was absolutely lost. I told her it's just the way he is."

All children are difficult some of the time. Some children are difficult all of the time. In *The Difficult Child*, Stanley Turecki maintains that 15 percent of all children are just plain difficult— ranging from "difficult some of the time" to "mother killers," a term that is self-explanatory. He argues that some kids are simply born that way; such children require a good deal more management than easy children and cause a good deal more grief. But they are normal.

According to Turecki, relief is in sight once you realize such children are not being difficult "to get you," that it's not a problem brought on by poor parenting, and that there are strategies to help manage them—but not necessarily the same strategies that work with less difficult kids. Firmness and authority, the formula for raising happy, compliant children, can backfire with difficult kids, who can turn a firm "no" into a major battle. So the old cliché "choose your battles" takes on great significance. With difficult kids, the appropriate response for a tantrum may be love and attention rather than the standard "no response."

Difficult kids can be unpredictable, finicky, loud, very active, or just plain negative—any or all of which makes them prime candidates for problems in group care. Some kids have particular difficulty with transitions and change; others are particularly sensitive to the feel of certain clothes or to certain tastes or smells. In other words, for some children, getting up and dressed and out to a child-care program can itself be a nightmare.[7]

What's All This Got to Do With Child Care?

Listen to what some of the providers I interviewed have to say about difficult kids: "We ask them to leave the program." "Their parents just aren't around enough to bring in the reins. No one is setting limits at home." "These kids don't want to be in day care. They want to be home." "Her parents aren't around enough to even care whether she's difficult. It doesn't affect their lives." "In the last center where I worked, they used to send difficult kids to the director's office, and they'd just sit there."

Now listen to some parents: "The day-care center says he's got a behavior problem, that this is serious. They called me several times. But when we sat down and talked about it, I realized that all his problems centered around the fact that he was unwilling to participate in morning group time. I just don't think they're flexible enough." "My first two kids were really easy children. My last two were really intense, much more difficult to handle. I had trouble holding on to a sitter. They just had more trouble with the kids." "He was kicked out of his last program. I was at my wit's

229

end. Then I put him in a preschool that focuses on the individual child, that understood *his* needs. They said, 'This is an enthusiastic, smart, active child. Let's work with him.' It was like night and day."

If you have a particularly difficult child, you need to tailor your child-care choices to meet that child's needs. For example, according to Turecki, some difficult kids jump from activity to activity until they "lock in" on something that captures their interest. Then it's near-impossible to pull them away. Imagine such a child in a group program in which kids are expected to drop everything at 10 A.M. and move on to the next activity. Other children may have extreme trouble with any kind of change in routine or transition—out to the playground, into the lunchroom, into group time. These kids are doomed to have problems in group care unless somebody's aware of their temperament. Still other children are simply loud or overexcitable or resistant to any new situation (even a trip to the supermarket).

If you're planning to introduce child care and your child has a difficult temperament, you should:

- start by pinpointing the problems, if you haven't already
- evaluate the appropriateness of the program on that basis
- make sure the caregiver or people running the program know about these problems
- find out in advance how they're going to handle specific situations
- work with the providers to get through any difficulties

If you don't deal with your child's difficulties head-on, the repercussions could be fairly substantial:

- Many providers and centers will kick a difficult child out rather than focus on solving the problem. In-home caregivers who can't handle a difficult child will simply quit.
- It will affect your relationship with the caregiver. Day-care workers and family day-care providers will assume that you're

a bad parent; once that notion is established, it will be tough to get beyond it.

- Chances are your child will spend a good bit of the day being punished, unless you've got trained people involved. Group care requires routines, rules, and compliance; most providers don't have the energy, knowledge, or incentive to deal with your child's problems individually.

- Finally, it's hard to like a difficult child who isn't your own. You can expect him to alienate peers and providers alike, setting off a vicious cycle of low self-esteem and poor peer relationships that may continue through the school years.

The easiest answer for parents with difficult kids is simply to hand them over to someone else and hope for the best. But that's not going to be the best solution for your child. What is best is finding a program in which providers are well trained in child development and sensitive to the needs of difficult children. I found one director who said she would never kick a child out of a program but would instead work with the child.

Turecki reminds parents that difficulties may be home centered or school centered. In other words, you may have more problems with your child at home than at school; or problems you've never encountered may surface during the first group-care experience, which may magnify them. Turecki notes that some parents may simply have to stop working during early childhood to resolve these behavioral problems. Other psychologists feel that getting a break from a difficult child is important for parents, who then approach the task with more patience and less frustration.

One longitudinal study of working mothers and their children found that mothers with easy children were more likely to work than mothers with difficult ones. Although these results are subject to a variety of interpretations, one thing is certain: You can go a long way toward preventing a major upheaval in your life by choosing child care with an eye toward your child's temperament.

Advice From Parents: The Finer Points of Making Child-Care Choices

Would that life were simple—that choosing child care meant only one visit to one place and using child care meant setting up just one arrangement. But in reality, child care can mean more than one arrangement: preschool and an after-school program or preschool combined with family day care, for example. And choosing care involves numerous considerations, including many that parents are unaware of. The following are some insights and cautionary notes—things to keep in mind when choosing child care:

Is it a nursery school or day care? Increasingly, the line between preschools and day-care centers is becoming blurred. Many day-care programs market themselves as preschools; numerous preschools, particularly in urban areas, have extended-day programs. You should be aware that in public schools that offer pre-K and kindergarten, many of these fee-based extended-day programs are run by private groups and operated under contract with the school.

When selecting such programs, a separate interview or visit to the extended-day program is essential. Any day-care center that operates a kindergarten should be accredited by the local board of education.

Piggybacking. When preschools offer no after-school care, parents are often forced to make elaborate plans to shuttle their kids between programs and providers. Some manage by using in-home care in combination with a preschool program. Others use family day-care providers who transport the child to and from school.

One mother I interviewed, Robin Latham, had her four-year-old in a preschool; she'd pick him up at noon and drop him at a family day-care provider's home three days a week. That fell apart relatively quickly. It's not easy for a three-year-old to say good-bye to his mother twice in one morning; nor is it easy to adjust to two dramatically different settings.

In *The Hurried Child*, David Elkind describes a jerry-rigged arrangement for a four-year-old named Peter. First, Peter goes to a neighbor's house, where he is picked up by a car pool and transported to nursery school. Then, after school, the child is picked up again by a car pool and dropped at his neighbor's house. Writes Elkind, "By the time he gets home, Peter has been out of the house for almost twelve hours and has adapted to a number of different places (neighbor's house, care, school) and a number of different people (neighbor, car pool person, teachers)." He continues, "This is a lot of adaptation for a four-year-old, and he has had to call upon his energy reserves in order to cope." Elkind calls this kind of setup "change overload." The result is a whiny, difficult, and unfocused kid.[8]

If you have one preschool-care arrangement, school, and an after-school arrangement for a preschool-age child, you are asking too much of that child. The most successful arrangements for piggybacking preschool and child care involve in-home sitters. Keep in mind, however, that most experts agree that no child *needs* to be in school before kindergarten—although children will need ample outside activities, friends, play groups, and playgrounds before then.

Part-time care. Children cherish the safety and predictability of a routine. If you have a part-time work arrangement, try to keep it simple, consistent, and sequential. A Tuesday, Wednesday, Thursday schedule is better than Monday, Wednesday, Friday because children get into a predictable rhythm. When they wake up, they're probably going to ask, "Is this a work day or a home day?" But it's easier for them to adapt if the days run in sequence. Providers, too, say children manage better if they are in care on sequential days.

Five 4-hour days are better than three 7-hour days—not just because the routine is more predictable (day care every morning) but because length of day is important for some children. Many providers tell me that once young children have spent six hours in care, they often are ready for the day to end. "They're not gaining anything from those afternoon hours," says one day-care director.

From a child's perspective, the shorter, the better. However, center care may not be the best arrangement for a part-timer. With most kids enrolled full time, a part-timer may feel like the odd kid out, unable to really get with the program.

Beware of too many special events. They sound good to parents but offer few benefits to children under age four. Special events—holiday parties, special guests, trips to the museum—can disrupt the routine and disturb very young children, and according to Lilian Katz of the University of Illinois, they are of little long-term value.[9]

At centers, be conscious of changing shifts. Most parents don't realize that when a child-care program is open nine or ten hours a day, there's going to be a shift change in there somewhere. Staff will work a standard eight hours and rotate in and out. Find out when the change occurs and how it works, and observe the transition if you can.

Drop in. Once you think you've found the right place, drop by unannounced two or three times—even during the same day—without your child. Ideal times for a visit include the lunch hour, nap times, and playground times. Says Judy Montgomery of Child Care Information, Inc., a Louisiana referral agency, "Lunchtime is where you find children who are cranky because they're hungry. . . . If they don't like what they're fed, they're unhappy. You'll see how a staff person interacts with a child under stress."

On the playground, the big issue is whether staff congregates together and chats or interacts with the kids. You're looking for the latter, although it's worth mentioning that even at some of the best centers, caregivers have a tendency to see "playground time" as a kind of break time. Fair enough—everyone needs a break. But are they paying attention? Are disputes passing unnoticed? Are children being pushed on swings? Is there some engagement? At nap time, you want to see the sleeping facilities, but also note how staff helps kids get settled and handles those who are not sleeping.

Don't stop dropping in once your child enters the program; as a general rule, plan to arrive late in the morning or do an early pick-up every now and then.

Talk to the teachers. Be wary of any program that doesn't encourage teacher-parent communication. Incredibly, there are such programs. Some require that all communications go through the director. That should be a red flag, because it means either the director doesn't trust her staff, the center has something to hide, or the staff has not been trained in how to deal with parents.

Sadly, day-care directors report that many parents are at best thoughtless and at worst downright rude when dealing with center staff. "These professional types will come in and start demanding things—'Where are his socks? Why is his shirt covered with paint? Did he take a nap?'—in a tone of voice that suggests 'You work for me,'" says one day-care director. "It really puts the assistant teachers off. Some of them get really upset, and they refuse to deal with the parents." But if you can't talk to the classroom teacher, the thread that connects home and day care will be lost.

Look for an open-door policy. Be particularly wary of a program that doesn't allow you to come by at any time. Of course, if you drop in unannounced, be prepared to take your child home with you when you leave. Coming and going without notice could be disruptive and disturbing to your child. But an open-door policy is essential.

Consider Little Rascals Day Care in Farmville, North Carolina, where the "Farmville Four," who ran and staffed the center, were indicted on 429 counts of sexual abuse. Only one mother interviewed in a recent documentary about the case was absolutely certain that no abuse had taken place.[10] Why? The only full-time working mother who used the center, she had an erratic schedule that meant picking up her child at odd hours, popping in and out of the center all the time with no prior notice. She knew, not only from her own daughter's behavior but also from her own experience, that the charges of bizarre and abusive behavior leveled against these providers were impossible.

Profit vs. Nonprofit Centers

Industrywide, studies tell us that for-profit centers pay their teachers less than anyone else in the industry and have higher turnover rates and lower staff-child ratios.[11] Why? For one thing, child care simply isn't a product that operates best on free-market principles. The bottom-line focus leads to high turnover, which is bad for kids. According to the National Child Care Staffing Study (1990), "Children in centers with higher turnover rates spent less time engaged in social activities with peers and more time in Aimless Wandering."[12] They were also found to have lower language skills. But it doesn't take a study to tell you that high turnover's bad for kids.

A second problem inherent in for-profit care: These programs have to depend exclusively on parent fees, while nonprofits have access to other income sources (grants, donations, government subsidies) to offset the high cost of delivering high-quality care. For-profits, in some cases, cost less than nonprofit centers. But in such cases you usually get what you pay for.

Some people claim the arguments against for-profit chains are purely ideological; that, in fact, for-profits often deliver programs that are "remarkably similar" to those of nonprofits. One study conducted in Connecticut found few differences between the two types of centers, but it did note that "where differences among the center types occurred, nonprofits were typically superior to for-profits." Where did the differences emerge? Among other issues, "Observations show that the nonprofit centers on average had environments that were more child-sensitive, more frequently had more materials in general and had more materials that encouraged creativity than did for-profit centers." Caregivers in nonprofits were "more frequently observed encouraging children to be involved with peers and materials" and were more likely to "establish rules that minimized disruption and disagreements."[13]

Barbara Willer, public affairs director for the National Association for the Education of Young Children, maintains that some nationwide chains have begun addressing the quality issue.

Kindercare, for example, "has recently beefed up its training program" and is trying to achieve accreditation. But Kindercare has a bad rep among child-care people for other reasons—notably its effort to sell Kindercare products to a captive audience of parents and kids, including life insurance for children.[14]

The bottom line on for-profit care: Let the buyer beware. What appears to be convenient, well-run, affordable care may look good to you but may not be good for kids. A long, hard look, a chat with the teachers, a series of drop-ins, and a few pointed questions can make all the difference. I found it interesting, for example, that the only day-care director I interviewed who objected to my encouraging parents to ask about staff salaries and benefits was the director of a for-profit center: "It's none of their business," she said pointedly. "I don't ask parents what they make." Her response made it clear that she missed the point altogether.

Choosing a Family Day-Care Provider

Family day care is one of the most popular child-care options in America, particularly for parents who work part time or have children under age three. It sounds ideal: a homelike setting, a dedicated mom caring for her own kids along with yours, plenty of freedom for the children, and flexibility for the parents (family day-care providers may have longer hours than centers and more flexible sick-care policies).

According to Susan Kontos, who made a study of the studies on family day care for her book *Family Day Care: Out of the Shadows and Into the Limelight*, family day care is not necessarily popular because parents prefer it over other forms of care; it's popular because it's available and accessible. There are probably 1.5 to 2 million family day-care providers minding over 5 million children in America today. According to the most reliable estimates, most of the homes—60 to 90 percent—are unlicensed and unregulated.[15]

I cannot in good conscience recommend signing up with an unlicensed provider who cares for groups large enough to require a license. It is illegal and risky; and from a political perspective, it encourages the continued growth of this vast underground network of unregulated providers. Studies have found that unlicensed providers are less apt to be caring and nurturing and more apt to deliver substandard care. But sadly, unregulated care is not the exception; in the world of family day care, it is the norm.

What you'll learn rather quickly when you begin looking at family day care is how varied it is. Some providers run what are essentially home-based preschool programs, often in expansive remodeled basements with kitchens, playrooms, and nap rooms. Others simply take in a few children, who have the run of the house. I met one provider who had given over the living room in her suburban home to child-size furniture and shelves full of toys. No parent passes beyond that point, except, occasionally, to fetch a child. "I got tired of parents coming into the family room and making themselves at home and staying until all hours of the night," the provider said. Others take on too many kids, have too little space, and offer little in the way of stimulation, activities, and toys.

A license does not mean a program is good; but good programs are more likely to be run by licensed providers.

Finding High-Quality Family Day Care

Mediocre family day care may be easy to find. High-quality care, however, is not; the search can be long. If you're going through a referral agency and making blind calls, expect to visit as many as ten homes before you come close to finding what you're after. Here are a few guidelines:

A good provider has a set interview process. For example, she might have parents come for an evening interview, then ask parents to visit during the program's hours *without* the child, then have parents visit with the child. A good provider will be screening you just as you're screening her. She'll be looking for parents and children who blend with her program. Once you've narrowed the field, you should spend at least part of the day observing the program and drop in (without your child) two or three times before making a final decision.

By the end of the interview, you should know about the basic philosophy, age mix, routine, activities, and general rules of the place. Are there paid holidays? Paid days when your child is sick? Is there vacation time? Is there a mechanism for backup care if the provider is ill? What is your child expected to bring (diapers, lunch, change of clothes) and allowed to bring (toys from home)? You'll want to ask many of the same questions that appear on page 191.

Look for signs of genuine warmth with children, not false warmth. Listen to the caregiver's story. (Ask her how long she's been in business and why she's involved in family day care.) Look for signs of a long-term commitment and an understanding of children. (Ask her to describe the other kids in care; how she handles conflicts; her views on discipline and punishment.) But remember, the research has shown that the best providers, the most caring and nurturing providers, are those who demonstrate their commitment to the field—by getting a license, by joining their local family day-care association or other professional groups, and by participating in training programs. Look for evidence of "intentionality." (See page 70.)

Ask about issues related to personal values. Such issues probably come up more when you are choosing family day care than when you choose any other form of care. That means questions about television and the type of television programming; nutritious foods; punishment; religion (some family day-care programs are religious). You'll find quirky providers out there who believe in one particular child-development theory and not another. You'll also find people who, like parents, fall into the common trap of assuming young children are ready to be in school before they're school age.

When a Washington, D.C., mother I'll call Eve Meadows was looking at family day care for her one-year-old, she interviewed a family day-care provider who'd left a corporate job to be home with her kids. The provider's style was professional (she had a resume, a handbook, references), but there was something that made Eve uncomfortable. At snack time the woman gave everybody an apple, sat them around a kitchen table, pulled out a chalkboard, and began a lecture about apples. Says Eve, "She was trying to present this educational program about apples, but the kids weren't paying attention. My son was only a year old. I was afraid he wasn't going to go with this game plan."

Look for flexibility. The routine in a family day-care home should be fluid enough to allow children to make choices about how they spend time. That, after all, is one of the biggest advantages of family day care vs. center care. But there should be a routine and a sense of order to the environment. You're looking for a place that's organized and neat, but not fastidiously clean.

"My sister is a neat nut," says one family day-care provider. "She put her two-year-old and five-year-old in a family day-care program that was meticulously neat. They seemed perfectly happy. When they visited me recently, I asked them what they did all day. The older sister told me that they all sat at the kitchen table all morning and worked on paper—writing. I told my sister to get the kids out of that place."

Ask about television and toys. The research on family day care raises red flags about too much TV and too little to do, so investigate. Ask how much television the children watch; if you suspect the television is on all day, stop by periodically before you make your final decision. Also ask what toys and equipment are available. Look for books, art supplies, games, and ample, sturdy toys. You'll want evidence that the provider invests time in caring for the kids and invests money in making sure they have something to do. Otherwise, your child is likely to spend the day fighting with Bobby over one Little Tikes bus or pushing Nancy off the only riding toy. Worse still, he might spend the day doing, essentially, nothing at all.

Ask about outings. Outings are an asset if they're age-appropriate. I encountered one provider who spent the morning taking her kids to a nearby shopping mall—fun for an occasional outing, but hardly a stimulating everyday activity for a child. Others make regular trips to the park. Some plan weekly outings to a restaurant, the supermarket, the paint store. One of the biggest advantages of family day care over center care is the ability to make regular forays into the real world.

Be direct and specific about certain issues; there are things a provider may not tell you unless you ask. She may drive a car pool every Thursday at 2 P.M. and plan to take your child along. She may keep three preschoolers in the morning, but six older children may arrive after school. She may be planning to take on an infant. She may go to a hair appointment every Tuesday afternoon while the kids are napping, leaving her teenage son to babysit. She may ask a neighbor to help out on a regular basis.

None of these facts should necessarily deter you from signing up, but they will certainly help you make a decision. Ask these questions: Will you be leaving my child with any other adults? Are there other adults in the house during the day? Will you be driving my child in your car? Will you be taking my child anywhere else during the day? How many children are currently in your care? Do you expect to increase the number of children? How many are you licensed to keep? What children are here at what times?

Ask about naps. The best time to call just about any family day-care provider is between 1 and 3 P.M.; that's downtime. Naps are essential in family day care; it's the only break a provider gets in a day that can stretch to ten or more hours. Be sure to find out what the nap situation is. Are the children sleeping in bedrooms? How long are they expected to nap? (One provider tells me she's got three- and four-year-olds sleeping for four hours every afternoon; another puts the kids in pajamas and has them go through a complete bedtime ritual: toothbrushing, bedtime story, lights out.) Consider how the nap schedule will mesh with your child's sleep patterns and whether she will adapt.

Check on policies regarding morning drop-off and evening pick-up. They may be out of sync with your expectations. Says one provider, "I don't let my parents come in at the end of the day. It's good-bye, get your coat, out you go. There might be some quick exchange like 'Jackie had a good day' or 'Janie was fussy.' But otherwise, the parents linger and the kids get into power plays between adults. Because of that, I have to let them drop in anytime they want. Otherwise, they'd never see the inside of the place." Be sure you're allowed in the program at some time.

Find out how communication takes place. It may be over the phone at nap time or at pick-up or drop-off. What you're looking for is evidence that communication *does* take place.

Ask about training. Ten hours of course work a year is considered the minimal standard for family day-care providers. But keep in mind that some of these hours are going to be in areas like "marketing your program" and "managing your business." Find out what child-development courses, if any, the provider has taken.

Realize that licensed providers want to be recognized as professionals. Some will expect you to sign a contract; others may have a handbook with rules, program logistics, and schedules.

Play it safe. With family day care, you've got to become the inspector. A home is going to be inherently more unsafe than an institution. Check to be sure that medicine cabinets are locked, cleansers and detergents are out of reach, and stairs are fenced off. Ask about emergency procedures and ask to see the first-aid kit.

Watch the provider's children. When observing family day care, you'll obviously want to watch the other children in the program, with an eye toward how they might mix with your own and how the provider engages them. But you'll also want to watch the *provider's* children. Some of them resent having their home invaded from nine to five every day. Says one grown daughter of a family day-care provider, "They actually used to sleep in my bed. I'd go to bed at night and it would be full of sand." I've seen providers' children who are genuinely abusive to their peers in family day care. One Maryland mother pulled her son out of a family day-care arrangement because the provider's child, who came home at 3 P.M., was picking on him. He was old enough to tell her what was going on.

Before you sign up, watch closely for signs of a problem. Those children are your window to a provider's child-rearing style. Says one mother, "I almost went with this one woman until I watched her with her own son. He was taking out the vacuum and pretending to vacuum, and she had told him many, many times to stop. She was trying to find ways to distract him. Finally, she got angry. She grabbed him harshly and yelled, 'Oh, you!' That one incident made my decision for me."

Be realistic. Say you find a warm, hearty soul who loves children, comes highly recommended, and has three or four kids in her care who are just the right age mix for your own. She gives over her kitchen to mixing dough and finger painting. She has a well-stocked toy shelf and a sprawling backyard full of climbing equipment and swings, and she spends countless hours reading, playing games, and engaging and stimulating her kids. But she gives them lollipops every day after lunch (and you don't like sweets), or they watch a one-hour Barney video every day (and you don't like any TV at all), or her grammar's not that great (and you are an English teacher), or there are no riding toys (and Janie loves riding toys). You can't have everything.

***

What to Remember

- *You're looking for the best care available in your community, so allow ample time—a month or more—to find it.* Remember, you're looking for a place where your child can potentially spend his or her preschool years.
- *Once you've narrowed the field, investigate carefully.* In addition to interviewing the provider, you should plan to spend a morning observing the program; then drop in several times, visiting during a nap session, during a meal, and, if staff rotates, during a shift change.
- *Key issues include staff turnover and training, ratios, and group size; but the number one concern should be how the caregivers interact with the children.* Look for signs of sensitivity to a child's needs

and an attitude of respect. Look at the program's history: Have the caregivers been there for many years? Do siblings tend to be enrolled? Have many of the five-year-olds been there since toddlerhood?

- A *license matters*. If you're looking at family day care, ask to see the license, and even though few centers and providers are accredited, ask about accreditation by NAEYC (for centers) and the National Association for Family Child Care. Unless parents begin to demand accreditation, it's not going to happen.

- *Look for a program that allows you to ease your child into care.* (See chapter nine.)

- *Find a situation you can trust so you can communicate that trust to your child and feel confident about your work arrangements.*

CHAPTER NINE

The Young Child

I have a secret dragon
Who is living in the tub,
It greets me when I take
   a bath,
And gives my back a scrub.
My parents cannot see it,
They don't suspect it's there,
They look in its direction,
And all they see is air.

—*From "I Have a Secret Dragon" in* The Dragons Are Singing Tonight, *by Jack Prelutsky*

Jennifer, age three, is sitting at the kitchen table drinking cranberry juice. She takes a sip, waits a moment, then spits it out. She picks up the cup again and repeats this procedure. And then does it again. I am watching Jennifer's mother. What is she going to do about this spitting? The possibilities are nearly endless:

1. She could remove the cup and say, matter-of-factly, "We don't spit juice at the table." That seems like a reasonable response.

2. She could slap Jennifer's hand and say, "No spitting." But then, physical punishment is never the best response.

3. She could scream and threaten, "If you spit your juice one more time, you are not ever getting any juice again for the rest of your life." Mom as child. No, this will never work.

4. She could calmly explain, "If everyone spit juice on the table, it would be sticky and messy," and hand Jennifer a sponge. A constructive approach, to be sure.

5. She could ignore it, which sometimes is the best approach of all. "Choose your battles" may well be the most useful adage for dealing with twos and threes.

But Jennifer's mother does something else. She says, "Jennifer, what are you doing?" And Jennifer replies, "I'm a baby beluga." Her mom laughs, wipes up the juice, and tells her,"That's a great game for the bathtub. Next time you take a bath, we'll try it. But not at the table, please." Jennifer stops spitting juice and picks up her sandwich.

Responses one and four would have been perfectly reasonable. But Jennifer's mother's response was downright brilliant. She decided to find out what was going on before doing anything else.

Of course, if Mom had been decked out for a morning meeting, packing Jennifer's lunch, gulping down her morning coffee, and calling out to Johnny in the other room to get dressed for school, her response might have been quite different. For one thing, she might not have noticed Jennifer spitting the juice at all. When her cuff slid through that puddle of juice, she may well have hit the ceiling. But in truth, none of those conditions would have prevented her from asking that simple question: What are you doing?

The best job description I've heard for a parent is, simply, "investigator." It was given to me by Dr. Robert Emde, a psychiatrist at the University of Colorado Medical School and president of the World Association for Infant Psychiatry. "Your child is like no other child in the world," says Emde, "and as a parent you are the expert in your child's individuality."

Consider this incident, which I witnessed at the home of a friend. Janice, age four, had decided not to wear a shirt. Alan, age four, wanted to play circus. Alan: "You have to wear a shirt to play circus." Janice: "I do not." Alan: "Do too. You can't play without a shirt." Janice: "My mother says I don't have to wear a shirt."

This goes on for several minutes, the kids facing each other in an absolute standoff, arguing. Both mothers are present. Neither says a word. Finally, Alan backs down. "Okay," he says. "But you have to wear a hat." Janice puts on a hat.

After the two kids leave the room, Alan's mother turns to Janice's. "I was terrified he was going to haul off and hit her," she says. Janice's mother laughs. "I just didn't want her to back down." Never mind that neither mother said a word. Both had agendas for their children, concerns based on their knowledge of them. Every kid has an M.O. And every kid needs someone in his corner. Tom gets hysterical by 5 P.M. if he doesn't have an afternoon nap; Mike is fearful of any new situation. Ciara whines; Bernard hits. Ella is strong-willed and defiant; Edgar placid and compliant.

The biggest job parents have is to help their kids build on their strengths and compensate for their weaknesses. It begins with understanding the M.O. It doesn't require a constant presence; it doesn't require constant intervention. But it requires sufficient understanding to make sound judgments—about child care, about home life, about routines, transitions, and change.

Bernard may be overstimulated in a big day-care center. Ella may go stir-crazy stuck in a one-room apartment with a sitter and a small infant. Mike will take a long time to adjust to a new child-care setting. Edgar will adapt nicely to just about any child-care setup. Ciara needs a rigid routine.

That process of getting to know your kid begins in infancy: You've got to figure out what that crying infant wants, but you've also got to figure out who that infant is. Is this child timid and fearful? Happy and outgoing? Eager to please and to connect? Easily excited or easily soothed? It's very much like solving a mystery or putting together a puzzle, only the process continues throughout the life of the child.

Being an investigator can be particularly tough for working parents. They simply aren't going to have as much time with their children; often, they have to put together bits of information from a third party. And they bring their own baggage to the process. "Amanda really prefers her father right now," says one mother. "I don't know if it's an age thing or a stage or it's because I'm at work so much and he's around more. He's much more relaxed with her. Maybe I just need to be more relaxed." And on and on it goes.

For working parents with toddlers and preschoolers, being an investigator is not always easy. It means not only second-guessing a child, but often doing so without adequate information. When you've been absent all day, connecting with a young child's immediate reality—what happened today?—can be hard. Question: It's 6:30 P.M. and Johnny's being difficult. Did he have a bad day? Is he tired? Did he miss lunch? Is he coming down with something? Does he just need some quiet time alone? Did he spend the whole day picking on Sandra in day care and getting punished with a series of time-outs? Did somebody pick on him? Did he spend the day with a substitute teacher he doesn't even know? Maybe, you think, we should read a book together. Or: Well, of course, he's just hungry, we'll make dinner, he'll feel better.

Meeting a Young Child's Needs

"Food and sleep," one parent told me, talking about what makes the biggest difference in her preschooler's temperament. "First things I ask myself if there's a problem: Is she tired? Is she hungry? Generally, it's one or the other."

That's as good a place as any to start. The weather's another big one. Kids who have been rained in or snowed in are bound to feel as constrained as you do. To diagnose any problem, even the most basic, requires information. Working parents have to work extra hard to get that information. How? For those with preschoolers in child care, that means:

Daily, ongoing communication with caregivers. At the very least, this will enable you to pick up where they left off. Communication means knowing the significant facts, which can generally be passed along in an instant. Johnny didn't eat today. His nose is running. I think he's getting sick. His best friend is leaving the center tomorrow; you should talk with him about it. Johnny's been cranky all day; I don't know what's up. Anything going on at home? That's the kind of dialogue that should go on between parents and caregivers. It doesn't have to take place every day (although for infants, schedule information is particularly critical). And it doesn't mean a long song and dance that covers the minutia of every moment. But it means getting a quick grasp of anything that might be significant.

"Sometimes parents don't tell us when one of them is out of town on business or there's been a death in the family," says the director of a Maryland day-care center. "They should tell us anything that could be important: He got his pant leg caught in this car door this morning; he lost his favorite toy; even, it was a really rough morning. It may seem minor to them, but it's major to the child."

Spending stretches of time with your child. The younger the child, the more uninterrupted time both parents need to catch up on her rhythms, developmental leaps, and capabilities. That means using your time not just to interact with your child but to be aware of her.

Making a connection between home and child care. Linger at the center whenever you can; go to the Thanksgiving party. Buy a birthday gift for your in-home sitter or your family day-care provider. Introduce your in-home caregiver to friends and neighbors. Introduce yourself to other parents at the day-care center; get to know the names of the children. A good child-care program will facilitate this process.

For a multitude of reasons, you should make an effort to promote friendships with other kids and parents in the same group-care program. It promotes a good relationship between

Toddler Talk: Why Communication Counts

Communication with center staff means crisp, meaningful messages. During the toddler years, a parent's insights can be particularly important. Consider the reasons, as described in this excerpt from *Nothing But the Best: Making Day Care Work for You and Your Child*, by Diane Lusk and Bruce McPherson (Quill; William/Morrow, 1992).

... Toddlers can actually "wake up on the wrong side of the bed." ... Teachers can't always change this mood weather, but your forecast makes a difference.

Good teachers handle toddlers in good and bad moods differently. A good-mood toddler might still blow up at a frustrating toy, throw it on the floor, and kick it around, yelling. A good teacher treats this as a "teaching opportunity." Here's a chance to teach, with questions and directions, what *else* to do when frustrated, what happens at day care after children throw things on the floor, how to get that toy to work. The basically good-mood toddler clears the air with the fit of frustration and stands ready for new thought; the coaching pays off. Try this with a miserable-mood toddler, and the small fit turns into a full-blown tantrum. Better to pack up toy and talk, and pack up the toddler to a couch for a snuggle or a book. Teachers need these two approaches, but don't want to mix them up too often. They don't want to drive the bad-mood toddler to rage and despair with educational questions, and they don't want to be teaching the good-mood toddler that people snuggle you on couches when you yell and throw things. [As a parent] your mood reports in the morning help teachers zero in on the sensible approach much faster.

Reprinted by permission of Diane Lusk and Bruce McPherson.

caregivers and parents; it enables your child to have a sense of community; it will give you access to people—other parents and trusted caregivers—who can help you if a problem arises in care; and, finally, it will enhance your kids' lives.

(Note: Parents tell me that choosing child care near work helps them stay in touch, but it can make it harder to, say, have your child's friends from child care over during the weekend. Says one mother, "My son's best friend from child care lives nearly an hour from our house. I don't know the parents, so we just haven't gotten them together.")

Allowing for downtime. Every child, at every age, needs downtime—time to relax, be alone, rest, snuggle, play quietly, watch a favorite television show. Your schedule may seem fine to you, but it may be too much to ask of your child. Day-care people tell me that some preschoolers—particularly those who can nap comfortably at the center—can get through nine-hour days on their own steam. Others find it difficult. Don't burden an already busy child with excessive weekend plans. Some working parents seem to feel that if they're not "doing something," they're not doing anything. Hanging around the house is a perfectly valuable way to spend your Saturdays.

Plenty of rest for your child. If I heard one complaint more than any other from child-care providers, it was this: Children do not get enough sleep. "When you bring a child who's not rested to day care, it's not fair to the child and it's not fair to the provider," says one family day-care provider.

Working parents can fall into the habit of keeping their children up late so they have time together. That's well and good if the child's being cared for at home and the schedule is flexible. But if you have to get your kid up and out by 7:30 A.M., putting him to bed at 10 or 11 P.M. is asking for trouble.

"Her parents don't give her enough sleep, so she comes here exhausted," says one provider, describing a three-year-old girl in her care. "Any little thing sets her off, and she starts sobbing hysterically." What do the parents have to say? "The story is that the mom has things to do and the dad's supposed to put her to bed. But the dad never does because he's watching TV or reading a book. And the mom can't because she's doing the laundry or whatever, so the child doesn't get to bed until 10 o'clock."

The Young Child at Home:
Creating a Place to Grow

In 1976, researchers at Harvard did an observational study of the kinds of home environments that produced the most competent infants and toddlers (meaning, in this case, children age three or younger). The following summary of those findings, from *Infants: Their Social Environments*, provides some useful insights on how to shape your home environment and what to look for in child care:

1. When babies were the most competent, the mother was a good organizer, arranger, and sharer of infant experiences and routines.
2. Homes of competent infants had toys that were typical of nursery school—crayons, paper, scissors, and such.
3. Competent children were allowed to help a lot with household chores—dusting, hammering, raking leaves, helping to sort laundry.
4. Fathers in the families of the competent babies spent more positive interaction time with their children. (All the families were two-parent families.)
5. Competent children were allowed access to what we would call more messy and perhaps even slightly dangerous items. There were blunt scissors in the homes for these children. Parents allowed their toddlers to help wash dishes even though a puddle might have to be sponged up from the kitchen floor. There is no one more enthusiastic at helping wash dishes than a two-year-old with soapsuds up to the shoulders!
6. Parents read to infants daily. Reading (with expression, interest, change of voice tone, and conversing about the story) correlates positively with later intellectual achievements in this and many other studies.
7. In the most competent children's home, TV was severely limited and supervised. The children could watch a one-

hour program such as *Sesame Street*. In the least competent infants' homes, children watched six hours of TV a day if they wished and viewed any program.

8. Parents of competent children *modeled* appropriate activities for them. If the parents wanted a child to do something, they showed her or him how.

9. Mothers of competent children were good *observers*. They kept an eye out to see where their child was developmentally and what the child was doing in which part of the house. The mother gauged her responses and activities according to her observations of the child's interests, abilities, and temperament.

10. When the mother was highly restrictive and punitive, the child's competence was severely damaged. Mothers of competent infants often *participated* with the child during activities—praising, encouraging, suggesting, permitting, and facilitating.

11. Competent children's parents had firm, consistent household rules and provided reasons for their rules.

12. The mothers of competent infants behaved as *teachers*. The mothers conversed, posed questions, transmitted information, and helped their children to solve problems. They helped their children to understand the unfamiliar.

13. Mothers of competent infants engaged in dramatic play. Did you ever play fantasy train trip with young children? Did you ever see your child hiding in your closet among your clothes and say, "Where's Joan? I've lost Joan! What will Daddy say when he comes home? Where can Joan be?" All the while Joan, in full visibility in the closet, is entranced with joy at this pretend game. Role-playing games help promote cognitive competence. Other games and entertainments of these parents often had intellectual content. Entertainment by parents of less competent infants often involved just physical, rough-and-tumble play.

Providers report that some children are simply exhausted after nine or ten hours in day care. Some centers and family day-care homes will not allow children to stay more than nine and a half hours. Others maintain that eight and a half hours should be the maximum time spent in group care.

"There's no reason for parents to drop off their children at 7 A.M. and pick them up at 6 P.M.," says one provider. "When that happens, I suggest they find a place closer to work." Says another, "Some children gain nothing from being here in the afternoon." Would she ever tell a parent that? "No. Of course not. They don't have any choice. I have to be realistic."

If you think the day is too long for your child, ask for insights from your provider and look for signs of exhaustion in your child. Then consider these options:

- Negotiate a flextime schedule. Shift work hours so that one parent starts work later or ends earlier to reduce your child's time in day care.
- Reduce your work hours. Some parents can cut back from full-time to part-time work.
- Reshuffle schedules. If one parent drops off and the other picks up, you may be able to cut down on your child-care hours.

Don't overreact. Kids have bad days, whether their parents are around or not. When that happens, they need understanding and patience. Some kids have bad days all the time. If your child is grumpy every night at 6 P.M., if the morning rush is excruciating, if bedtime is a nightmare, it's time for a change. Start by analyzing specific behaviors that have sparked your concern, then ask yourself:

- Is this an age thing? A stage? A good provider should be able to help you figure that out.
- Is this a chronic problem? If the behavior is consistent and predictable, you're going to have to devise a strategy for changing it.

How Much Sleep Do Children Need?

That, of course, depends on the child. In his book *Solve Your Child's Sleep Problems*, Dr. Richard Ferber, director of the Center for Pediatric Sleep Disorders at Children's Hospital in Boston, offers these guidelines:

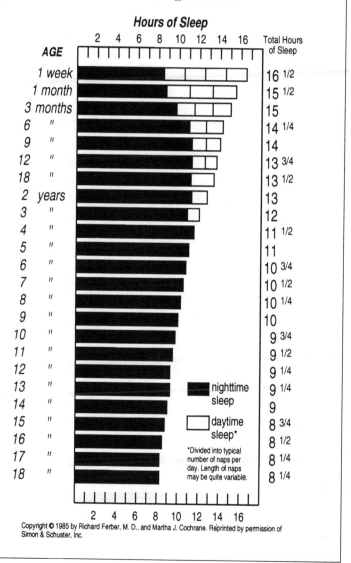

Hours of Sleep

AGE	Total Hours of Sleep
1 week	16 1/2
1 month	15 1/2
3 months	15
6 "	14 1/4
9 "	14
12 "	13 3/4
18 "	13 1/2
2 years	13
3 "	12
4 "	11 1/2
5 "	11
6 "	10 3/4
7 "	10 1/2
8 "	10 1/4
9 "	10
10 "	9 3/4
11 "	9 1/2
12 "	9 1/4
13 "	9 1/4
14 "	9
15 "	8 3/4
16 "	8 1/2
17 "	8 1/4
18 "	8 1/4

■ nighttime sleep

□ daytime sleep*

*Divided into typical number of naps per day. Length of naps may be quite variable.

Try to focus on the specific issue rather than initiating sweeping changes.

Don't operate in a vacuum. We learn by observing, but working parents have fewer opportunities to observe how other parents handle various situations; how other children behave; how their own children deal with other kids. Says one at-home mom, "I have a friend who works. She calls me all the time with questions—what books to buy, what toys to get. She asks me what my son likes to do, because she has no idea anymore what's going on at this age."

A family day-care provider recounts this tale, with some amusement: "One of my mothers asked me one day, 'How do you keep her from throwing food?' It seemed so simple to me. I give her limited amounts. When she throws it, I assume she's finished eating and I take the food away. She doesn't throw food here."

You need to make the time at home and create the time at work. Set up weekend play dates with other parents. Get your child into a play group for children of working parents. Volunteer to work for an hour or two a week at your child's day-care program. Set up a discussion group at work. A local branch of the Women's Bar Association reports the single biggest issue these lawyers want to discuss is child rearing. Some child-care centers offer workshops for parents. If none of these options are available, you may have to create your own learning opportunities.

Accept the fact that your child will sometimes embarrass you. Your child says "shut up" to you in the checkout line of the supermarket; pitches a fit in a restaurant; hurts another child; sticks out her tongue at your parents; pulls up her dress or pulls down his pants in public; screams in terror instead of hopping onto Santa's lap. And suddenly everybody starts staring at you.

One parent tells this story: "One day, when my daughter was three, she was waiting for me with her grandfather outside the supermarket. When I came out of the store, she started yelling, 'That's not my mother. That's not my mother.'" Naturally, people started staring at the mother suspiciously. "One woman really gave me the evil eye," she recalls. "It was bizarre."

Normal kids do bizarre things. And most parents are, at one time or another, embarrassed by their children's behavior. Yet for reasons equally bizarre, adults act as if it is somehow the parents' fault or it's abnormal or they've never seen such a thing before in their lives. We live in a culture that's not particularly tolerant of the idiosyncrasies of childhood. Don't let your embarrassment get in the way of being an effective parent. Sometimes parents overreact, delivering severe reprimands for behavior that is, well, simply childish. Other times they ignore inappropriate behavior because they're uncomfortable disciplining or reprimanding their kids in public.

Such advice is particularly relevant within the context of child care. Recognize that your provider will probably see your child at his best *and* at his worst. Be aware that when parent and provider are both present, it's prime time for acting out. "It's a power play," says one provider. "I think when we're both present, it's not clear who has the authority," says another. If your child's acting crazy at pick-up time, either take charge or encourage the provider to intercede. And try not to be too judgmental of other parents. Remember, most do the best they can.

The Young Child at Home: Strategies That Work

Here follows some of the best advice I have encountered on how to deal with young children. You may want to use it as a guide for setting the tone of your home life, for evaluating child care, and for meshing the two worlds.

Don't be afraid to say no. Young children need to know the boundaries. "You are not allowed to climb on the dining room table." "You can watch TV for one hour a day." "You may not throw toys at your sister." "Play-doh belongs only in the kitchen." Whatever your house rules, make them clear and stick to them. "Say what you mean, and mean what you say," writes Penelope

Leach.[1] But don't make so many rules that they demand constant enforcement.

It can be particularly hard for working parents, who spend less time with their children than they might like, to say "no." But the general consensus is that children feel more secure when they know the limits; safer when their parents enforce them; and happier when the rules are clear and consistent. Says Mitzi Ross, a clinical social worker who conducts workshops for family day-care providers, "Parents who work tend to overcompensate by being indulgent. They seem to feel somehow saying 'no' is being mean or that it's somehow depriving the child of something. But they pay a big price." Failing to set limits makes children feel they have too much power, and that can be frightening. "They're searching for the limits," says Ross. "They may pout for a minute, but they're also likely to feel relieved."

Present options. "You can't climb on the living room sofa with your shoes on, so why don't we just take them off?" "We can't go outside right now; how about a game of hide and seek?" Don't say, "Do you want to get dressed?," but "Would you rather wear the red pants or the blue pants?"

Arrange things so you don't have to say "don't" all the time. Create a child-safe environment in your home so you don't have to repeatedly tell your child, "Don't do that." One measure researchers use to gauge the quality of a child-care setting is the number of times caregivers have to say "don't." The more "don'ts"—don't touch, don't run, don't climb on that—the worse the setting.

Promote competence and independence. It can be easier for working parents to dress the child, put on the coat and hat, and grab the lunch box themselves. But that really puts a check on a child's ability to develop a sense of responsibility. Allow more responsibility and control as your child ages. Working parents can easily fall out of step with developmental leaps. Twos can empty a dishwasher and fold laundry. Threes can help set the table or help clip an overgrown bush in the yard. Fours can help rake the leaves, feed the cat, and make their bed. They're also perfectly capable of putting together a pizza pie and claiming responsibility for an entire meal.

Try giving a two-year-old a cabinet of his own in the kitchen so he can get out his own pots and pans to play with. Give a three-year-old a stool so she can actually reach the bathroom sink and wash her own hands. Keep a stack of paper cups within reach of a four-year-old so he can pour himself a glass of juice from the refrigerator. Every child needs a sense of mastery.

Preschoolers love to do chores, provided they're presented as a form of entertainment as well as a responsibility. In *The Mother's Almanac* (1975), Marguerite Kelly and Elia Parsons offer a laundry list of tasks that preschoolers are perfectly capable of doing. They include dusting, polishing silver and furniture, washing windows, getting fingerprints off woodwork, cleaning up spills, and folding and sorting laundry. Start around one and a half, the authors advise, when a child is capable of getting the morning paper and helping you unpack a few groceries.[2]

Explain the consequences. As soon as your child is able to understand words, your "no" should be accompanied by a simple explanation of why: "If you throw that ashtray across the room, it will break and it could hurt someone." "If you get water all over the floor, you could slip and hurt yourself." The best lesson, of course, comes when precisely what you predicted actually happens. But don't fall into the trap of explaining everything to death. Stanley Turecki, in *The Difficult Child* (1985), maintains that "because I said so" and "no means no"—phrases that new-generation parents appear to deplore—are perfectly valid approaches for setting limits and establishing authority.

But how do you discipline—and should you punish? "Discipline is an attitude, not a technique," says David Elkind in *Miseducation: Preschoolers at Risk*, noting, "When we as parents feel that we are in charge of the situation, we communicate this sense of being in charge to our child."[3] If we don't feel in charge, he notes, we communicate that as well.

Given that, here are a few strategies effective parents and caregivers recommend:

- Give warnings: "You get one warning"—not empty threats: "If you do that, you may never have another candy bar for the rest of your life."
- Count to ten, and tell them what you expect to happen by the time you get there: "You'll be out of the bathtub"—not what will happen *to* them.
- Revoke privileges: "That's two warnings; one more and you lose your TV privileges." Time-out and banishing a child to her room work for some children, but they are best when not used as a punishment but as a chance to step away from a stressful situation. One of the most effective techniques I've used when emotions begin to spin out of control is putting *myself* in time-out: "You're getting out of hand and I am about to get very angry. I am going into the other room. I need a time-out."

About spanking. There's general agreement that spanking doesn't work to improve behavior, although it may have the immediate effect of stopping the behavior. The consensus seems to be that spanking builds up anger and resentment; that it's frightening to children; and that if your authority is based on force, it isn't on very firm footing. Nevertheless, there are times when children push or test the limits so much that parents react—often in anger—with a smack on the behind.

In all the child-rearing books I've read, I've encountered only two that condone spanking, and only under very specific conditions. I won't even cite the sources, because to take their words out of context would be a disservice to the authors. But in each case spanking is mentioned—not recommended—as a last resort and part of a broad and detailed child-rearing program.

In contrast, most child-rearing experts will tell you, flat out, "Never spank a child." Spanking may clear the air, defuse tension, shock the child, or reestablish your authority; it may be your ultimate weapon in the war against unruly children. But it has never been shown that spanking is an effective discipline method in child-care situations or at home. Never, ever, should another adult be allowed to inflict physical punishment on your child. Incredibly, some states allow physical punishment in day care—with a note of permission from the parents—and some providers tell me that they've been instructed by parents to spank their children.

Sharing: The great misnomer. Usually, when parents ask a toddler to "share," they are asking her to give something up. The best lessons in sharing involve actual sharing: "Let's share this snack by splitting it in half." Generally, when parents say "share," they should say "Please take turns" or "Since we have a guest, we should let her play with our toys." Kids are capable of taking turns at a very early age; but they're not so good at sharing until about age four.

I've seen people take a toy from one child and give it to another in the name of "sharing." As a general rule, "whoever had it first" is the fairest policy. You wouldn't expect an adult to give something up just because someone else wants it. Don't expect more from a young child.

Let the punishment fit the crime. If two toddlers can't take turns ("two minutes for Jane, two minutes for Mitzi"), put the toy away. "You used crayon on the walls; you need to clean it up." "You smashed Jane over the head with the baseball bat; the bat gets put away." So the child-rearing experts advise. If your child-care program uses time-out as a universal response to every infraction, you might want to speak with someone about it; not in an accusatory way: "Why do you use time-out so much?"—but diplomatically: "I've found 'time-out' doesn't always work with Rebecca; can we talk about using some other strategies?"

Dealing with a child's aggression. When one of my children was about 18 months old, he started hitting in play group. I was stunned and couldn't figure out where it was coming from. Concerned, I turned first to the baby books and looked up aggression. I found a philosophical treatise on guns in Dr. Spock, and in another child-rearing book I found the Pollyanna suggestion that hitting was learned behavior and no child would hit unless he'd been hit. I talked with my son's babysitter: Had anybody been hitting him? Had she been trying to discipline him with a smack on the wrist? Absolutely not, she said.

When the behavior persisted, I called a friend, a child psychologist. "Stop taking him to play group," he advised. "If it's becoming a pattern, you should remove him from the situation." He also noted that there was no reason for any 18-month-old to spend time with other children. Although that struck me as curious, I followed his advice.

Only now, having spoken with countless people in the field, do I find that my son's behavior was normal, even common for that age. And there are a number of ways to deal with it, none of which include giving up and taking the child out of play group. "Aggression is the job description for toddlers," says child development consultant Phylis Benner.

What's the best way to deal with it? Here's some of the best advice I've now encountered: Comfort the wounded first. That sends a signal that the aggressor doesn't get the attention. Then, if you know what happened, explain other options to the child: "When Simcha's in your way, just ask her to move."

For toddlers, experts advise removing the child from the immediate situation (not the play group itself), distracting her, and explaining, simply, "We don't hurt others" or "Hitting is not allowed." For older twos and threes, again, comfort the wounded. If the victim is crying, show the aggressor that he hurt someone. Encourage the hitter or biter to apologize, even to comfort the other child. Don't make too big a deal out of it, or hitting can turn into an attention-getting behavior.

I pass these lessons along only because I had so much trouble learning them myself and as a reminder that many professionals genuinely believe that children should be insulated during the early years—an attitude that is of little value to working parents who aren't able to "just take him out of play group."

Adjusting to Child Care: Getting Off to a Good Start

Adapting to a new child-care situation can be a big job for a small child. Very few studies have examined the process by which children adapt to child care, although there's a general consensus that most kids adapt well to high-quality group care. Here are some insights, gathered from parents, providers, day-care directors, and other people in the child-care field.

Easing Into Care

A good program recognizes that all children need time to get used to a new setting and that some children take longer than others. Any good program allows parents—even invites and encourages them—to spend time at the center or family day-care home with their child during the first week or so.

The transition into care might stretch over a week or more. Maybe parent and child will spend two hours together at the center the first day and leave together. Maybe they'll stay a bit longer on the second day. On day three, Mom or Dad might stay 30 or 40 minutes, then leave Junior for two or three hours. Gail Solit, director of the Gallaudet Child Development Center in Washington, D.C., encourages such transitions: "Some kids take three days. Some kids take two weeks." Indeed, sometimes it's the parents who need time to adjust to the separation and get comfortable with the center.

The advantages of a gradual transition are numerous. Aside from helping parents and child, it enables the parents to get to know the other children and the caregivers, so they can connect with the child's experience. Says Solit, "I would distrust any program that doesn't allow you to ease into care."

Yet when I sat in a room one night with four of the best family day-care providers in my area, they almost unanimously agreed that easing a child into care was unnecessary. "It's for the parents, not the child," said one. "Children need to get used to the routine," said another. "If you leave them one day for an hour, the next day for two hours, and then for an entire day, they find it confusing." Just as important, these providers, many of whom seem to cherish a certain level of control of their programs and a fair amount of privacy ("I don't let parents wander all over my house"), felt easing children into care would be disruptive to their routines and to the other kids. All of which means there are different philosophies regarding this subject.

Perhaps the wisest statement I heard was this: "It depends on the parent, and it depends on the child." You know your child. If she's been through frequent child-care changes, adapting may be more difficult. It may also be difficult if your child has been cared for almost exclusively by you before starting child care.

It also depends on the child's age and stage. "Any program where they say, 'Come in the first morning and drop your two-year-old off and then just leave,'" says Solit, "they're nuts. They do not understand little kids." According to Solit there are at least two things going on. First, the child has to get used to the place, to start trusting the new adult, to learn about the environment. "The other piece of big work is separating from Mommy and Daddy and knowing that Mommy or Daddy is going to come back," she says.

Here's the plan Solit generally proposes, particularly for two-year-olds:

> Week one, day one: Child comes to the center with Mom, Dad, or caregiver. Both stay about two hours.
> Day two: Both stay through lunch.
> Day three: Adult stays 20 to 40 minutes, leaves child for the morning, and returns in the early afternoon. This is repeated as needed until the child seems comfortable with the leave-takings and the setting.
> Days four and five: Parent drops child off, and child stays through early afternoon.
> Week two: Child begins child care in earnest.

From the standpoint of the child, this approach makes perfect sense. Yet in my experience, allowing for a gradual transition in the world of child care is the exception, not the norm. I have to believe that's because it's inconvenient for adults—meaning caregivers and parents alike.

Tell a new caregiver everything you can about your child. Caregivers in a good program want to know whether your child is shy and slow to warm to a new situation; aggressive with other children; fond of blocks or books. They'll also ask what other child-care situations she has been in. For your child's sake, arm them with information.

How Children Adapt to Child Care

Few studies have addressed the question of how children adapt to child care. But anecdotal evidence suggests that although it takes some longer than others, the vast majority of children adapt well to high-quality care. Some kids are more flexible than others. I remember an 18-month-old whose parents dropped her at my house in a pinch (their in-home provider had called in sick); she didn't bat an eye. She apparently adjusted just as easily to the neighborhood day-care center, where she stayed periodically when the in-home child-care situation broke down. She was, I thought, an unusually self-contained child.

That said, I've also seen children of the same age wail for 10, 15, or 20 minutes after the morning drop-off—a process that went on for nearly a year.

Said one mother of two college-age boys, "My first one walked into any new situation perfectly happy, said good-bye, and that was it. With the second, there was always some hesitation. It's just a matter of their personalities. Even today, when the younger one goes off to college, I can see him pulling back, holding on just a little bit. He still has difficulty letting go."

If your child has difficulty letting go, be sure to find a program that allows for a gradual transition and allows you to be present for a time until he begins to adjust.

If you decide to go the cold-turkey route, expect four possible responses:

- The norm: Your child cries when you say good-bye but stops within minutes of your departure. Teachers tell me it generally takes about two weeks (ten days) for children to adjust to a new program. Try to be chipper about the whole thing: Keep your good-bye brief—"I'm going to work; I'll be back after nap time" or "Have a good day"—and if necessary, literally place your child in the arms of the teacher/caregiver. Feel free to call when you get to work and double-check. In fact, a good center will encourage you to call and will appreciate the fact that you do.
- The lag effect: Your child is fine at first; then the crying begins on day two, three, or four. It may go on each morning for a few days or a few weeks. Some kids seem to do fine at first, then it dawns on them that this is for real—this is how it's going to be every day from now on.
- No tears: Your child seems perfectly happy, says good-bye, and takes off. If this is your child, count yourself among the lucky. Don't follow her, linger, or try to elicit a response. Say good-bye and go.
- Major trauma: Your child just cries and cries. It's rare, but it happens, particularly if your child is under age three. Virginia Spitler, a family day-care provider with 20 years' experience, has been through this once, with a two-year-old boy who had been home with his mother "all his life." He cried all day the first day, and it went on for the entire week. "At the end of the first week, I told his mother, 'This might not work,'" says Spitler. "It was very disturbing. He'd stop to eat, and then he'd start up again." Finally, after two weeks of nonstop tears, Spitler told the mother it wasn't going to work out. "She said, 'Please, let's try it for one more week.'" On the Monday of week three, when they arrived at Spitler's house, the little boy jumped out of the car, said good-bye, ran in the house, and never cried again. "He's been fine ever since," says Spitler. Two weeks on the nose.

How do you handle a problem like this? Talk it through with the provider, wait it out, and try to be understanding with your child. Don't say, "Isn't day care fun?" when you know full well your child isn't having fun yet. Try to be encouraging: "Once you get used to it, I think you're going to like it" or "I really like Ms. Spitler. Let's give it another try." Be supportive and acknowledge your child's feelings: "It's hard for me to say good-bye too" or "I miss you too."

This is when trusting your child-care choice and knowing your child makes all the difference. In chapter two I mentioned one of my temporary family day-care situations that lasted little more than a week—the one in which I found my son napping on a dining room rug, with a lollipop in his mouth. This was his second day-care experience. The tip-off that something might be wrong came when he cried intensely every morning for a week. It wasn't just the crying that suggested a problem; it was the character of the crying. It had an almost desperate quality. That was what led me to drop in unexpectedly and, ultimately, pull him out of the program. When I moved him to a high-quality center where we'd been awaiting an opening, the crying at drop-off stopped altogether.

A Washington, D.C., mother had a similar, though less disturbing, experience when she put her son in a family day-care home at 13 months. She had looked at seven other family day-care homes, and this one was spacious, open, and organized. There were plenty of toys; the kids seemed happy and the caregiver warm and friendly. But every day the number of children in care seemed to grow; the place just kept getting bigger and bigger. Her child cried every day at drop-off for a month; but 13 months is a sensitive age, and he'd been cared for exclusively at home, so she expected an adjustment.

Yet the mother's confidence in the program was beginning to wane. She decided to spend some time there. What did she notice? For one thing, her son's personality was dramatically different at the provider's. "He was very quiet and restrained at the place. At home he was active and bubbly and happy, but there he just wasn't himself," she says. "What broke my heart was when I saw him playing with a puzzle; then he got up and very neatly put it back on the shelf. That just didn't seem right to me—that a boy 13 months old should be expected to do that. I do think kids need structure. But the structure of the program was so unlike home. He just seemed very unhappy and confused." She moved him to a much smaller provider, a woman who kept several kids in addition to her own; and both she and her son were happier.

Constructive strategies for dealing with adjustment. My own belief is that easing a child into care goes a long way toward easing adjustment problems. The brunt of helping a child adapt falls to the caregiver. You can help by arming the caregiver with all the information you have about your child's personality and interests.

In general, the child who's going to have the hardest time adjusting is one who *(a)* is generally fearful of new situations, *(b)* has had frequent child-care changes, or *(c)* has been in the near-exclusive care of one person all her life. A difficult child may also have trouble adjusting to a particular program. You can make it easier by:

- maintaining confidence in the child-care situation. Studies show that even infants can read anxiety in their parents' facial expressions.
- enlisting the caregiver's help in facilitating transitions
- telling your child, "I know it's hard to get used to it." Don't belittle the child's feelings by saying, "Oh, come on now. It's not so bad" or offering false cheer: "This is a great place! Have a great day!" Be sympathetic.

Transitions

One Monday morning last year, my then three-year-old started complaining at breakfast. "I don't want to go to school," he said, an unfamiliar remark that was to become a refrain. "Why?" I asked. Stopped in his tracks, he searched for the answer. "Tommy is bothering me," he said. We talked a little bit about Tommy, and then we went off to school. Later, when I picked him up, I asked him about his day. "It was great," he said enthusiastically. But on

Tuesday, again, he didn't want to go to school. This time he said Jimmy was bothering him. On Wednesday, it happened again. Yet every afternoon he said school was "great."

I called his teacher, who saw no apparent need for concern but said she'd keep an eye on things. His father spoke with him. "It seems like every morning you don't want to go to school, but every afternoon you say it was great," said his father. "What do you think about that?" My son had no answer.

Finally, on Thursday morning, when he announced that he didn't want to go to school, I asked him the same question his father had asked. He sat still for a moment, as if contemplating the problem. Finally, slowly and painstakingly, he said, "It's just such a great distance." A five-minute ride, but an enormous journey.

Transitions are tough. They're tough for children. And they're tough for parents. Amy Voorhes, a mother in Silver Spring, Maryland, tells of the time her son was in the hospital. She was working on a major project several miles away, and she and her husband would split shifts at the hospital. "I was fine at work. I was fine once I got to the hospital. But in between, I was a wreck."

For kids, anxiety over separation rears its head, off and on, throughout the preschool years. Caregivers tell me that kids have the most difficulty separating on Monday mornings (no surprise), after holidays, and when they are coming down with something.

Saying Good-bye

There's no shortage of studies on what works best for the morning drop-off. One 1977 study examined three basic styles for saying good-bye. The first group of parents left without a word to the child. The second group told their children they were leaving, said a short and sweet good-bye, and departed. Group three talked more extensively to their children about where they were going, when they'd be back, what they'd be doing. Children reacted with the least distress to style number two: Keep it short and sweet, and never leave without saying good-bye.[4]

In another study, researchers enlisted mothers' involvement to compare the difference between a brief good-bye (10 seconds) and a long one (40 seconds). Again, the short good-bye won out.[5]

What else can we learn from the research? For whatever reasons, boys appear to have more difficulty separating from their mothers than do girls, though they don't have a problem separating from their fathers.[6] For obvious reasons, infants separate more easily when they are going to the arms of a familiar, rather than an unfamiliar, caregiver.[7]

Studies show that when parents linger, children cry.[8] Basically, the inference is that if you're ambivalent about leaving, your child will pick up on it. But that raises a chicken-and-egg question. Does the child cry because the parent lingers? Or does the parent linger because the child tends to cry? Some children do have more trouble separating, and it's intensified at various ages and stages.

No matter how you look at it, a nice, crisp good-bye does the job best, with one caveat: If your child is having a tough morning or is going through a clingy phase, there's no harm in staying for a few minutes, *if you make it clear that's what you're doing.* Create a line of demarcation if you can. Take off your coat. Read a book. Do a puzzle. Before you begin, say that you'll be staying for five minutes or ten minutes.

One mother shares the tale of her 14-month-old, who cried when dropped off at family day care. "I started bringing his favorite book every morning," she says. "I'd tell him, 'I'm going to read this story, and then I have to go. Then Nancy will read to you.'" It worked. He knew precisely what to expect. The crying stopped immediately.

Aside from the peak separation phases (the last half of the first and second years), toddlers cry the most. Threes (often prone to fears) may go through crying phases. By four, most kids who have been in group care are pretty savvy about saying good-bye, but even fours go through a clingly phase.

Most providers will tell you to kiss and go. Here are some successful strategies parents have used to ease the morning split:

• As mentioned above, always say good-bye. Never sneak out.

- Find a good-bye window. If there's a spot where your child can look out a window, encourage her to look out as you wave good-bye. I've seen it work wonders.
- Find a transition person. For center care, enlist someone (the same person every day) to take your child from front door to classroom.
- Create a good-bye ritual. Butterfly kisses; a special word; a consistent morning routine—any of these can make the good-bye easier.
- Provide easy reference points. As any parent knows, young children have no sense of time. Saying you'll be back at one o'clock is as meaningful to a two-year-old as saying Halloween's in October. So say, "I'll be back after nap" or "I'll be back to get you before dinner."
- Set aside extra time. The Gabbetts, who live in Raritan, New Jersey, have a choice: They can either spend 30 minutes in heavy traffic by leaving home at 7:30 or drive to day care at 7:10 and have breakfast with their son, Christopher. The latter helps ease him into a morning routine.
- Make a switch. If little Jimmy cries when Mom drops him off, switch drop-offs to Dad, if he's available. That may be enough to break a cycle.

What to Expect at the End of the Day

Some kids in group care are not eager to leave at the end of the day; they're having a good time. Sometimes parents feel rejected and upset, or they're in too much of a hurry to linger and wait. What do you do?

- Shift gears before walking in the door. Remind yourself that while you may be on your way, your child doesn't know it. He may well be engaged in something else—and that's as it should be. Be prepared to linger to give him time to finish up. It may be an ideal time to become more familiar with the center.

- Set a deadline for your child: "After you finish that game, we have to go" or "Five more minutes. I'll let you know when time's up."
- Make a connection to something positive: "How'd you like to help me make a pizza?" or "Did you make anything to take home today?"
- Enlist the help of the caregiver to get the child to the front door or even to the car.
- Develop some rituals. Bring a special toy or snack in the car for the ride home. A favorite musical tape makes any ride a pleasure.
- Talk about this transition with your child. You'd be surprised how open some children are to discussing such an issue. Tell a three- or four-year-old that you need her help in getting home at the end of the day, that you'd appreciate some cooperation.
- Head for the door. Most children will fall right in step.
- When all else fails: Pick the child up and leave.

Venting

A common reaction for preschoolers when they first see their parents at the end of the day is to unload all their most intense feelings at once. It can happen with the provider, on the way home, or after you arrive. But you can't miss it, whether it takes the form of anger, hysteria, tears, or a tantrum (depending on the age of the child). Rest assured, it's not the least bit uncommon. I call it venting.

Here's how Lorraine Coffey, a Silver Spring, Maryland, mother, describes her two-year-old's venting episodes: "When she first greets me, she's always very sweet and loving. And it takes about 15 minutes. She starts totally—I want to say 'acting out,' but that has the implication of bad behavior. It's just everything. If I want to diaper her, there's no way. If I want to do something, there's no way. She's usually very gentle, but when she gets wound up or very tired, she'll squeeze or hit." Says Lorraine's mother, Beatrice Pecarsky, who serves as her granddaughter's caregiver, "It's like she's saying, 'Look, here's the sum total of my personality. We haven't got much time. Let's just do it all at once.' "

In fact, venting, according to the experts, is rather like a backhanded compliment. T. Berry Brazelton explains it as "saving up one's strongest feelings." Look at it this way: It may take every ounce of energy your child has to get through an eight- or nine-hour day in group care. It may take just as much to spend the day in the care of someone other than Mom or Dad—always the most significant people in any child's life. Venting is a kind of outpouring of feeling, often coupled with end-of-the-day exhaustion.

How do you deal with it? Whatever you do, don't take it personally. Patience and calm are in order here—the ultimate demonstration of parental love. Don't force things. There's no rule that says you have to be completely focused on your child from the minute you get home. Try stepping back a bit.

Business Trips: Helping Children Deal With Your Absence

Travel means more than the absence of a parent; it means a break in the routine. Some parents turn that to their advantage and make one parent's business trip the other's (and the children's) adventure. Make the most of the change; the older the kids, the better this works. You can do something special like having dinner out or bringing home take-out food, taking a picnic to the park, or going to a ball game. With younger children, many parents maintain that sticking to the normal schedule is what gets them through.

Says one dad, describing life with his three-year-old and six-year-old when his wife's on the road, "Life is like a conveyor belt. First breakfast, then get on the bus, come home. They're allowed to watch one television program, then they come in and poke

---

Getting Up and Out in the Morning

Getting dressed in the morning, eating breakfast, getting teeth brushed, and getting out the door all pose big challenges for working parents. Pleading, cajoling, and yelling are quick fixes that can just as quickly ruin your day. Here are some other options:

For fours and fives, a get-dressed race: "I'll shut my eyes, and when I get to 25 you'll have your shirt and pants on."

For threes and fours, a race to the car: "Whoever gets there first wins."

For twos and threes, rhymes, songs, or riddles—anything that's distracting enough to get the clothes, the coat, the shoes on. For fours and fives, try guessing games.

For any problem you want to resolve, post a star chart. It can turn a problem into a challenge. Ten stars (for getting dressed on time; using the potty; brushing teeth) mean a special outing, lunch out on Saturday, a baseball game—whatever your child likes best.

---

around with what I'm cooking. After dinner, which takes anywhere from 40 minutes to an hour, it's upstairs for bath and story and bed by 8 P.M. It's tough for me because there's no downtime. It's much smoother than when their mother is here. The kids do fine; they just move from activity to activity to activity. But if she's gone more than five days, they start to miss her. That's an entire week of school. Then it begins to wear on them."

Your travel can be enriching for your kids, says an article in *Working Mother* magazine.[9] I agree. I know a woman who travels internationally on a fairly regular basis. Her family's Christmas tree is covered with ornaments from around the world. She brings home gifts for the kids that are representative of other cultures. They talk about where she's going—Australia or Israel, Japan or Russia—for weeks in advance; they talk about what she might bring back; and in the process they learn about these other cultures. She takes pictures and shows the slides in each of their classrooms. Her travel has become an integral part of their lives. And it has unquestionably enriched them. Both her sons, now 9 and 13, share her enthusiasm for travel and have a sense of the broader world.

But it works, in large part, because her husband is already very involved with every aspect of their lives. The couple has one of the few truly 50-50 parenting setups I know of. (I can say the same of the conveyor-belt couple I spoke of earlier.) Even so, before every trip she takes, the mother in this family lays out her children's clothes for every day of the week and packs the nonperishables in a series of lunch bags lined up on her kitchen counter. Each time her kids get dressed and grab their lunches, they know exactly how many days remain until her return. "It makes it that much easier for my husband," she says.

Making It Easier on Your Children

When parents with young children travel, the key seems to be keeping everything else in the kids' routine relatively stable. The rules are much the same as those for short-term separations: Always say good-bye. Give them ample time to prepare (a few days for a two-year-old). Find a way to communicate how long you'll be gone. Your attitude is important; keep your explanations simple and try not to communicate concern. Ellen Galinsky, in *Working Mother* magazine, warns that an overly emotional heart-to-heart talk could convey the idea that something terrible is about to happen.[10]

Phone home daily if you must, but recognize that young children may find it disturbing to talk with you long-distance; be prepared for pleas for your return or tears as you hang up. Some young children are upset by phone calls from a traveling parent. ("I never call home," says one mother. "I don't want to disturb the equilibrium.") Older children, on the other hand, are not always eager to talk at the time of your call. Brace yourself for disinterest or lack of enthusiasm from older kids if you catch them in the middle of their favorite TV show.

Preparing Preschoolers for Your Absence

Here are some projects for traveling parents, from *The Preschool Years*, by Ellen Galinsky and Judy David (Ballantine Books, 1988), that can make it easier for your preschool children when you're away:

- A map with stick-on dots showing where you are going. Even though your children may not understand all of this, it is comforting for them to compare where you live with where you are going.
- A calendar on the wall or refrigerator with pictures of the major activities for your children while you're away and a pencil nearby to X out each day until you return.
- A packet of something special (a book of stickers or Lifesavers) that contains the same number of items as days that you will be gone. Your children can take one a day and see or count how many are left until you return.
- A series of notes with a message for each day to be read to the children in the morning. Again, the number of notes remaining will serve as a reminder of how soon you will come home.
- A photograph of you for your child to keep in his room or take to school. Let your children know that you also carry photographs of them with you wherever you go.
- A "surprise package" for you made by your children. You can encourage them to put together a collection of drawings or messages, one for each day you will be gone.

Try to keep travel to a minimum during phases when your child is particularly sensitive to separation.

Always tell your child's day-care center or provider when a parent—either parent—is away on business. Unless they're informed, they don't know precisely how to respond when your three-year-old cries, "I miss Daddy." Your child may need some extra strokes in day care. Says one day-care teacher, "We have a little boy in our class right now, and his mom went away for training and was due back, but she didn't come back when she was supposed to. Obviously that makes a big difference in his life. But no one even told us she was gone; it took about a week to pick up the fact that his mom was out of town. We could have reassured him. We could have talked about it. There are books we could have read."

When you return from a trip, young children may be withdrawn or angry. That's a perfectly normal and common response. Recognize that this too will pass.

Should You Take the Kids Along?

I cannot imagine why anyone would take their children along on a business trip. It seems analogous to parents who take their kids to cocktail parties on Friday nights because they feel guilty about their absence all week long. Cocktail parties and business meetings don't make for quality time; nobody will enjoy themselves. Better to stay home, I say.

But then I heard Andrea Zintz's story, and it changed my perspective. She was still nursing her eight-month-old daughter when a major weeklong conference came up; as a vice president and management board member, she was required to attend. She approached her supervisor about bringing her husband and daughter. Bad precedent, he responded. She offered to put them up in a hotel, separate from the conference, and, of course, pay their way. Can't do it, he replied, suggesting she simply skip the meeting. When forced to choose between continuing to nurse and her job responsibilities, she went with the job. She weaned the baby. The entire incident speaks volumes about the inflexibility of businesses as regards family-related issues. If your career involves travel, be aware that there will be times when your job will have to come first.

Developmental Changes: A Different Kind of Transition

Weaning, potty training, giving up a pacifier, moving from a crib to a big bed: All of these are major changes in the lives of children. Your child must be your guide to when these changes should be made. If you wait for signals from your child, the process will be that much easier. Parents are sometimes astonished at how readily children give up something we imagine they still cherish. It's easy *because they're ready*. A bottle, for instance: "I just put it in the cupboard when she was about 18 months old." Or a pacifier: "He marched over to the garbage and threw it away. He never asked for it again."

Such decisions should not be made without the involvement of your child's caregiver. Before throwing away the diapers or putting up the bottle, talk with your provider. Does she think the child's ready? What approach will you take together? Is anything else going on that might impede the child's progress (a new caregiver in day care; a room or schedule change; a friend leaving the program)? "My son entered a day-care program when he was nearly three; a month later, they shifted him to a new room. He had to be potty trained all over again," says one mother.

You don't want to arrive at day care one day, training pants in hand, and announce that it's time to potty train. You must recognize that while you, as the parent, make the final call, your provider's involvement is essential. This is a not a decision that you should make alone.

When talking with your child's caregiver, put out feelers that allow the provider to have an opinion. Don't say, "I think it's time to wean him." Say, "Do you think we should begin weaning?"

Toilet Training Advice

Somewhere between the ages of two and a half and three (girls are generally ready before boys), children are ready to give up diapers. If they are physically ready, it should be fairly easy to make this leap. Often it's easier to potty train children in group care; other children in the group who have already given up diapers can be powerful teachers. And it's not uncommon for a provider to tell a parent that she thinks your child is ready. Some things to keep in mind:

- Check your own schedule. Don't plan any major transition when you're facing a stressful deadline, planning a business trip, or expecting to work late for several nights.
- Give your child time to adjust to the idea. Put a child-size toilet in the bathroom and tell her what it's for, inviting her to give it a try. Remind her, "Soon, you'll be using the potty."
- Even if your child's ready, there will be accidents. It takes a fair amount of commitment on the part of parents and providers to help children remember what to do and approach accidents with good humor (no reprimands or punishment). False starts are not uncommon.
- Don't be afraid to retrench. If it becomes obvious that your child is not ready, give it up and wait another month or so. Don't force it; don't make too much of it; and do be sure you and your provider are working together.

Toilet training and other developmental changes can bring on disagreements and tension between parents and their in-home caregivers. These are often due to cultural differences. I met an in-home provider who routinely placed a one-year-old on the toilet for long stretches of time in order to train him—a physical impossibility. A caregiver may tease or reprimand a child for failing to use the toilet. She may have a dramatically different style from your own. One caregiver may be punitive, for example, when a child doesn't make it to the potty. Another may shrink from the challenge of giving up that nap-time bottle or starting potty training because it makes her job that much more difficult.

Toilet Training: What *Not* to Do

From *Sharing the Caring*, by Amy Laura Dombro and Patty Bryan (Simon & Schuster/Fireside, 1991), comes this scenario, a lesson in how *not* to approach issues like potty training:

> "Hi. I began toilet training Lenny [two years of age] over the weekend. I brought these in case he has an accident."
>
> Fran, Lenny's mom, hands Alice, a family child-care provider, a stack of five pairs of underpants and pants.
>
> That afternoon Alice hands Fran a large plastic garbage bag filled with wet clothes.

How would you feel if you came to pick up your child at child care and found him wearing diapers the first day you sent him to child care wearing underpants? How would you feel about spending a large part of your day wiping up puddles from your living room rug and having to change a child six times? How do you think it would feel to find yourself soaking wet and have someone interrupt your jumping on pillows and building with blocks six times in order to change all your clothes?

There are several possibilities of what has gone wrong and it is up to the adults to figure out the best way of handling the situation.

Perhaps Lenny did use the toilet successfully at home over the weekend and today had a bad day, or simply found it to be too much to keep up a new skill at child care where there were other people and activities to distract him from remembering to use the toilet. Maybe at home he depended on his mother's constant reminders, which his caregiver was too busy to reinforce.

Perhaps Lenny's mother was ready for Lenny to be toilet trained before he was. Toilet training has certain prerequisites: the cognitive ability to recognize signals, the physical maturity to control muscles, and on the emotional side, self-control. It's very common for parents and caregivers, in their eagerness to be through with wet, smelly diapers and struggles with changing uncooperative two-year-olds, to decide the time for toilet training has come before a child is ready.

The task of the adults is to figure [out] what is happening. To do this, they need to talk together. Alice needs to know exactly what Fran means when she says she began toilet training. Was Lenny able to say he needed to go to the potty, a sign that all systems are go? Or did Lenny spend the weekend sitting on the toilet at regular intervals, so that he happened to be there when he had to urinate or defecate—a sign that Fran, not Lenny, is ready for toilet training?

Fran and Alice may each need a little more information about toilet training to decide if Lenny is indeed ready to wear underpants. They may find some books and articles helpful, or talking with a pediatrician or the mother of a recently toilet trained child.

Taking everything into account, the two adults will come up with a plan. Perhaps they might decide to give Lenny another day wearing underpants, or perhaps what they find out about toilet training will lead them to wait for Lenny to tell them he's ready. Another day of puddles that ends with a mountain of wet clothes is a vote for waiting.

Reprinted by permission from Amy Laura Dombro and Patty Bryan.

The keys to working out these issues are *(a)* frank and open communication, *(b)* waiting until the child is ready, and *(c)* listening to what the caregiver has to say (she may, after all, be right). Talk with your pediatrician and other parents, and check the baby books when questions arise.

When to Change Your Child Care

Nothing is more disturbing to a parent than the suspicion that something is wrong with a child-care arrangement. And let's be honest: It may not be just because you're concerned about your kids. It may also be because you face the prospect of having to find child care all over again. Says one family day-care provider who's also a mother and has used day care herself, "People wait a long time to make changes, because even if they don't like what's happening, at least they *know* what's happening."

Keep in mind that change, if it doesn't happen too often, can be a healthy thing. If all the other elements in a child's life remain constant, learning to adjust to a child-care change can actually have positive effects. Neil Bernstein, a Washington, D.C.–based child psychologist, told *Child* magazine, "A child who learns to adapt to different situations will usually be a happy child. When parents take children through change successfully, the kids build self-esteem."[11]

But knowing when and whether to make a change is something else altogether.

If Something Awful Happens

If a serious incident occurs, you've got to ask yourself four questions: Why did it happen—e.g., does a policy need changing? How did the center or provider handle it? Will it happen again? And could it happen anywhere? Then you be the judge of whether the answers are satisfactory.

A couple of years ago, the people at an East Coast child-care center left an infant inside when they locked up for the night. The child was asleep, covered by a quilt, and slept through the incident, which lasted only a few minutes because Dad arrived and discovered what had happened.

Every center, of course, should have a sign-out sheet. But that's not the real lesson of this tale. The real lesson lies in the way this potentially very dangerous situation was handled. The center's director responded immediately to the father's call and got the baby out. She then proceeded to call the state authorities herself to report the incident and called every parent who used the center to tell them what had happened.

The baby's parents kept their child at the center; so did all the other parents. Why? The director's honesty, for one thing. She says, "The only way parents are going to have complete faith in you is if you're honest. If you screw up—and you're going to screw up—you've got to tell them. You forget to give [the child] medicine. If they fall, you have to tell [parents] how the kid fell. You have to tell them if a kid gets bitten. These things are going to happen. If you're honest, then it's up to the parents to make a decision."

Contrast the forgotten-infant incident with a similar one that occurred in the Southeast ten years ago. Day-care workers left a toddler locked in the center while they went on a trip to the park. Within months of this episode, the center had to shut down. Why? The director didn't tell anyone about it, which means the rumor mill took hold. People pulled their kids out, and the center, which had been operating for more than a decade, never recovered.

If the Situation Isn't Working Anymore

It's particularly hard to make the move from the first child-care situation—often designed to suit the needs of an infant—to the second, in which the physical environment plays an enormous role for a toddler.

Consider the case of a little boy I'll call Matt. Matt began going to a sitter's house at 11 months and, according to his mother, adapted well. The sitter, a registered nurse, was not a professional caregiver by any stretch. When she agreed to watch Matt she was awaiting the arrival of her adopted child; as it turned out, her baby never arrived, but she agreed to keep caring for Matt. After less than a year, she appeared to lose interest in the arrangement. "She seemed great at first," says Matt's mother. "Then she wanted time off. She'd call and say, 'I have to go to the doctor or I have to go this place or that place, and my friend so-and-so can watch him. Is that okay?'"

It wasn't okay. Worse still, Matt, approaching two, became increasingly unhappy with the arrangement. He was being cared for alone in an apartment by a person who had grown less than enthusiastic about this particular job. "For the last month or two when I took him, he would hold on to the door frame and I would have to push him in," says Matt's mother, wincing. When a child-care arrangement is breaking down, you'll know it.

If Your Child Has Outgrown the Situation

Sometimes parents hold on to an infant-care arrangement longer than they should in the name of attachment: They don't want to break the tie between child and caregiver. Such parental concerns may be unwarranted, as was the case with a child I'll call Rob, now a very active four-year-old. When Rob was 11 weeks old, his parents signed him up with a family day-care provider. She keeps a handful of children, some of them relatives, in an apartment in Washington, D.C. Although the provider has a reputation as an extraordinary caregiver—patient, thoughtful, articulate, loving—the apartment, accessible only by elevator, is poorly suited to the needs of growing toddlers and preschoolers. It consists, basically, of a single small room dominated by a television set and a playpen. When I visited, four children were rustling through a single box of toys. Trips to the park are limited to times when another adult—the caregiver's daughter—is present or when the infants aren't napping.

What may be an acceptable setup for an infant is not really appropriate for a toddler. But Rob's parents kept him in the "program" until he was three and a half—an age when many children are already in preschool and most kids need a fair amount of stimulation and outdoor play. "I really thought he was going to miss her," Rob's mother says of the caregiver. "I scheduled his move to a day-care center, but for the first week I paid for both because I didn't know how he was going to react. Boy, was I wrong. He walked into the center and was ecstatic. He was overjoyed. He never looked back."

How Do You Know if There's Really a Problem?

Every parent I spoke to who'd made a child-care change because they had misgivings about the care said they suspected a problem *and* saw evidence of it in their child's behavior. The child did not always tell them what was wrong, but after more than a month in the program, crying and clinging intensified; or they began saying, for the first time, "I don't want to go" or "Don't leave me here."

A mother I'll call Mary tells of a share-care arrangement that broke down after a month. Bad feelings were generated when Mary, who was paying the share-care parents, learned that they hadn't increased the caregiver's salary even though she was now caring for two children. But more important, Mary's son simply didn't adapt. "My kid didn't really like it. Right from the beginning he'd cry when I brought him and cry when I picked him up. He'd cry on the way in the car. I thought maybe he just didn't like being separated from me," she recalls. But when she switched to a family day-care provider, he adapted almost immediately.

Another mother tells of an arrangement in which, unbeknownst to her, her two-and-a-half-year-old son was required to sit on a couch all day and watch television. "He was hysterical when I left him there in the morning," says his mom. "I didn't know until later what was going on. He told his new sitter. He never told me."

A clinical social worker reports a case in which a little girl began saying, "I'm not a bad girl, Mommy," words her mother had never heard her say at home. Her mother's ears pricked up; she looked into the care situation and found that the provider was absent for long stretches of time.

Good child care/bad attitude. If your child is unhappy with a child-care program, examine your own attitudes. If you don't trust the care arrangement, you may be projecting that distrust to the child, undermining his ability to adapt.

Says day-care director Gail Solit, "Unless a child has special needs, I find if they have trouble adjusting it's usually because the parents are ambivalent or there's someone in the family who doesn't want the child to be in child care. If the parent distrusts the place, the child is going to distrust the place"—even if it's a good program. Day-care operator Neesy DeCherney seconds this: "A lot of moms don't want to go back to work. They look for an excuse in the caregiver."

If you want to make a change because you're unhappy. Ask yourself: Is this my problem? Or my child's problem? A Pennsylvania woman I'll call Rebecca tells the story of her two-year-old daughter, who started family day care at 20 months. About two months after she started, Rebecca discovered that the day-care provider was routinely playing host to a mentally retarded neighbor. She was miffed that she was never informed of his presence: "We were really upset at first," says Rebecca. "We talked to the other parents. We've spent time around this man now. We don't think it's harmful in any way for Sarah. But it upset us that we hadn't been told." Rebecca, who describes the provider in glowing terms and says her daughter is "absolutely happy" in her care, says, "Ultimately, I decided to keep her in. It was an adult issue; it was our problem; my daughter's fine."

Troubleshooting: What's Normal? What's Not?

Basically, you know what's normal for your child and what's not. It's normal for a ten-month-old to cling and cry when you say good-bye; normal for a two-year-old to balk and test the limits; normal for a three- or four-year-old to dissolve into tears when disappointed (no apple juice in the refrigerator!), to experience fear over things that go bump in the night, or to want to "play baby"; normal for a four-year-old to be fascinated with bodily functions and to say, "I want to do it myself." It's normal for kids to vacillate between a preference for one parent or the other throughout their lives, and it's normal for any preschooler to regress, particularly under stress.

Some parents report that when their au pairs depart, a potty-trained child will stop using the potty, start waking suddenly in the night, or become whiny and tearful. When a child moves from one room in day care to another, you may see the same kind of behavior. Expressing your understanding—by spending more time with your child, giving her more attention, nurturing and snuggling, talking—is the best response.

The difficulty for working parents is knowing what's "normal" and what's not. How do you tell if your child has a problem that merits attention? Here's what I find in the child-rearing books:

- Most behavior—tantrums, crying jags, aggression, defiance, fearfulness, shyness—falls well into the range of normal behavior. Growing kids are going through an arduous and sometimes painful process. Here's where knowing your own child comes in. Most children will send signals if there's something wrong, but you have to have your eyes and ears open.

- If a child at any age says, "I hate myself" or "I'm bad" or "I'm evil," it's cause for concern.

- If a child is disruptive in group care or providers report behavior problems, prick up your ears. If the problems occur only at child care or in school, they may be program-related (too much structure, not the right structure, a dramatic style difference between home and the program), but not necessarily. If the problems occur at home *and* in care, you may need some professional help.

- By their very nature, children are changelings; not every change is a symptom of a problem. Working parents may overreact to minor changes if they fall out of step with their children's everyday rhythms. Children go through periods of regression before they make big developmental leaps, as T. Berry Brazelton points out in his 1992 book, *Touchpoints*. This is a pattern that any alert parent can observe: I have seen my children's sleep patterns, energy levels, and temperaments seem to change right before they take a big step forward. *Touchpoints* is the best reference I've seen to help parents negotiate their way through the emotional leaps and bounds of early childhood.

If you suspect a serious problem such as depression, hyperactivity, or a sleep or eating disorder, ask your child-care provider about it; then get help from your pediatrician or a mental health professional.

Dealing With Caregivers

Caregivers are your link to your child. However, those who aren't trained in the fine art of working with harried parents, such as assistants and aides, family day-care providers who don't participate in workshops and support groups, or in-home providers with little experience, may be ill-prepared to deal with your parental concerns.

Research has uncovered a vast gulf between providers and parents. (See page 79.) Some providers genuinely feel that parents should be home with their children, that they are relinquishing their responsibilities as parents. These caregivers have a keen eye for parents who they believe are irresponsible: those who rush in and out; who always arrive right when the center's closing down; who don't give them the information they need. Others see themselves as child-rearing experts and feel undervalued. If your child has a behavior problem, such caregivers may assume it's the result of inadequate parenting rather than a matter of the child's temperament.

To counter such assumptions, you can begin by being sensitive to the stresses caregivers experience and by establishing your own credibility as a parent. That means focusing on the real needs of your children.

Show caregivers you care about your child—and about them. This is the best way to establish a healthy relationship with caregivers. Be on time; call if you won't be. Bring your child directly to the door; don't drop her off at the curb. Call if you're concerned.

Show caregivers you appreciate their work. Say thank you to the people in day care; let them know you value what they're doing. Says one family day-care provider, "My parents are wonderful. They send me little notes. They tell me they appreciate my help. They remember my birthday." A little appreciation goes a long way.

Introduce yourself. You should know the names of everyone who cares for your child. Period. If a new caregiver joins the center staff, put out your hand and introduce yourself. A lot of parents are timid in a child-care setting: They're uncomfortable about who's in charge; they're embarrassed by perfectly normal behavior on the part of their children. If you feel uncomfortable talking with the people who take care of your children, then that in itself is a problem. If you have strategies that work with your child, pass them along: "I find this works . . . " or "She seems to respond really well to. . . ."

Be realistic. Providers complain about parents who make unreasonable demands. An in-home caregiver told me about a father who berated her for comforting a baby while his two-year-old was calling her from another room. From a family day-care provider I heard the tale of a father who arrived to pick up his son and was furious that the boy hadn't been "cleaned up to go home." "I had six children outside playing," she says. "Was I supposed to leave them to clean this child up so he could be presentable for his father?"

Defer—but not too much. Naturally, if you trust the child-care situation, you're going to ask for a caregiver's advice. That's as it should be. But don't defer too much. Says one day-care director, "I have this parent who's always asking me to diagnose her kid. She calls me Dr. Mary. I'm not a doctor. I don't want that responsibility."

Put yourself in the provider's shoes. It's 6 P.M. and you arrive to pick up your child. You're manicured, your husband's dressed for success, and the family day-care provider is wearing jeans and a T-shirt. She hasn't had a chance to comb her hair all day because she's been on duty. She's ready to close up. But you decide to come in and sit down for a chat, parking yourselves on her living room sofa. Her own kids, who by now crave her full attention, are acting out. Your child, who hasn't seen you all day, wants your attention. This is not the time to talk. Even if the children are happy and engaged, you shouldn't stay unless you specifically ask, "Is this a good time?" Some providers find it hard to draw the line with parents. Don't make it any harder.

It's the Friday after Thanksgiving, and you want a day off. So does your provider. Don't ask if you can bring your child by on a holiday. Your child is sick; you have to stay home with him. Don't expect to dock your provider's pay. You decide to drop in and see how the child-care situation is going. Don't get up to leave without your child if that child is upset about being left behind. All of these are real-life situations encountered by providers I've spoken with.

A good caregiver is investing an enormous amount of energy in helping you raise your child. Parents need to recognize the value of that job. Do call if you're going to be late. Do be appreciative, empathetic ("Looks like you had a rough day"), diplomatic ("I've been trying to work on his whining—any suggestions?" vs. "Can't you do anything about his whining?").

What difference does all this make? If your child has a problem, it will enable you to work with the caregivers to address it. If you have a complaint or concern, the day-care people will be far more sympathetic if you've established a healthy relationship with them. And that relationship begins on day one.

***

What to Remember

During the preschool years, young children go through so many changes, phases, leaps, and lapses that it's sometimes hard to keep up, especially for working parents. Here's some of the best advice I heard from parents, caregivers, and experts in the field of child development on how to keep the process running smoothly:

- *Keep the lines of communication with caregivers open and monitor care by dropping by occasionally for an early pick-up.*
- *Talk with your child often.* Spend time with her—at least 20 minutes of focused time a day—so you become an expert on your child, so you know what she's thinking about and how she is emotionally. That will increase your ability to spot problems, to adapt your home life (rules, activities, chores) and adjust your expectations (what's age-appropriate?) to your child's personality, interests, and capabilities.
- *Don't be afraid to set limits*—a common pitfall for working parents.
- *Be sensitive to your child's feelings.* Recognize that a lost toy, a new caregiver, your business trip, or the anxieties you feel can all have implications for your child.

CHAPTER TEN

After Five: The School Years

The summer that I was eight
Can it really be that long ago?
For it seems like yesterday.

The headdress comes out of the bag
And onto my head.
Kitchen knives come out of the drawer
And into the hands of a warrior.
I go outside.
I am a true Sioux
Dancing and killing all the cowboys
Who hang around my house.

Oh, how I loved the little me.

—Justin Taylor, as an eighth grader at the Grace St. Luke's School

In September 1993, less than a week before the fall semester was scheduled to begin, public school officials in two of America's largest cities, Chicago and New York, announced that schools would not open as expected. In New York, the holdup involved a delayed asbestos inspection; in Chicago, budget problems and contract negotiations were to blame. Millions of American school-children were left in limbo as parents scrambled to make special child-care arrangements to fill the weeks between *other* special child-care arrangements and the start of school. That same week, schools in Montgomery County, Maryland, closed two hours early, without notice, because of the heat. Thousands of elementary schoolchildren were simply sent home, regardless of whether an adult was there to care for them. These incidents drove home a point many working parents are well aware of: You can't rely on school as a substitute for child care.

Most school-age children have working parents; many public schools, however, are barely willing to acknowledge that fact. Others do so only grudgingly, allowing but not embracing after-school programs run by outside agencies that make use of their gyms, cafeterias, and empty classrooms.

Only about one-fourth of all formal before- and after-school programs are located in public schools; among those, fully half are operated by outside agencies.[1] Put another way, only 18 percent of all formal after-school programs are actually operated in and sponsored by public schools. Yet public schools are the ideal sites for such programs. Says Tracey Ballas, president of the National School-Age Child Care Alliance, "Taxpayer dollars are paying for those buildings 24 hours a day. Yet they're only being used eight hours a day." They have gyms, playgrounds, libraries, and the best homework rooms available. But in many school-based programs, kids are restricted to a cafeteria or a single classroom; adequate storage space for supplies is not provided; and kids have no access to computer rooms or libraries.

Some parents imagine that when their child enters school, their child-care woes are over. School-age child care, at an average cost of $1.77 an hour,[2] should take up a lesser share of the family budget than before; children are more mature and independent, able to adapt to changes more easily, able talk about what goes on in day care, able to help make choices about child care. And in many respects, life *is* simpler. It's much easier to evaluate an after-school program than a day-care center, much easier to select a summer camp for an eight-year-old than hire a nanny for an infant, and far easier to tell whether a seven-year-old is sick enough to stay home from school (colds no longer count) than to make the same decision about a two-year-old. But recognize that as your child grows, your child-care needs will grow increasingly complex—as will your job as a parent.

The biggest problems with school-age care include: gaps between school schedules and summer camp schedules; the lack of school-age programs designed for children from third through sixth grade; and few options for adult supervision during middle school, junior high, and high school—when many children still need supervision. On the most basic level, one of the biggest adjustments you'll have to make is to the fact that your child will spend more time out of school than in school. That means finding programs and child care not only for before and after school but for holidays, summer, snow days, teacher in-service days, and sick days. While the majority of school-age child-care programs operate when school is closed (around 80 percent, according to national studies), those based in public schools are least likely to stay open.

Daily schedules can pose problems. Many school systems operate during hours that are in conflict with standard area work schedules—opening at 9 A.M., say, in regions where businesses routinely open at 8:30. As a result, children as young as five and six are too often left alone for 20, 30, or 40 minutes in the morning—minutes that can seem like hours to a young child. First, second, and third graders can be seen every morning in school yards around the country, rain or shine, waiting, unsupervised, outside locked buildings. Yet this problem could be easily solved by simply shifting school and business hours so that schools routinely open 30 minutes before the workday begins—a reform that child-care advocates have been proposing for a decade and that Attorney General Janet Reno has been advocating of late.

To make matters more complex, you can expect your school-age child to develop interests and have opinions of her own. "I hate the after-school program. It's boring." "I don't want to get on the Kindercare bus anymore. I feel like a baby." "I want to play soccer." "Can I please take piano lessons . . . go to Zachary's house after school . . . go to camp with Elizabeth?" Things really heat up around third grade, when sports kick in, along with your child's craving for more autonomy. As kids age, their lives, and the logistics of working while raising them, become more complicated. Gone are the days when you could bundle Jennifer up, drop her at day care, and pick her up at 6 P.M.

Here's how a Chicago mother with a full-time job, an after-school babysitter, and a husband with flexible hours describes the schedules of her two children, Jenny, 12, and Matthew, 9. "On Monday Jenny has problem solving after school. On Tuesday she has an hour between school and Hebrew School. On Wednesday she has Earth Club. She also has soccer once a week. Matthew has soccer after school as well and a game on the weekends. On Thursday Jenny is in a Great Literature for Children program; they do a competition every other week with another school. That's after school." Many schools offer such enrichment programs from first grade on up; it's generally possible to enroll your child every day. But the activities are not child-care programs.

The backbreaking straw, for many parents, is transportation. Referral services tell this story: "We see six- and seven-year-olds walking themselves home to an empty house." "A lot of areas around our schools are unsafe. That's a big issue for working parents." "We get a lot of calls from parents who can't get their child from point A to point B. We try to help, but transportation is hard to find." Transportation services have failed to materialize in many communities because of the high cost of liability insurance. Some day-care centers pick up and deliver, as do some special programs, but charges for the entire package may run as high as $270 a month in major cities.

Is your child old enough to walk herself to the family day-care home? Old enough to take a bus to soccer practice? Old enough to care for herself every day after school for three or four hours? Those answers depend on your child, your community, your values, and the insights you get from other parents with whom your child connects.

"You just know when your child is ready for something," says one mother. At a certain moment, you realize it's safe for your child to take a bath alone; at another, you realize she's perfectly capable of riding around the block on her bike alone; at another, you know she's old enough to babysit. The law tells us when our children are old enough to drive cars and when they are required to enter school. (There are also municipal laws, of which most parents are unaware, governing how much, at what ages, and even at what times of day a child can be left alone—before or after dark, for example.) But beyond that, decisions regarding our children's safety and independence are ours alone. "Usually, circumstances force the issue," says one parent. "Say Mark wants to go over to Robert's house and I can't give him a ride. It suddenly dawns on me that Mark is old enough to cross the street and get himself to Robert's, and that he's responsible enough to get himself home by whatever time I say. Maybe the first time I tell him to call me when he gets there. Maybe not."

Unfortunately, circumstances related to a parent's work schedule often force such issues before a child is ready. There's no question that too many American kids are left alone, for too long, while their parents are at work. Estimates of the number of kids who routinely care for themselves while their parents work range from two million to ten million. People in the field believe it's closer to the latter figure and that about one out of every three school-age children with working parents, across all age groups, spends at least part of his time home alone. There's plenty of evidence that many of these children are under 12; one study of middle-class third-graders in Texas found that one-third of the kids had no adult supervision after school. The numbers are hard to pin down for obvious reasons: Parents don't want to report that their six-, seven-, and eight-year-olds are staying home alone.

Many of these children are caring for younger brothers and sisters. Statistics on sibling care are in short supply; no nationwide figures exist. But for an article entitled "Kids Taking Care of

Kids," reporter Linda L. Creighton of *U.S. News & World Report* found two studies on sibling care that provide a sense of the depth of the problem. The first, a reader survey by the school-age publication *Weekly Reader*, found that 7,000 of the 30,000 12-year-olds surveyed—nearly one-fourth—were home alone with a sibling after school. The second, a survey of school-age care in Baltimore, found that "of the [city's] 90,000 schoolchildren, almost half are latchkey. Most go home with a brother or sister." Writes Creighton, "Parents, teachers, psychiatrists, and children say this is America's big secret: that millions of children are left in charge because there is no one else."[3]

Although the issue of sibling care has received scant attention, public awareness of the latchkey crisis has grown considerably over the past decade, stimulating discussion about the role of schools in providing care, developing child-care programs for older kids (meaning ages ten and up), and creating special check-in programs for adolescents and teenagers.

There are lots of reasons for the latchkey problem. One is money: School-age child care is almost exclusively funded by parent fees. Some parents simply can't afford it (organized care generally runs from $25 to $50 a week); others are unwilling to pay. A national survey of parents with latchkey kids, conducted by Phone Friend, a support line for children at home alone, found most parents were not willing to pay even a dollar an hour for a "block mother" or neighborhood checkpoint for their elementary school children. But money isn't the only issue: There simply aren't enough good programs for all age ranges.

Most child-care programs are not designed to accommodate older kids. The first child-care crunch comes at around age eight or nine. According to the 1993 National Study of Before and After School Programs, the first major study of school-age programs, there's a dramatic decline in attendance at formal programs around those ages, and a corresponding increase in the number of kids who care for themselves: "By age 10, as many as 60 percent [of school-age children] are on their own for at least some portion of their after-school hours."[4] According to Louise Guerney, one of the co-founders of Phone Friend, most of the calls coming into the support line are from seven- and eight-year-olds. Why are these kids home alone? Because in many cases that's the best option—or the only option. By age eight or nine, some kids are champing at the bit to get out of after-school programs that are designed for younger kids. That's the age when parents begin to hear kids use the words "babyish" and "boring" to describe such programs.

Once a child hits middle school, he may be too old for child care and, according to many experts, too young to be without adult supervision. A sixth-grader clearly does not want to have a babysitter. When officials in Arlington, Virginia, set up a task force on middle-school child care (for grades six through eight), they included children on their planning committee. "The kids said, 'For crying out loud, don't let our parents walk in with their checkbooks,'" says Tracey Ballas, president of the National School-Age Child Care Alliance. "They said, 'This is going to be our club. We'd feel like it was babysitting or child care.'"

By age 12, most kids have outgrown child care as we know it. Often they have other activities that make after-school programs too restrictive: soccer practice every Tuesday, a paper to research at the local library, after-school enrichment on Friday. According to Deborah Belle of Boston University's psychology department, who spent four years studying Boston schoolchildren in various child-care situations, self-care can be a suitable option for some children. "I came to understand why some parents took their kids out of supervised settings," she says, describing her findings. "Some kids thrived in unsupervised settings. Others did very badly. But supervision did not guarantee that a child would do well. Some children were quite unhappy in supervised settings." The problem, according to Belle, lies with the quality of school-age care: "The range of what's available is inadequate—clearly inadequate."

Still, most experts agree that no child is ready for routine self-care until at least age 12. They warn that no child should be charged with caring for another child until both are old enough for self-care—meaning no child under 12 should be left in the care of another child. Yet in today's child-care environment, such guidelines seem hopelessly unrealistic.

Given that and the quality of care available, how do you evaluate formal settings and gauge your child's readiness for self-care? Those questions, along with the developmental issues of the early school years and the relationship between your work and your child's world, are covered in this chapter.

Formal Child-Care Programs for School-Age Kids

Parent advocacy and community activism have played an enormous role in reforming school-age child care over the past decade. The change has been dramatic. Twenty years ago, there were virtually no extended-day programs in American schools. As of 1993, when the first national study of school-age child care was released, there were nearly 50,000 formal programs, with 1.7 million kids in attendance—although, again, many of these programs are not based in schools.

Consider the transformation our society has undergone. In 1986, when community leaders in Zanesville, Ohio, sat down to map out a plan for attracting new business to the town, an outside consultant told them one of the biggest steps they'd have to take was to set up some school-age child-care programs. At the time there were none. The local Soroptimist Club, a women's group, picked up the ball, researching the options, and programs began in collaboration with the Zanesville city schools. In 1983, when Louise Guerney and her co-founders set up the first Phone Friend support line for latchkey kids in State College, Pennsylvania, there were no formal school-age child-care programs in this college town of 40,000 full-time residents and 8,000 school-age kids. Today there are half a dozen such programs in the town. Phone Friend, which now has 300 independently operated lines in the U.S. and Canada, helped spark widespread advocacy for school-age care by attracting a lot of media attention, much of it focused on the alarming rise in the rate of latchkey care for seven-, eight-, and nine-year-olds. Many school-based programs began when parents petitioned schools for space.

The field of school-age child care is still new and changing rapidly. National standards for such programs—guidelines for setting up and evaluating them—were not completed until 1991. In August 1994, for the first time in history, professionals in the nascent field of middle-school child care held a national meeting to talk about providing care for kids over age 12. And at this writing, the Wellesley School-Age Child Care Project is preparing to unveil an accreditation program for school-age care and spearheading efforts to establishing a degree program for school-age child-care professionals.

Private schools were among the first to pick up the school-age child-care ball. Programs based in private schools are, on average, eight years older than those based in public schools.[5] And today private schools are far more likely to offer a wide range of enrichment programs and to be open on nonschool days— holidays, snow days, summer days. In the affluent town of Wilmington, Delaware, 25 percent of the city's children attend private schools,[6] which routinely offer all manner of enrichment programs and are open, according to one parent, "just about all the time." They have to do it, she says, to compete for the children of two-income couples.

The Search for School-Age Care

What's available to you and your family will depend largely on what you can afford and where you live. Take my experience as an example: When my older son attended a private day school in the South during pre-K and kindergarten back in 1983, child care was no problem. The school offered before- and after-school programs that had access to all the school's facilities and were age-appropriate, staffed by teachers, and full of his friends.

In 1985, when we moved to the Northeast and he entered public school as a first grader, school-based care was available, but we were put on the waiting list. The after-school program (ASP) was operated by a parent-run board, which had petitioned the school for space a few years earlier but had no formal links to the school administration. Kids in kindergarten through fourth grade (there may have been a few fifth and sixth graders) were crowded into a single, dismal room that was used by the school during the day. Supplies were crammed into a metal cabinet. When the school's own after-school enrichment program, run by the PTA and open to all, made use of the Main Hall (which functioned as a makeshift gym for the ASP kids on rainy days), that space was no longer available for the regular program. During our first year there, no homework room existed. Although the staff—headed up by someone with a background in recreation—made an enormous effort to plan activities and work with the kids, the space was inadequate and the program had a chaotic, overcrowded feel to it.

Had our house been a block farther east, we would have been in another school district and would have had access to an after-school program housed in its own large, sunny space—stocked with toys and equipment and carpeted wall to wall—run by a trained professional with a background in child development.

But we still hadn't experienced the worst of after-school care. That happened in 1989, when my son, then in fourth grade, transferred from one public school to another. His new school's program was housed in the gymnasium, where kids ranging from kindergarten to grade four had the option of sitting on the gym floor and doing homework, playing a game of cards, or going out onto the blacktop and running around. There were no activities provided—no art, no clubs, no games, no drama, no field trips, no options. Most accurately described as warehousing, this type of custodial after-school program is still very much with us, in gymnasiums, cafeterias, and empty classrooms.

My family's experience, I find, is typical. School-based child care runs the gamut from outstanding to dismal. Again, what you get will depend on where you live and where your child goes to school.

How to Evaluate a School-Based Program

Evaluating a school-based before- or after-school program is pretty straightforward. An hour or two spent in a typical after-school program will tell you most of what you need to know about staff attitudes, activities, and the feel of the program. From the standpoint of selection, accreditation and licensing are minor issues. Most school-age programs comply with local regulations; accreditation generally means a program is accredited as part of the school accreditation process. Quality standards for school-age care are relatively new, and at this writing national accreditation processes specifically designed for school-age care do not exist.

What are you looking for? The essentials include:

- space—a quiet place for homework, space to play indoors (a gym or big room) and out (a playground, park, or sports field), and activity space (for games, art projects, science experiments)
- kids your child's age
- available adults (most school-age programs offer a good ratio of adults to kids)
- safety (sign-in sheets and sign-out sheets, permission slips for trips to the library, clear rules about when your child can leave and with whom)
- equipment and supplies

Good signs. A good program also has:

- a parent-advisory board
- a mechanism for communicating with parents (such as a bulletin board or newsletter—conferences are rare) and for fostering communication among parents (look for monthly dinners, annual picnics, special gatherings)

- a cooperative relationship with the program site (school, church, YMCA). Talk with other parents; in some schools there's an openly hostile relationship between working and nonworking parents or between school officials and the program.
- genuine enrichment opportunities (drama and chess clubs, cooking projects, field trips, and access to swim classes, piano lessons, karate classes, or dance classes through the facility in which the program is located)
- creative programs
- access to a library or computer room for older children

Choices. Look for a program in which your child is free to pick and choose. What school-age kids *don't* need is to be herded from one activity to another. When Tracey Ballas, president of the National School-Age Child Care Alliance, trains providers, she talks about lap kids, nap kids, snack kids, and rap kids. Lap kids, she says, need to run around after school—climb, jump rope, play soccer or catch. (But according to the National Study of Before and After School Programs, only 27 percent of school-age child-care programs have access to outdoor space.) Nap kids (a term not to be taken literally) need to rest, veg out, and wind down—by reading a book, doing a puzzle, playing a board game. Then there are the snackers. "Some kids are absolutely starving when they first come in. Not only do they need food, they need enough of it, and it has to be very nutritious," says Ballas. Some kids are rap kids—they want to talk to an adult or a friend. They need to process what went on that day. "All these kids have different needs, and they come in at the same time," she says. You want a program that can accommodate everybody but that suits *your* child.

Looking Beyond the School for Child Care

If your school has no program, or an inadequate one, where do you turn? It may be possible to continue your current child-care arrangements if you have a trusted in-home caregiver, family day-care provider, or center that offers after-school care. Some day-care centers—particularly for-profit centers—offer school-age programs; 35 percent of school-based programs are in centers that serve younger children but have separate school-age programs. Many such slots are filled by kids who graduated from the early-childhood program and are bused back by van for school-age care. For example, at the Yuk Yau Child Development Center in Oakland, California, a model program whose waiting list for day care had over 500 names on it in 1991, all the children who left for kindergarten that year stayed on at the center's school-age program.[7]

Family day-care providers based near schools may be a possibility; talk to school officials and parents or contact the resource and referral service in your area. Remember Maryanne Lazarchick, the model provider who appeared in chapter three? Most of her kids stay with her through the elementary school years, and some stay until junior high. Some referral agencies endeavor to link parents with family day-care providers who offer transportation to and from their home.

Churches, synagogues, community centers, recreation centers, Boys and Girls Clubs of America, and YMCAs and YWCAs are also common sites for before- and after-school care.

Working With Providers

The golden rule for working with school-age child-care providers is *communicate*—but not too much. If something major is going on in your child's life, the people in his before- and after-school programs should know: "Johnny is on medication." "We're getting a divorce." "Marcia knows we're moving at the end of the school year, and she's upset." "Eleanor needs some extra help in math."

However, bonding with your school-age providers to the point where you're sharing the details of your life and keeping providers at work beyond reasonable hours is inappropriate. "I've seen parents so bonded to the staff that they would consume us until 9 P.M.," says Tracey Ballas. The solution? Providers should promote parent-to-parent communication so parents can talk to one another about developmental and social issues facing their kids. Ballas offers these ideas (all of which have been put into practice) from various school-age programs throughout the country, aimed at helping parents connect with other parents and have more time for their kids—both of which are good for children:

Put up a bulletin board for parent-to-parent communication—sharing information on transportation needs, sports programs, babysitting coops, bikes for sale, community activities. Says Ballas, "At one of our programs we set up a parent corner with a comfortable chair, a coffeepot, and the bulletin board." Information on area social services, provided through the United Way, was there for the taking.

Initiate parent-child activities in which the kids play with the kids and the parents talk to the parents. One example is a dance in the gym, with parents rotating in and out as chaperones and playing cards in an adjacent room. "Whoever loses the hand goes back in to chaperone and taps another parent to return to the card room," says Ballas. A sporting event or a field day at which kids play, parents visit with one another, and referees rotate in and out is another option.

Make picnics and dinners more than annual events to bring families together with other families more frequently. In one of Ballas's programs, which had access to a full kitchen, the kids cooked a spaghetti dinner for their families on a regular basis, creating goodwill all around.

Use services that save parents time. At one of Ballas's programs, a dry-cleaning delivery service made a regular pickup at the after-school program for parents' convenience. Parents could put in orders for deli dinners in the morning and pick them up at child care at the end of the day.

One of the best ideas I've heard: A barber and beautician regularly visited one of Ballas's after-school programs, eliminating the need for a long Saturday wait at the haircutter's. Parents left their money in an envelope, along with specific instructions, if necessary (no crew cuts, longer bangs this time). "The kids really enjoyed watching other kids get their haircuts," says Ballas.

Find Out What You Can Do

The best way to open the lines of communication with providers is to empathize and ask them what kind of support they need. Many school-based programs suffer from a lack of space, supplies, storage space, and indoor play areas for bad-weather days. Ask the people in your program what you can do for them. What supplies do you have at home? Old newspapers for papier-mâché projects; old magazines for collages; old clothes for costumes; games your children have outgrown; a video camera to lend for a movie-making project; a tape recorder to lend for a "radio broadcast"; a computer to help fledgling reporters put together a newspaper or newsletter? What do you have access to at work? Computer paper for drawing; out-of-date office equipment that's being discarded; fabrics; clay; an ideal site for a field trip? Better to start talking with caregivers by proposing some constructive ideas than to have your first conversation when a problem comes up.

Fixing a School-Age Program

Have you heard the one about the mother who joined the board of directors at her son's after-school program to make it better and ended up nearly destroying it? I certainly hope not, because that mother was me. When my oldest son was eight years old and enrolled in a program at his public school, I had some concerns about the program; for example, the before-school program engaged in the questionable practice of playing loud rock music and feeding the kids donuts. That, I thought, was hardly the best way to start the school day: hyped up on sugar and music. I felt compelled to get involved, if only to find out what was going on and who was running the show. I plowed ahead naively at my first board meeting, expressing my concerns to the board members and director. The next day the director, much loved by the kids, resigned. Shortly thereafter, most of the rest of the staff left.

The board managed to pick up the pieces; however, there was no question I had screwed up by failing to follow some of the basic rules of advocacy: Find some allies and build a consensus before plowing ahead. Walk gently; many times providers are victims of the same limitations that plague programs (no space, no storage, no money, no equipment, pent-up kids with no place to run, tired kids with no way to rest). When your concerns involve a school-based program, approaching the school principal can turn things around. Says Ellen Gannett, associate director of the School-Age Child Care Project at the Wellesley Center for Research on Women, "I have talked to principals who have no idea what's going on in their before- and after-school programs because they have no responsibility for those programs. Then some parent comes up and complains, and all of a sudden they say, 'What's going on in that basement?' They take a look, and they don't like what they see." But again, before approaching the principal, don't forget to enlist someone else's support; talk with providers and people who run your program first.

Starting a School-Age Program

Grass-roots activism is the name of the game in school-age child care. To find out how to start or fund a program, contact the School-Age Child Care Project at the Wellesley Center for Research on Women, Wellesley, Massachusetts 02181-8295. It publishes a book entitled *School-Age Child Care: An Action Manual for the '90s and Beyond*, available for $19.95 plus $3.00 shipping and handling, which provides detailed guidelines on how to organize parents, approach school officials, obtain funding, and set up programs.

Between Home and School: What Children Need

Lest you imagine you know what goes on in the minds of school-age children, consider this: When asked to rank potentially stressful life events, adults generally rate birth, death, divorce, and moving as the big-ticket items. When the National Association of School Psychologists asked children ages 6 to 11 to do a similar ranking, the results were surprising. The children agreed with their parents that the death of a family member is the number one stressor. But second on their list was "fear of going blind." Other fears included "being rejected or humiliated by wetting their pants in class," "being sent to the principal's office," or failing to be promoted to the next grade in school.

During the early school years, kids are finding their place in the world. The task of separation that occupied the preschool years will resolve itself in kindergarten, when children begin to see themselves as truly separate and distinct from their parents. But until about third grade, they are still very much at the center of their own universe. Then the bad news hits them and a new preoccupation takes hold: If I'm not the center of the universe, where the hell do I fit in? Kids will get no shortage of cues from their environment about where they belong. They are rated, ranked, graded, and tracked; chosen or not chosen for sports teams; invited or not invited to birthday parties; included or excluded from "out" groups and "in" groups. A minor incident on the playground can be a major source of stress. Issues related to achievement, competition, friendship, and peer relations as they affect the evolving sense of self will become the central focus of their lives.

What can you do to make your child's school life easier? For one thing, you can help him become organized. With school comes a host of new challenges related to managing your child's time. That means creating space and time for homework, scheduling after-school activities and play arrangements, facilitating friendships by extending invitations, making sure your child is enrolled in the programs he wants to attend, and making suitable arrangements for getting him there. Managing the life of a school-age child is no small task. Add more kids and it's an executive-level job, one that takes a good deal of planning and organization. Some of the essentials:

Keep a family calendar. All school holidays, school conferences, special programs, sporting events, after-school activities, play arrangements, transportation, and social activities should be on paper in one place, accessible to all.

Learn to be an advance planner. "Yesterday I took my son to his tennis clinic wearing cowboy boots. He didn't have a racket," one mother told me. "The coach looked at me like I was crazy." They had discovered just that morning that his sneakers were too small and the tennis racket had been lost in a recent move. "I spend my life feeling like an inadequate mother," said the woman. But imagine how her son felt.

The best way to avoid bad feelings all around is to plan ahead. That means learning to count backwards. Enrollment for June summer camp begins in March and April; sign-up for fall ballet classes may begin in August; the check for spring soccer has to be in the mail by March 15, which means you have to call in February to get the enrollment form. The Halloween costume that's needed for the school party on October 29 must be bought, borrowed, or, worse still, created a week ahead. If the science fair is in November, you'd better get started in October. These are the kinds of plans that fall through the cracks and can cost your kid valuable experiences.

Create a time and space for homework. Be it a desk in the bedroom, a spot at the kitchen table, or a homework room in an after-school program, make sure your child has a place and time to get homework done. Scores of studies support the notion that parents who spend more time helping with schoolwork and reviewing homework have kids who do better in school. That's a far more successful strategy than reviewing report cards and meting out praise or punishment for grades. If you're genuinely involved with your child's academic efforts, report cards won't come as a surprise.

Get involved in the school. No other bit of advice may be more crucial to your child's ability to adapt to and succeed in school. At least *50 studies* have confirmed that parents who are involved with their children's schools—through fundraising efforts, parent-teacher conferences, PTA meetings, and special events—have kids who do better in school; and schools—both private and public—with high levels of parental involvement are better schools. But school involvement does more than promote academic achievement. Parents who are active in schools connect with other parents, which facilitates friendships between kids and provides a link when you need advice on what's age-appropriate. Involved parents are more apt to get positive feedback from teachers and school officials when a problem comes up, and, I've found from my experience, they can resolve difficulties more easily.

Between Home and Work: Special Concerns for Working Parents

As your children age, your work takes on a different meaning to them. A preschooler needs to know where you are during the day; a visit to your workplace satisfies more than curiosity. It gives her an image to grab on to, as in, "Ah, so this is what you're talking about when you go to work." At the elementary school level, most kids take pride in their parents' achievements; they want to know what you do and how you do it. Career days at school are nice; so is Take Our Daughters to Work Day. "I love my work" may be an important message to send to your kids. But it's far more important that you become aware of their world than that they become aware of yours; your interest in their schoolwork is more important than their interest in your job.

Be aware that as children move from kindergarten through elementary school, they will become increasingly aware of how much your work affects their lives. Here are some issues that may come up:

The fact that you work may make your child feel he's at a disadvantage. For many children with working parents, school is the first time it becomes clear that some other kids have at-home moms and that there are advantages to the arrangement. "Why can't you pick me up?" can become a familiar refrain. As kids

311

mature, they're perfectly capable of accepting the truth: You have to go to work to make money. Explain to them that you love your work just as they enjoy school, gymnastics, or sports.

If the problem becomes chronic, look closely at your child-care arrangements. Does your child have access to his friends? Are there plenty of activities to keep him interested? Does he have time to veg out? At-home care may be preferable to outside care. And for some parents, an abbreviated work schedule may represent more than a gesture—it may make it easier for your child to be with friends, play basketball, practice piano, or get homework done.

If you're not careful, your work will invade your child's life: "I have an early-morning meeting." "I'll be home late tomorrow." "I'm having a problem at the office." "I'm on deadline."

Don't let work problems be a dinnertime topic. Constantly reminding your child of the stresses of your work situation sends a clear message: My work is the most important thing. Worse still, you risk conveying the impression that work is, basically, a stressful, unpleasant experience.

Dealing With Other Parents

The battle between at-home moms and working moms takes many forms. Pettiness abounds on both sides. Each can be judgmental of the other. ("I think my neighbor's jealous because I go to work," one working mother told me. Said another, "One parent I know is very self-righteous. She makes it clear that she's home because she believes it's important to be there for her kids.") Truth is, a lot of mothers are working who'd rather be home, and a lot of stay-at-home moms would rather be working.

Women who stay home are under constant pressure to justify their decision ("it's good for the kids") to husbands, friends, and other mothers. In contrast, working mothers spend endless hours dealing with guilt and justifying *their* choice—if indeed it is a choice—to themselves. A surprising number of women I interviewed worked only because their husbands insisted on it—a sad commentary on contemporary feminism. It seems to me some understanding and support are needed all around.

312

A Sick Kid Can Mean Panic for a Working Parent

"My parents treat my getting sick like a major crime. They don't even stay home with me but they try to make me feel guilty for getting sick. My dad's a lawyer and he talks to me like he's examining a witness in a case. He says things like 'How come you were well enough to go out all weekend but are sick now?' How am I supposed to know?"
—*Walter, age 13, quoted in* The Working Parent Dilemma

I doubt most working parents would subject their child to such a grilling, but the basic message well-meaning parents convey to sick kids may be the same: How can you do this to me?

I know the feeling all too well. As the thermometer rises on Tuesday night, you're thinking about your Wednesday schedule and struggling for the right words: "I'm sure it'll pass by morning." Some employers now have sick child–care policies that allow parents to take personal time off; others provide access to sick child–care centers or sick-care sitter services. But for most parents, the available options are to stay home themselves, ask a relative to help out, or leave the child alone—not an advisable solution for children under age 12. Pediatricians report that illness sends working parents into a panic—a panic that's easily conveyed to their children.[8]

Working transforms parents in curious ways. When my son runs out the door without his sweater, I know the appropriate response is to let him get cold and come back in for it when he's ready. But I'm thinking: He's going to get a chill; he's going to get sick; *I'm going to miss work*. The process has turned me into an incorrigible nag. Don't let "You mean he can't go to school tomorrow?" be your first response when the doctor orders bed rest. Your kid is sick! A little empathy is in order.

Sometimes school-related activities—PTA meetings, picnics, school fairs—break down into two camps, with employment status determining which corner you're in. If you can, try to bridge the gap. But be aware that parents with flexibility are witness to a good deal of irresponsibility on the part of full-time working parents with demanding schedules. They see the kids standing out in the rain before the school doors are unlocked in the morning; the kids who are left to make their own transportation arrangements; the kids who, to all appearances, are not thriving in child care. They take the calls from working parents who can't get away in time to pick up Susie or Tim. *They don't understand the desperate pinch you're in because they live in another world.* One mother tells me, "I feel free to comment on my friend's child-care arrangements because I'm the one who takes her kids everywhere and I'm the one who has to make arrangements with this babysitter who can barely speak English." Says another mother, who hired an in-home caregiver and returned to work after 11 years at home, "I learned that mothers often apply harsher standards to another person's caregiver than they apply to their own."

Problems between moms-at-home and moms-at-work take on greater significance when these conflicts get in the way of children's activities and friendships. "I don't let my child visit a friend's house after school unless the mother's there or I know the babysitter," says one at-home mom. A number of parents told me their kids were unable to sustain friendships with the children of nonworking parents; there was too much resentment flowing both ways for the parents to work out the logistics involved in keeping the friendship alive. Says one mother of a fourth-grade boy, "My son lost a friend because his mother's at home and I'm at work. We simply could never get them together. She was unwilling to drive both ways on weekdays so my son could visit." Unfortunately, in such cases the responsibility for fixing things falls to the working parent. If it's important to your child, put on your thickest skin, pick up the phone, and call the other parent to try to work it out. If you can't, the best you can offer your kid is an honest explanation—and a lesson in bending.

If you rely on parents who are home, be sure to reciprocate. Says one father, a man with a flexible job who is room parent at his daughter's school, "I'm the 'mother' who can get off from work and take the kids to the parties and drop them off and stuff like that. . . . So I'm pretty resentful at times. You would think just because of the gender strangeness of it, people would think twice about dumping their kids on me!" If you have to ask an at-home parent for help, do your best to reciprocate when you can. "We always had elaborate carpool arrangements for Hebrew school," says the mother of a teenager, who worked throughout her daughter's life. "I remember feeling beholden because I couldn't do my share. So I always drove on Sundays." Make it a rule to keep a mental count of the favors done for you and repay them in kind.

Get Past the Guilt

"What advice do you have for working parents?" I asked people this question at the end of every interview I conducted for this book. "I would urge working parents not to feel guilty," said one high school principal. "Working parents are taking the rap for problems they haven't created," said an educational consultant who deals with many learning-disabled kids. "Tell them you just have to relax and know that you love your kid and you're doing what's best," said another.

If it's any reassurance, studies show that working mothers are more concerned about their child's education and more involved with homework than nonworking mothers; they even carry more of the transportation load than their nonworking counterparts. Working parents are also just as involved in school activities as nonworking parents, and they compensate, even overcompensate, for their absences. "Just as many children are sent to my office who have mothers at home as those with mothers at work," says one school principal.

Going Back to Work

Some parents wait until their children hit school to go back to work or scale up to full-time employment. "I'll never forget the night my mother told me she was going back to work," says a woman who's now a mother herself. "She came up to my room before bed and gave me a pack of gum as a gift along with the news. I was devastated." Says another mother, who recently returned to work after 11 years at home, "My daughter, who's seven, misses me a lot. She's very clingy. I spend a lot of time with her in the evenings." Some people might imagine that the ideal time to return to work is when your child begins school. However, ages five to six, when kids are beginning to transfer their affections and allegiances from family to friends, are tough times for a kid to adjust to a major change. In contrast, older children, say eight and up, are eager for autonomy. They may be ready for the independence your new job allows.

But think carefully, and don't expect a bonanza. Judy Saks decided to go back to work as an editor when her daughter was 7 and her son was 11. In retrospect, she feels she should have given it a little more thought. "I should have put a calculator to it," she says; despite earnings of $47,000 a year, once she deducted taxes, social security, the cost of in-home care (at $265 a week), plus commuting costs and lunch, she ended up netting $15,000 a year. But what she really should have added up, she says, was the commuting time. "It takes me an hour in the morning and an hour and a half in the evening," she says. "I can leave the office at 5:30 and I'm not home until 7." Generally, she says, she's absent from 8 A.M., leaving the house before her kids go to school, until 6:30 at night. She notes, "I didn't calculate the physical exhaustion of the commute," which gives her not only less time but less energy for her kids.

Should I Quit My Job?

Obviously, this question is more likely to be raised by mothers than fathers. The logistics of school-age child care get increasingly complex as children grow. Should your child have a parent at home? The answer may be yes if:

- you can afford it
- your child is losing out on valuable opportunities because of your work schedule. Baseball, piano, ballet, or computer club may not be an option because there's no way to get there. I interviewed a mother who was simply unable to find a way to get her son to soccer practice every afternoon. Once is okay, but if it becomes a habit, you may be working to your child's detriment.
- academic problems can be traced to your work schedule. Is homework slipping because the after-school setting doesn't provide adequate time and space? Is your child exhausted because of your work schedule? I cut back to a six-hour workday when my oldest son's schedule made homework time a virtual impossibility. Sports started at 5 P.M. and ended at 7; the after-school program, from 3 to 5 P.M., was too distracting. And nights were turning into homework marathons. My new work schedule opened up time for him.
- you feel too stressed to offer support to your kids
- the child care available is inappropriate and your child is too young to be home alone. Before considering a job change, take a few days off and look into it. Call other parents, referral services, and local agencies; talk to the school. If the situation is desperate, call the United Way and find out what agencies to contact.
- your child has a problem that must be dealt with. Studies show that parents whose children are doing well are more likely to remain in the workforce than those whose children are having problems. If you have a school-age child who's experiencing social, emotional, behavioral, medical, or academic problems, quitting work may not be the solution, but it may be the only avenue for solving the problem. Think carefully. Does you child need services that will require the money or health insurance your job provides—for medical care, therapy, or tutoring?

This Matter of Time

There is a big snowstorm toward the end of the children's picture book *Take Time to Relax*, by Nancy Carlson, which captures the pace of modern life. It's a picture book about a family of gophers in which both parents work and, like their daughter, attend all manner of enrichment programs. Nature forces the snowbound family to stay home for a day to tell stories, sing songs, pop popcorn, and sit by the fire. Once the snowplows arrive, they elect to remain at home instead of going to the office, computer club, and aerobics. "We're having too much fun!" say Mom and Dad. The moral of this fable, of course, is that it's worthwhile to take time out from the hustle-bustle of family life, 90s-style, to be together.

At one end of the child-care spectrum are school-age children warehoused in custodial programs or left alone at home with the television and a bag of chips for too many hours. Child-care advocates are concerned about the time that's left unfilled and the learning opportunities that are lost to these children. At the other end of the spectrum are the hurried, harried children of affluent parents who fill their hours with an endless round of programs, programs, programs, to the point where it seems a 12-year-old cannot organize himself without a Filofax. " 'Veg out' was a phrase I heard a lot," says Boston University psychologist Deborah Belle of her interviews with school-age children. "These kids want time to veg out." To get your kids off the treadmill, you may have to get yourself off first.

The time shortage is one of the biggest issues facing American workers, and working parents are among its greatest victims. They want to downshift, scale back, and hop on Parent Tracks, but they are competing in the real world, where the American work ethic has become the American overwork ethic. In *The Overworked American*, author and economist Juliet B. Schor paints a dismal picture of the dramatic decline in America's nonworking hours; in 1987, American workers put in an average of 163 more hours apiece than did workers in 1969—"the equivalent of an extra month a year."[9] That holds true, Schor says, across income groups, industries, and family types (including those with and without children). In 1990, she writes, "one-fourth of all full-time workers spent forty-nine or more hours on a job each week. Of these, almost half were at work sixty hours or more."[10] Americans are working more overtime hours, taking shorter vacations, and, increasingly, working more than one job, trapped in what Schor calls "the insidious cycle of work-and-spend."

According to time studies, as children age, parents spend less and less time with them. It's easy to imagine that a seven-year-old or ten-year-old who's absorbed in activities, friendships, sports, music, and dance has little need for focused time with Mom and Dad. But that assumption couldn't be further from the truth. If there's one thing on which all the experts in the field of child development agree, be they pediatricians, psychologists, psychiatrists, educators, or child-care experts, it's this: Children thrive in families that are loving and supportive, with parents who are available (meaning *present*), who keep the lines of communication open, and who show that they care—all of which takes time. For working parents, that means:

Finding time for conversation. If you've got a rapper, you're in luck. But some kids don't volunteer information easily. Adolescents are renowned for clamming up. When my older son was in child care, he tended to share his thoughts and feelings at bedtime. When he was in elementary school, the car seemed to be the best vehicle for deep discussions—about death, about sex, about friendships and conflicts—perhaps on the way to the barbershop or the supermarket. Sometimes I'd make him come shopping just to get him in the car. Says Beatrice Tier, who has two school-age kids, "You can spend time with your kids but not really discuss things. The challenge is getting to the heart of the matter, and that means knowing your child and picking up the cues. I could spend a whole day with Matthew, and he waits until 8 P.M. to bring up something that's been bothering him all day. That's just his way. The important thing is finding those private moments when they might open up."

This advice takes on added significance if you're considering letting your child stay home alone before or after school. Deborah Belle of the psychology department at Boston University tells of a child who became truly anxious when caring for himself every day for long hours between school and his mother's arrival home. He was unable to do his homework; he could read fiction or watch television, but he was simply too anxious to focus on his work. She muses at the fact that he readily volunteered this information to her. What must his mother be thinking? she wondered. "We realized some parents had never asked the child how they felt," she says. "Kids will let you know how they feel if you give them the opportunity." Not, however, if they think what they have to say is not what you want to hear.

Start listening and stop lecturing. A parent told me about discovering her teenage son's journal, written for school when he was in third grade. "My mom's okay," he had written. "But sometimes when I tell her stuff, she always comes up with what I should have done. It gets on my nerves." It's easy for parents to dish out advice, scold, reprimand, and lecture. What can be harder is to keep quiet, listen, and offer encouragement.

In a series of books—*Liberated Parents: Liberated Children, How to Talk so Kids Will Listen & Listen so Kids Will Talk, Siblings Without Rivalry,* and *How to Be the Parent You Always Wanted to Be*—authors Adele Faber and Elaine Mazlish have developed some guidelines that really work for facilitating communication. The basis of the system is listening. The quickest ways to cut off communication are precisely the routes most parents take.

Connect with your child's world. "Remember when Dan Quayle became vice president?" asks Nancy P., a lawyer who gave up a high-powered job to be with her school-age kids. "Someone asked Marilyn Quayle what she missed most from her former life, and she said, 'I miss car pools.' I thought, this woman is sick!" But, Nancy now realizes, car pools were Marilyn Quayle's window into her children's lives. "That's when she cued into what was going on," says Nancy. "Now I do the same thing. I realize Marilyn Quayle was right." A car pool is an extraordinary opportunity to eavesdrop on a child's world. "In a car pool, children think you're deaf," Nancy remarks. "They talk about all sorts of things that they'd never mention to you. I will pick up something that I heard in a car pool and use it as a discussion."

For most working parents, the days of the car pool are long gone (unless you count weekend rides to sports). What strategies do the parents I interviewed use to keep up with their kids? "At the end of every day, I ask, 'What's the best thing that happened today? What's the worst thing that happened?' " says one mother. "We do a round robin around the dinner table: 'What happened in your day?' " says another. When the search for information turns into a daily grilling and the feedback you're getting is basically "uh-uh" and "not really," experts advise that you ask specific questions, not general ones; not "How was your day?" but "Did you get a chance to spend any time with Marcia today?" or "Who did you sit next to at lunch?" or "How did the science project go?" Anything that will spark a memory helps. But while that's fine for general information, finding out if there's a problem brewing or an issue your child needs to talk about sometimes takes more.

Spend focused time with your child. In his book *Playground Politics*, psychiatrist and author Stanley Turecki advises parents to set aside 20 or 30 minutes a day of focused time with each of your children. That may mean just lying down on their bed and sitting and listening. It may mean awkward silences if your primary contact with your children has been passing each other in the hall. "When parents bring their children for a consultation," he recently told a group of parents, "I tell them, 'First, spend 20 or 30 minutes with them every day.' Most parents come back two weeks later and they haven't done it." At first it may be hard, maintains Turecki, but determination pays off. You get to know your child better, you open the way for communication, and you convey the fact that you care.

Ideally, a parent will find something to do with a child that they both actually enjoy. Not long ago, there was a very personal piece in the *Washington Post* by a young woman who had jogged daily with her father for years. That ritual became the foundation for her memories of him and the context for their conversations. Whatever it is you enjoy—fishing, gardening, building, cooking, road trips, collecting, concerts, movies, sports—give your children a chance to try doing it with you. That can be the point at which you connect.

Be supportive but realistic. On the subject of self-esteem, Stanley Turecki offers this jewel: Stop the self-image commercials! Stop telling your kids how great they are all the time. Why? Says Turecki, "Self-image commercials don't work."[11] You can't give a child self-esteem; that comes from within. It also comes from genuine accomplishment. When they do well, tell them they've done well. When they do poorly, don't berate them. Encourage them to keep trying. Studies of winners of MacArthur Foundation grants, people with high creativity, high motivation, and high achievement, determined that support and encouragement from parents was a much more important factor in developing those qualities than demands or pressure for superior performance.[12] What motivates children is the genuine interest and involvement of their parents.

Carve out family time. Studies of national merit scholar finalists tell us that the single trait these kids have in common is this: Their families sat down together for dinner during their school years. Family time gives children a sense of belonging, the critical stepping-stone to self-esteem, according to Abraham Maslow's theories—wherein lie the roots of our current preoccupation with self-esteem. Says Anne Gay, principal of the Janney School in Washington, D.C., "Everyone tries to teach self-esteem, to tell kids, 'You're wonderful, you're great, you're terrific,' instead of saying, 'You're part of us. You're in this family. You're connected with us. You can take a risk and you can fail, and that isn't going to affect your status.'" This, says Gay, should be the message of home and school: You belong.

Come home. The National Study of the Changing Workforce, released by the Families and Work Institute in 1993, found that when there's a pull between work and home, work usually wins. It's families who are doing most of the changing, the accommodating, to adapt to the needs of business, when it should be the other way around. Saying no to a supervisor who needs more of your time and more energy than you can give is far more difficult than saying no to a school-age child who awaits your return. By comparison to both, saying no to a spouse is a piece of cake.

Many of the studies I've read for this book support the notion that intact families are good for kids. If you have to choose between working late and spending time with your kids, go for the kids. If you have to choose between working late and going to a movie with your family, go for the movie—for your kids' sake as well as your own. If more employees said no to unreasonable hours, the trend toward 50-hour workweeks might be reversed.

Self-Care and Latchkey Kids: Is Your Child Ready?

I recall a morning at work when I overheard a conversation between a secretary at my office and her six-year-old daughter. "Just unplug it," the secretary was saying into the phone. "Everything will be all right. Your daddy should be there any minute." She told me her daughter was home alone from 8 A.M., when she left for work, until about 8:30, when her husband returned from his night job to take the child to school. On this morning, Dad was late and the fish tank had stopped bubbling. Her daughter was worried about her fish, and the breakdown had caused her to panic. Should she put her hand in the tank? What could she do to get the bubbles back? Were the fish going to die? Her mother, sitting at a desk ten minutes from home, had no option but to attempt to soothe her over the phone. Little things, however minor they seem to an adult, can be frightening to a young child. But even a child of 10, 11, or 12 can be frightened in an empty house.

Authors Earl Grollman and Gerri Sweder, experts in crisis management and child development, interviewed 400 school-age kids for their book, *The Working Parent Dilemma*. They heard this comment from a 12-year-old: "I was all by myself when it started thundering. I didn't know if it was a hurricane or what. It sounded bad."[13] And this from an 11-year-old: "I answered [the phone] and the person just hung up. It really scared me."[14] In *Child Care Choices*, by Edward F. Zigler and Mary E. Lang, the authors cite testimony before the Select Committee on Children, Youth and Families in the U.S. House of Representatives during hearings on latchkey kids, including this comment from a ten-year-old girl: "Some things scare me when I'm alone, like the wind, the door creaking and the sky getting dark fast. This may not seem scary to you, but it is to young people who are alone."[15]

We live in a culture that breeds fear into our children. If television and newspapers are an accurate guide to our cultural preoccupations, serial murders and bizarre crimes are among our favorite topics. Fear of strangers is bred into children as young as two and three, who are instructed to 'Never talk to strangers' despite the fact that no two- or three-year-old should ever be out in public without a familiar hand to hold. So it's not surprising that when left alone, some children develop a fear of sexual abuse or kidnapping along with the natural fears that come with being a child: fear of thunderstorms, fear of intruders, fear when the phone or doorbell rings.

The consensus among pediatricians, child-care researchers, and psychologists is that no child should be in self-care before age 12, and many kids aren't ready even then. The reasons, which couldn't be more basic, include:

The ability to respond in an emergency. Being able to respond appropriately in a crisis is the chief prerequisite for self-care—and that's not possible until most children are at least 12, according to Dr. Eli H. Newberger, a pediatrician at Children's Hospital in Boston and president of the Massachusetts Committee for Children and Youth. Until children reach age 12 or 13, Newberger told a reporter from the *Boston Globe*,[16] they're not capable of "formal operational thinking," which, according to this newspaper report, "enables them to review alternative actions and quickly choose the best.... If a fire breaks out, what do you do first? Get everyone out of the house? Find the cat? Try to put out the fire? Call 911?" According to Newberger, "These are the choices a more mature person can sort out with alacrity, and with accuracy, whereas kids younger than 12 or 13 often are bewildered and confused." Even at 12 or 13, it depends on the child. Some might not have the maturity to deal with a crisis.

The emotional consequences. Too much responsibility too soon can cause stress. When Phone Friend, the national support line for latchkey children, conducted a nationwide survey of why kids call in, the top reasons were boredom and loneliness. These kids, most of them in the eight-to-ten age range, just wanted someone to talk to. The next most common reason was a particular problem—"Mother's late" . . . "The dog ran away" . . . "I broke a glass" . . . "I can't find the book I need to do my homework." According to Louise Guerney, a founder of Phone Friend, a common concern among children is how the parent will respond. "They say, 'My mother's going to be really mad because I'm supposed to do my homework and I forgot my book,'" reports Guerney. "They say, 'My mother's going to be really mad because I shouldn't have gotten this glass out, and now it's broken' or 'I didn't get the dog walked today.' They're concerned that they haven't fulfilled their obligations or complied with parental wishes." For children with a sense of responsibility, independence can be stressful. They call Phone Friend, in many cases, out of concern that they are going to get in trouble. The issue is pretty straightforward: They need an adult's support, and there's no adult around.

What the Research Says

The research on the effects of various after-school arrangements is scant and inconclusive. But like the research on early child care, it suggests that children in high-quality after-school programs can be enriched by such programs—and that children in mediocre and poor arrangements do less well.

What about latchkey kids? The research on self-care presents a mixed picture. Some studies suggest that latchkey kids have lower self-esteem and school performance and higher anxiety levels; that they tend to watch too much television and snack too much; and that they are prone to worrying. However, other studies suggest that there's a self-selection factor: Among older children (third grade and above), those in self-care may be *more responsible, high-achieving, and independent* than those who remain in after-school programs.

Researchers point out that some kids enjoy the independence and freedom that self-care provides, a view supported by studies that conclude that under the "right conditions"—if they are well prepared and their parents are generally involved and supportive— children in self-care benefit from higher self-esteem and "a sense of control over their world."[17]

For example, a study of 347 middle-class third-graders in Texas, conducted by Deborah Vandell and Mary Anne Corasaniti in 1988, found that middle-class suburban kids in self-care or home with their parents after school appeared to be better adjusted, have better peer relationships, and be more advanced cognitively than the children in organized but poorly run after-school programs and children cared for by in-home sitters. According to Vandell, self-selection may be an important factor here. With so few child-care options for school-age kids, middle-class parents with responsible, mature, and high-achieving kids are more likely to put them in self-care, while kids with problems in one area or another are more likely to stay in child care.

Rules are important. Perhaps the most interesting study, however, was the one that concluded that kids who do best in self-care are those with parents who practice an affectionate and firm parenting style. (See page 156 for a description.) In other words, kids who are doing well in general, because they have supportive, loving families who teach responsibility, are more able to take on personal responsibility, to feel safe, and to be independent when the time comes. Being in a self-care arrangement, with rules and responsibilities, is quite different from being left to wander the neighborhood with few restrictions.[18]

Piling bad after-school care on top of poor early care. Given so few child-care options and so few programs tailored to the needs of kids in third grade and up, it's quite possible that the children who are most likely to be in child care past age nine or ten are those who need to be in child care the most: those who are less responsible, do less well in school, and have a greater need for adult supervision. There's the possibility, too, that some kids are suffering from the cumulative effect of too much lousy child care and that, ultimately, these kids find themselves in poorly run after-school programs.

I asked school principal Anne Gay of the Janney School in Washington, D.C., which serves a middle- and upper-middle-class neighborhood, whether she sees any differences among the children who have been in group day care when they arrive in first grade. "Some," she says. "Kids from *some* programs behave more like pack animals." These are the children, she says, from programs that stress peer interaction over adult interaction. "They don't make connections with adults," she says. "They make connections with their peers." These are kids who have been socialized, to a large extent, by other kids. They tend to have conduct problems in school and authority problems with teachers. Then they move on to group after-school care.

Consider, for example, how Kathy Wright, who operates eight after-school programs in public schools in an affluent Maryland county, describes those programs: "The kids don't want to be there; they're tired and they want to go home. They don't behave well. The use foul language." On the one hand, the kids are difficult to control. On the other, they're obviously not engaged by the program. Viewed from just about any perspective, such programs can be a nightmare for kids who want out.

What Are the Other Options for After-School Care?

In communities where the only options are inadequate after-school programs or self-care, parents would seem to have no options at all. But people can and do find babysitters to mind their children and transport them in the afternoons. These may be college or graduate students, retired people, other parents, or people who need part-time work. In some communities, kids check in with "block mothers" and family day-care providers. The Reston Children's Center, in Reston, Virginia, is frequently cited as a model program; the day-care center serves as a base for after-school care and for training and linking family day-care providers, and, beyond that, as a school-age checkpoint. But according to people in the field, Reston represents the exception rather than the rule.

Seek out the resources in your community. Parent support groups, school newsletters, neighborhood newspapers, community centers, child-care referral services—all can provide leads on finding in-home care, advertising for a share-care arrangement, or finding family day care. In some communities, librarians, overwhelmed by the number of unsupervised kids arriving at their doorstep every afternoon, have set up organized after-school programs. And businesses, overwhelmed by a rash of phone calls between 3 and 5 P.M., have grown increasingly concerned about the latchkey problem and are beginning to get into the act. If you work for a large company, your human resources department may have information on area programs.

Evaluating the Options

Sitter arrangements are often imperfect. The sitter the kids like may not be the same one you like. Some parents report that sitters are simply unable to establish authority with older children; in such cases, they may take the approach one takes with grandparents: a little spoiling doesn't hurt. Says one parent, "The rules are just more lax. I know that. The kids know that. They can deal with it." But those imperfections are minor if the only other option is a self-care arrangement before a child's old enough.

Formal arrangements between and among parents appear to be uncommon. It is hard enough, it seems, for families to manage their own lives without taking another child on board—a sad commentary on our times, perhaps.

According to Deborah Belle of Boston University, it's common for kids to have varied arrangements that change from day to day: On Monday, a friend comes over. On Tuesday, Mom comes home early. On Wednesday, take the bus to soccer and hop a ride home. On Thursday, the library. If your child is mature enough to handle the independence and your neighborhood is safe enough to facilitate these transitions, a varied schedule combined with self-care can be a great arrangement. But those are two important "ifs."

How Can You Tell if Your Child is Ready for Self-Care?

Ask yourself these questions:

- Is she responsible enough to babysit for younger children?
- Is she doing well in school?
- Do I trust her to follow the rules?
- Is she capable of dealing with any emergency?
- Is she a happy kid?
- Is she communicative? Does she tell me what's going on at school, with friends, in her life? Does she talk honestly about her feelings? In other words, will she tell me if it's not working out?
- Is she able to take public transportation alone?

If you answer yes to all of the above questions, your child may be ready for self-care.

Look closely at the environment:

- Is there an adult always available in the neighborhood during the hours of self-care?
- Will your child have access to activities outside the home and be able to get to and from those activities?
- Is the neighborhood safe?
- Are any of his friends in self-care?
- Is one parent available to take phone calls during self-care hours?
- Is emergency assistance adequate in your community?

• Is there a nearby park, community center, or friend your child can go to for companionship, or will he be locked in every day for three hours? "I'd never have let Daniel come home alone if there hadn't been plenty of adults in the neighborhood who were home during the day," says one mother of her eighth-grade son.

Some kids are made for self-care. If Stephanie loves practicing the piano for hours, she can do so without interruption in self-care. If Harold's a computer nut and wants time to monopolize the family computer, self-care will give him the opportunity. If Janice has soccer practice every afternoon until 5 P.M. and then gets a ride home, and Dad is home at 5:30, self-care makes sense. For other kids, even into the teenage years, self-care is a risky prospect.

Into Adolescence

"I think eighth grade is the scariest time for the kids and the parents. At that age, they need all the structure they can get," says Renee Brimfield, assistant principal at Poolesville Middle Senior High School and mother of a 17-year-old. "I think it's *more* important to have child care when the kid is older than when they're younger." Some studies of adolescents in self-care are disturbing. One highly publicized study of nearly 5,000 eighth graders in Los Angeles and San Diego found that kids who spent 11 or more hours a week caring for themselves were more likely to try drugs, alcohol, and tobacco. The findings held true for lower-, middle-, and upper-class kids, and the researchers determined that self-care was the single most consistent correlate of the study. However, they cautioned that "parenting styles or strategies of self-care, rather than self-care per se, might increase or reduce the risk, particularly the amount of parental guidance over the time spent alone (clear rules, lists of chores, calling in, etc.)."[19]

By the time your child hits 13, you should have a pretty good sense of whether she is apt to use the latchkey hours to smoke, drink, and party or to study and relax. Questions related to self-care will be no more or less perplexing than questions related to curfews, overnights, and parental supervision in general and should be considered in light of your own child and her network of friends.

How to Prepare for Self-Care

There are plenty of books, pamphlets, and videotapes designed to tell parents how to judge their children's capacity for self-care and teach them how to train their kids; there are even guides for kids themselves. I reviewed a number of them in the course of my research and can't in good conscience recommend any. My feeling is that if a child has to take a crash course in safety procedures or needs a reference book to handle an emergency, that child isn't ready for self-care; if parents need guidance on what rules to establish, those parents are not ready to put their kids in self-care.

Preparing a child for self-care is not unlike preparing him for adulthood. It should begin with basic safety lessons, starting in toddlerhood and continuing through adolescence. Many of the rules relate to telephone use (never tell a caller there are no adults at home), locking doors and windows, answering the door (either never answer the door or answer only if you know the person on the other side), guests (many parents say no visitors, but some researchers believe that two responsible friends left together are better off than one left alone), transportation, chores, cooking (don't or do use the stove), checking in, and when (and when not) to call you at work. The impulse for many parents is, essentially, to lock their child in—no visitors, no excursions, no exceptions; but such arrangements can be isolating and particularly disturbing for children.

Saying "Only call me in an emergency" makes sense to most parents. But children under 12 may not be able to distinguish an emergency from a non-emergency. According to Louise Guerney, calls come in frequently to the Phone Friend line from kids seeking advice on precisely that question—which tells me these kids shouldn't be home alone.

If you're considering letting your child care for herself, give it a trial run and then ask her how she feels about it. Check out the special services in your area designed for latchkey kids. Emergency hotlines, free community services such as Phone Friend, and paid phone services for latchkey kids are available in many communities. Leave the door open for a different plan.

***

What to Remember

- *Don't assume that your school's before- and after-school programs are good ones.* Many are operated by outside agencies and have no affiliation with the school. Stop in for a visit before enrolling your child.
- *Get involved with the school.* The research is conclusive and consistent: Parents who are involved with their children's schools have children who do better in school.
- *If your child's interest in her after-school program begins to wane at age eight or nine, look into other options in your community before trying self-care.* Many experts feel that routine self-care is inappropriate for any child under age 12, and may be inappropriate even then.
- *No child should stay alone at home unless the neighborhood is safe and there is a friend or neighbor nearby*—ideally, plenty of friends and neighbors nearby—to whom she can turn for help when she needs it.
- *If inadequate school-age care is all that's available for your child, consider taking an activist role.* Unlike early child care, after-school programs have been founded and run by parents and community groups from the start. But in many communities, the work has yet to be done.
- *Resist the temptation to assume that your child needs you less as the years pass.* Although the desire for autonomy increases from year to year, from toddlerhood on, children need your time, interest, encouragement, and support as much at age 12 as at age 2.

Notes

Chapter One

[1]Cheryl D. Hayes, John L. Palmer, and Martha J. Zaslow (eds.), *Who Cares for America's Children?* (Washington, D.C.: National Academy Press, 1990), p. 17.

[2]Telephone interview, U.S. Bureau of the Census, May 1994.

[3]*Beyond Rhetoric, Final Report of the National Commission on Children* (Washington, D.C.: National Commission on Children, 1991), p. 7.

[4]Carin Rubenstein, "What Pediatricians *Really* Think About Working Mothers," *Working Mother,* April 1990, p. 40.

[5]Ellen Galinsky, *Work and Family: 1992 Status Report and Outlook* (New York: Families and Work Institute, 1992), p. 12.

[6]Susan Faludi, "The Kids Are All Right," *Utne Reader,* May/June 1993, pp. 68-70.

[7]Etzioni Amitai, "Children of the Universe," *Utne Reader,* May/June 1993, pp. 52-61, excerpted from Amitai Etzioni, *The Spirit of Community: Rights, Responsibilities and the Communitarian Agenda* (New York: Crown Publishers, 1993).

[8]Carollee Howes (ed.), *Keeping Current in Child Care Research: An Annotated Bibliography* (Washington, D.C.: National Association for the Education of Young Children, 1990).

[9]Mary Frances Berry, *The Politics of Parenthood* (New York: Viking Penguin, 1993), p. 32.

Chapter Two

[1]Personal interview, Angelina Vaulx, Tennessee Dept. of Human Services, Memphis, February 8, 1994.

[2]Current Population Survey, U.S. Bureau of the Census, June 1992.

[3]Ellen Galinsky, *The Cost of Not Providing Quality Early Childhood Programs* (New York: Families and Work Institute, 1988).

[4]1991 figures, U.S. Bureau of the Census, telephone interview, May 23, 1994.

[5]*1993 Child Day Care Licensing Study* (Washington, D.C.: The Children's Foundation, 1993).

[6]Personal interview, Barbara Willer, Director of Public Affairs, National Association for the Education of Young Children, July 22, 1993.

[7]Cheryl D. Hayes, John L. Palmer, and Martha J. Zaslow (eds.), *Who Cares for America's Children?* (Washington, D.C.: National Academy Press, 1990), p. 151.

[8]Barbara Willer et al., *The Demand and Supply of Child Care in 1990, Joint Findings from the National Child Care Survey 1990 and A Profile of Child Care Settings* (Washington, D.C.: National Association for the Education of Young Children, 1991), p. 59, and Cheryl D. Hayes, John L. Palmer, and Martha J. Zaslow (eds.), *Who Cares for America's Children?* (Washington, D.C.: National Academy Press, 1990), p. 151.

[9]Personal interview, Elaine Piper, National Association for Family Child Care, May 19, 1994.

[10]*1993 Family Day Care Licensing Study*, Family Day Care Advocacy Project (Washington, D.C.: The Children's Foundation, 1993).

[11]Cheryl D. Hayes, John L. Palmer, and Martha J. Zaslow (eds.), *Who Cares for America's Children?* (Washington, D.C.: National Academy Press, 1990), p. 131.

[12]Based on findings from Sandra Hofferth et al., *National Child Care Survey 1990* (Washington, D.C.: Urban Institute, 1991).

[13]According to a report on *All Things Considered*, National Public Radio, January 4, 1994.

[14]M. Whitebook, C. Howes, and D. Phillips, *Executive Summary: National Child Care Staffing Study* (Oakland, CA: Child Care Employee Project, 1989), p. 16.

[15]Ellen Galinsky, Carollee Howes, Susan Kontos, and Marybeth Shinn, *The Study of Children in Family Child Care and Relative Care: Highlights of Findings* (New York: Families and Work Institute, 1994), p. 81.

[16]Ibid, p. 47, and personal interview, Ellen Galinsky, January 11, 1994.

[17]*The Changing Workforce: Highlights of the National Study* (New York: Families and Work Institute, 1993).

[18]Ellen Galinsky, Carollee Howes, Susan Kontos, and Marybeth Shinn, *The Study of Children in Family Child Care and Relative Care:*

Highlights of Findings (New York: Families and Work Institute, 1994), p. 4.

[19]"Choosing Quality Child Care: Topline of Findings," prepared by EDK Associates, New York, for the Child Care Action Campaign, September 1991.

[20]Anonymous, "Nanny: Confessions of an 'Illegal' Caregiver," *Mother Jones*, May/June 1991, p. 75.

[21]Cheryl D. Hayes, John L. Palmer, and Martha J. Zaslow (eds.), *Who Cares for America's Children?* (Washington, D.C.: National Academy Press, 1990), p. 239.

[22]K. Alison Clarke-Stewart and Christian P. Gruber, "Day Care Forms and Features," in R. C. Ainslie (ed.), *The Child and the Day Care Setting* (New York: Praeger Publishers, 1984), p. 40.

[23]K. Alison Clarke-Stewart, "Predicting Child Development From Child Care Forms and Features: The Chicago Study," in Deborah Phillips (ed.), *Quality In Child Care: What Does Research Tell Us?* (Washington, D.C.: National Association for the Education of Young Children, 1987), pp. 21-41.

[24]Ellen Galinsky, Carollee Howes, Susan Kontos, and Marybeth Shinn, *The Study of Children in Family Child Care and Relative Care: Highlights of Findings* (New York: Families and Work Institute, 1994), p. 8, citing Hofferth et al., *National Child Care Survey 1990* (Washington, D.C.: Urban Institute, 1991).

[25]Barbara Willer, "The Full Cost of Quality Must be Paid," in Barbara Willer, *Reaching the Full Cost of Quality in Early Childhood Programs* (Washington, D.C.: National Association for the Education of Young Children, 1990), p. 15.

[26]M. Whitebook, C. Howes, and D. Phillips, *Executive Summary: National Child Care Staffing Study* (Oakland, CA: Child Care Employee Project, 1989), p. 3.

[27]Ibid, p. 4.

[28]Cheryl D. Hayes, John L. Palmer, and Martha J. Zaslow (eds.), *Who Cares for America's Children?* (Washington, D.C.: National Academy Press, 1990), p. 113.

[29]Stephen B. Thacker, et al., "Infectious Diseases and Injuries in Child Day Care," *JAMA*, vol. 268, no. 13, October 7, 1992, pp. 1720-1726.

[30]Deborah Phillips and Carollee Howes, "Indicators of Quality in Child Care: Review of Research," in Deborah Phillips (ed.), *Quality In*

Child Care: What Does Research Tell Us? (Washington, D.C.: National Association for the Education of Young Children, 1987), p. 11.

[31]Ibid.

[32]Personal interview, Howard Hayghe, U.S. Bureau of Labor Statistics, March 1994.

[33]Barbara Willer et al., *The Demand and Supply of Child Care in 1990, Joint Findings from the National Child Care Survey 1990 and A Profile of Child Care Settings* (Washington, D.C.: National Association for the Education of Young Children, 1991), p. 47.

[34]M. Whitebook, C. Howes, and D. Phillips, *Executive Summary: National Child Care Staffing Study* (Oakland, CA: Child Care Employee Project, 1989), p. 10.

[35]Barbara Willer et al., *The Demand and Supply of Child Care in 1990, Joint Findings from the National Child Care Survey 1990 and A Profile of Child Care Settings* (Washington, D.C.: National Association for the Education of Young Children, 1991), p. 35.

[36]Ibid.

[37]Ibid.

[38]Ellen Galinsky, Carollee Howes, Susan Kontos, and Marybeth Shinn, *The Study of Children in Family Child Care and Relative Care: Highlights of Findings* (New York: Families and Work Institute, 1994), p. 74.

[39]Ibid, p. 83.

[40]Marybeth Shinn, Deborah Phillips, Carollee Howes, Ellen Galinsky, and Marcy Whitebook, *Correspondence Between Mothers' Perceptions and Observer Ratings of Quality in Child Care Centers* (New York: Families and Work Institute, 1990).

[41]Barbara Willer (ed.), *Reaching the Full Cost of Quality* (Washington, D.C.: National Association for the Education of Young Children, 1990), p. 33.

Chapter Three

[1]Personal interview, Martin O'Connell, U.S. Bureau of the Census, May 1994.

[2]Ellen Galinsky, Carollee Howes, Susan Kontos, and Marybeth Shinn, *The Study of Children in Family Child Care and Relative Care: Highlights of Findings* (New York: Families and Work Institute, 1994),

p. 8, citing Sandra Hofferth et al., *National Child Care Survey 1990* (Washington, D.C.: Urban Institute, 1991).

[3]Tiffany Field, "Quality of Infant Day Care and Grade School Behavior and Performance," *Child Development*, vol. 62, no. 4, August 1991, pp. 863-870.

[4]Deborah Lowe Vandell and Mary Anne Corasaniti, "Variations in Early Child Care: Do They Predict Subsequent Social, Emotional and Cognitive Differences?" *Early Childhood Research Quarterly*, vol. 5, no. 4, December 1990, pp. 555-572.

[5]Ibid, p. 555.

[6]Ron Haskins, "Public School Aggression Among Children with Varying Day Care Experience," *Child Development*, vol. 56, no. 3, June 1985, pp. 689-703.

[7]Neal W. Finkelstein, "Aggression: Is It Stimulated by Day Care?" *Young Children*, vol. 37, September 1992, pp. 3-12, and personal interview, Dr. Francis Campbell, Frank Porter Graham Child Development Center, March 1994.

[8]Susan M. Hegland and Mary K. Rix, "Aggression and Assertiveness in Kindergarten Children Differing in Day Care Experiences," *Early Childhood Research Quarterly*, vol. 5, no. 1, March 1990, p. 109.

[9]Ibid, p. 106.

[10]C. Howes, "Can the Age of Entry Into Child Care and the Quality of Child Care Predict Adjustment in Kindergarten?" *Developmental Psychology*, vol. 26, no. 2, 1990, pp. 292-293.

[11]Tiffany Field, "Quality of Infant Day Care and Grade School Behavior and Performance," *Child Development*, vol. 62, no. 4, August 1991, pp. 863-870.

[12]Marybeth Shinn, D. Phillips, Carollee Howes, Ellen Galinsky, and Marcy Whitebook, *Correspondence Between Mothers' Perceptions and Observer Ratings of Quality in Child Care Centers* (New York: Families and Work Institute, 1990).

[13]E. Schliecker, D. R. White, and E. Jacobs, "Predicting Preschool Language Comprehension From SES, Family Structure and Day Care Quality," paper presented at the biennial meeting of the Society for Research in Child Development, Kansas City, MO, April 1989, as summarized in *Keeping Current in Child Care Research*, compiled by C. Howes for the National Association for the Education of Young Children (Washington, D.C.: National Association for the Education of Young Children, 1990).

[14]Deborah A. Phillips, S. Scarr, and K. McCartney, "Child Care Quality and Children's Social Development," *Developmental Psychology*, vol. 23, no. 4, July 1987, pp. 537-539.

[15]C. Howes, C. Rodning, D. Galluzzo, and L. Myers, "Attachment and Child Care: Relationships with Mother and Caregiver," *Early Childhood Research Quarterly*, vol. 3, no. 4, 1988, pp. 403-416.

[16]K. Alison Clarke-Stewart, "Predicting Child Development From Child Care Forms and Features: The Chicago Study," in Deborah Phillips, *Quality In Child Care: What Does Research Tell Us?* (Washington, D.C.: National Association for the Education of Young Children, 1987), pp. 21-41, and *Keeping Current in Child Care Research*, compiled by C. Howes for the National Association for the Education of Young Children (Washington, D.C.: National Association for the Education of Young Children, 1988).

[17]Deborah Lowe Vandell, V. Kay Henderson, and Kathy Shore Wilson, "A Longitudinal Study of Children with Day-Care Experiences of Varying Quality," *Child Development*, vol. 59, 1988, pp. 1286-1292.

[18]Ellen Galinsky, Carollee Howes, Susan Kontos, and Marybeth Shinn, *The Study of Children in Family Child Care and Relative Care: Highlights of Findings* (New York: Families and Work Institute, 1994), and personal interview, Carollee Howes, Feb. 17, 1994.

[19]K. Alison Clarke-Stewart and Christan P. Gruber, "Day Care Forms and Features," in Ricardo C. Ainslie (ed.), *The Child and the Day Care Setting: Qualitative Variations and Development* (New York: Praeger Publishers, 1984), pp. 35-62, and K. Alison Clarke-Stewart, "Predicting Child Development From Child Care Forms and Features: The Chicago Study," in Deborah A. Phillips, *Quality In Child Care: What Does Research Tell Us?* (Washington, D.C.: National Association for the Education of Young Children, 1988), pp. 21-41.

[20]*The Study of Children in Family Child Care and Relative Care* (New York: Families and Work Institute, 1994).

[21]Brenda Krause Eheart and Robin Lynn Leavitt, "Family Day Care: Discrepancies Between Intended and Observed Caregiving Practices," *Early Childhood Research Quarterly*, vol. 4, no. 1, March 1989, pp. 145-162.

[22]"Quality Child Care Lasts a Lifetime," *Family Day Care Survey Results*, Child Care Connection, Montgomery County, Maryland, 1993.

[23]Alice M. Atkinson, "Stress Levels of Family Day Care Providers, Mothers Employed Outside the Home, and Mothers at Home," *Journal of Marriage and the Family*, May 1992, pp. 379-386.

[24]Personal interview, Ellen Galinsky, Families and Work Institute, Jan. 11, 1994.

[25]Susan Kontos, *Family Day Care: Out of the Shadows and Into the Limelight* (Washington, D.C.: National Association for the Education of Young Children, 1993), p. 86.

[26]Ibid, p. 87.

[27]R. Innes and S. Innes, "A Qualitative Study of Caregivers' Attitudes About Child Care," *Early Child Development and Care*, vol. 15, 1984, p. 134.

Chapter Four

[1]Penelope Leach, *Children First* (New York: Alfred A. Knopf, 1994), p. 83.

[2]Ibid, p. 87.

[3]Selma Fraiberg, *Every Child's Birthright* (New York: Basic Books, 1977), p. 82.

[4]Anita Shreve, *Remaking Motherhood* (New York: Fawcett Columbine, 1987), p. 163.

[5]T. Berry Brazelton, *Touchpoints* (Reading, MA: Addison-Wesley Publishing Co., 1992), p. 80.

[6]Ibid, p. 81.

[7]Sandra Scarr, *Mother Care/Other Care* (New York: Warner Books, 1985), p. 153.

[8]*Starting Points: Meeting the Needs of Our Youngest Children* (New York: Carnegie Corporation of America, 1994), pp. 8-9.

[9]Personal interview, Sarah Friedman, National Institutes of Child Health and Human Development, April 1994.

[10]Robert Karen, "Becoming Attached: What Children Need," *Atlantic Monthly*, February 1990, pp. 35-70.

[11]Sirgay Sanger and John Kelly, *The Woman Who Works, The Parent Who Cares* (Boston: Little, Brown & Co., 1987), p. 19.

[12]David Elkind, *Miseducation: Preschoolers at Risk* (New York: Alfred A. Knopf, 1987), p. 53.

[13]Diane E. Eyer, *Mother-Infant Bonding: A Scientific Fiction* (New Haven: Yale University Press, 1992), p. 6.

[14]*Diane Rehm Show*, WAMU-FM Radio, April 2, 1994.

[15]Deborah A. Phillips, "Infants and Child Care: The New Controversy," *Child Care Information Exchange*, vol. 58, 1987, pp. 19-22.

[16]Robert Karen, "Becoming Attached: What Children Need," *Atlantic Monthly*, February 1990, pp. 35-70.

[17]U. Bronfenbrenner, "Who Cares for America's Children?" in V. C. Vaughan and T. B. Brazelton (eds.), *The Family—Can It Be Saved?* (Chicago: Chicago Yearbook Medical Publishers, 1976), cited in Laura L. Dittmann, "Where Have All the Mothers Gone, and What Difference Does It Make?" in Bernice Weissbourd and Judith Musick (eds.), *Infants: Their Social Environments* (Washington, D.C.: National Association for the Education of Young Children, 1981).

[18]M. Rutter, *Maternal Deprivation Reassessed*, second ed., (Middlesex, England: Penguin Books, 1981), p. 160, cited in T. Field, W. Masi, S. Goldstein, S. Perry, and P. Silke, "Infant Day Care Facilitates Preschool Social Behavior," *Early Childhood Research Quarterly*, vol. 3, 1988, pp. 341-359.

[19]Robert Karen, "Becoming Attached: What Children Need," *Atlantic Monthly*, February 1990, pp. 35-70.

[20]Jay Belsky, "Infant Day Care: A Cause for Concern?" (September 1986), in *The Zero to Three Child Care Anthology, 1984-1992* (Arlington, VA: National Center for Clinical Infant Programs, 1992), pp. 108-116.

[21]Robert Karen, *Becoming Attached* (New York: Warner Books, 1994), p. 328.

[22]Personal interview, U.S. Bureau of the Census, May 1994.

[23]T. Gamble and E. Zigler, "Effects of Infant Day Care: Another Look at the Evidence," in E. Zigler (ed.), *The Parental Leave Crisis* (New Haven: Yale University Press, 1988; originally published in the *American Journal of Orthopsychiatry*, vol. 56, no. 1, January 1986.

[24]Pat Wingert and Barbara Kantrowitz, "The Day Care Generation," *Newsweek Special Edition: The 21st Century Family*, Winter/Spring 1990.

[25]Deborah Phillips, "Infants and Child Care: The New Controversy," *Child Care Information Exchange*, no. 58, 1987, p. 20.

[26]Ellen Galinsky and Judy David, *The Preschool Years* (New York: Ballantine Books, 1988), p. 369.

[27]Jay Belsky and Michael J. Rovine, "Nonmaternal Care in the First Year of Life and the Security of Infant-Parent Attachment," *Child Development*, vol. 59, 1988, p. 161.

[28]K. Alison Clarke-Stewart, "The 'Effects' of Infant Day Care Reconsidered: Risks for Parents, Children and Researchers," *Early Childhood Research Quarterly*, vol. 3, no. 3, September 1988, p. 307.

[29]B. E. Vaughn, K. E. Deane, and E. Waters, "The Impact of Out-of-Home Care on Child-Mother Attachment Quality: Another Look at Some Enduring Questions" (1985), in I. Bretherton and E. Waters (eds.), *Growing Points in Attachment Theory and Research*, Monographs of the Society for Research in Child Development, 50 (1-2, Serial No. 209). Cited in M. Weinraub, E. Jaeger, and L. Hoffman, "Predicting Infant Outcomes in Families of Employed and Nonemployed Mothers," *Early Childhood Research Quarterly*, vol. 3, 1988, pp. 361-387.

[30]M. E. Lamb, K. J. Sternberg, and M. Prodromidis, "Nonmaternal Care and the Security of Infant-Mother Attachment: A Reanalysis of the Data," *Infant Behavior and Development*, vol. 15, 1992, pp. 71-83, and K. A. Clarke-Stewart, "Infant Day Care: Maligned or Malignant?" *American Psychologist*, vol. 44, 1989, pp. 266-273.

[31]Margaret Tresch Owen and Martha J. Cox, "Maternal Employment and the Transition to Parenthood," in A. E. Gottfried and A. W. Gottfried (eds.), *Maternal Employment and Children's Development: Longitudinal Research* (New York: Plenum Press, 1988), p. 104.

[32]J. Jacobson and D. Willie, "Influence of Attachment and Separation Experience on Separation Distress at 18 Months," *Developmental Psychology*, May 1984, pp. 477-484.

[33]Thomas J. Gamble and Edward Zigler, "Effects of Infant Day Care: Another Look at the Evidence," in E. Zigler (ed.), *The Parental Leave Crisis* (New Haven: Yale University Press, 1988), p. 86.

[34]Rita K. Benn, "Factors Promoting Secure Attachment Relationships Between Employed Mothers and Their Sons," *Child Development*, vol. 57, 1986, pp. 1224-1231.

[35]P. Barglow, B. Vaughn, and N. Molitor, "Effects of Maternal Absence Due to Employment on the Quality of Infant-Mother Attachment in a Low-Risk Sample," *Child Development*, vol. 58, 1987, p. 952.

[36]Robert Karen, *Becoming Attached* (New York: Warner Books, 1994), p. 341.

Chapter Five

[1]Louise Erdrich, "A Woman's Work," in *Harper's Magazine*, May 1993.

[2]E. Trzcinski and W. T. Alpert, "Leave Policies in Small Business: Findings from the U.S. Small Business Administration Employee Leave Survey," Washington, D.C., October 1990, in J. T. Bond, E. Galinsky,

M. Lord, G. Staines, and K. Brown, *Beyond the Parental Leave Debate* (New York: Families and Work Institute, 1991), p. 4.

[3]Ellen A. Farber et al., "Managing Work and Family," in Edward Zigler and Meryl Frank (eds.), *The Parental Leave Crisis* (New Haven: Yale University Press, 1988), p. 167.

[4]Beverly Birns and Niza Ben-Ner, "Psychoanalysis Constructs Motherhood," in Beverly Birns and Dale Hay, *The Different Faces of Motherhood* (New York: Plenum Press, 1988), p. 62.

[5]Margaret Tresh Owen and Martha J. Cox, "Maternal Employment and the Transition to Parenthood," in A. E. Gottfried and A. W. Gottfried (eds.), *Maternal Employment and Children's Development: Longitudinal Research* (New York: Plenum Press, 1988; 1994).

[6]Michael E. Lamb, "The Changing Role of Fathers," in Michael E. Lamb (ed.), *The Father's Role: Applied Perspectives* (New York: John Wiley & Sons, 1986), p. 9.

[7]Joseph Pleck, "Are 'Family-Supportive' Employer Policies Relevant to Men?" prepared for Jane C. Hood (ed.), *Work, Family and Masculinities*, in press.

[8]Ellen Galinsky, *Work and Family: 1992 Status Report and Outlook* (New York: Families and Work Institute, 1992).

[9]"Mothers in the Workplace Working Paper: The Role of Managers/Supervisors in Easing Work/Family Strain," National Council of Jewish Women, Center for the Child, December 1988, cited in S. B. Dynerman and L. Hayes, *The Best Jobs in America for Parents* (New York: Rawson/Macmillan, 1991), p. 71.

[10]T. Field, W. Masi, S. Goldstein, S. Perry, and S. Parl, "Infant Day Care Facilitates Preschool Social Behavior," *Early Childhood Research Quarterly*, vol. 3, 1988, p. 357.

[11]Sandra Scarr, *Mother Care/Other Care* (New York: Warner Books, 1985), p. 153.

[12]Kathleen McCartney and Deborah Phillips, "Motherhood and Child Care," in Beverly Birns and Dale F. Hay, *The Different Faces of Motherhood* (New York: Plenum Press, 1988), p. 164.

[13]Sarah Hall Sternglanz and Alison Nash, "Ethological Contributions to the Study of Human Motherhood," in Beverly Birns and Dale F. Hay, *The Different Faces of Motherhood* (New York: Plenum Press, 1988), p. 31; and personal interview, Janet Mann, October 1994.

[14]T. Field, W. Masi, S. Goldstein, S. Perry, and P. Silke, "Infant Day Care Facilitates Preschool Social Behavior," *Early Childhood Research Quarterly*, vol. 3, 1988, pp. 341-359.

[15]Wendy A. Goldberg and M. Ann Easterbrooks, "Maternal Employment When Children Are Toddlers and Kindergartners," in A. E. Gottfried and A. W. Gottfried (eds.), *Maternal Employment and Children's Development: Longitudinal Research* (New York: Plenum Press, 1988), pp. 121-151.

[16]Kathy R. Thornburg et al., "Development of Kindergarten Children Based on Child Care Arrangement," *Early Childhood Research Quarterly*, vol. 5, no. 1, March 1990, pp. 27-42.

[17]T. Berry Brazelton, *Touchpoints* (Reading, MA: Addison-Wesley Publishing Co., 1992), p. 369.

[18]Robert Karen, *Becoming Attached* (New York: Warner Books, 1994), pp. 344-345.

Chapter Six

[1]A. E. Gottfried and A. W. Gottfried, "Maternal Employment and Children's Development: An Integration of Longitudinal Findings with Implications for Social Policy," in A. E. Gottfried and A. W. Gottfried (eds.), *Maternal Employment and Children's Development: Longitudinal Research* (New York: Plenum Press, 1988), pp. 269-270.

[2]Lois Wladis Hoffman, "Effects of Maternal Employment in the Two-Parent Family," *American Psychologist*, February 1989, p. 289.

[3]Ibid, p. 290.

[4]A. E. Gottfried, A. W. Gottfried, and K. Bathurst, "Maternal Employment, Family Environment, and Children's Development: Infancy through the School Years," in A. E. Gottfried and A. W. Gottfried (eds.), *Maternal Employment and Children's Development: Longitudinal Research* (New York: Plenum Press, 1988), pp. 11-58.

[5]A. E. Gottfried and A. W. Gottfried, "Maternal Employment and Children's Development: An Integration of Longitudinal Findings with Implications for Social Policy," in A. E. Gottfried and A. W. Gottfried (eds.), *Maternal Employment and Children's Development: Longitudinal Research* (New York: Plenum Press, 1988), p. 270.

[6]Ibid, pp. 270-272.

[7]1991 figures, U.S. Bureau of the Census, phone interview, May 1994.

[8]*Starting Points: Meeting the Needs of Our Youngest Children* (New York: Carnegie Corporation of New York, 1994), p. 13.

[9]Cheryl D. Hayes and Sheila B. Kamerman (eds.), *Children of Working Parents: Experiences and Outcomes* (Washington, D.C.: National Academy Press, 1983), p. 227.

[10]Thomas J. Berndt, "Peer Relationships in Children of Working Parents: A Theoretical Analysis and Some Conclusions," in Geryl D. Hayes and Sheila B. Kamerman (eds.), *Children of Working Parents, Experiences and Outcomes* (Washington, D.C.: National Academy Press, 1983), p. 22.

[11]John P. Robinson, "About Time: Caring for Kids," *American Demographics*, July 1989, p. 52.

[12]Personal interview, Martin O'Connell, U.S. Bureau of the Census, July 6, 1993.

[13]*National Work-at-Home Survey*, Link Resources, New York, 1993.

[14]Paula Ries and Anne J. Stone (eds.), *The American Woman 1992-1993—A Status Report*, Women's Research and Education Institute (New York: W. W. Norton, 1992), p. 347.

[15]"Catalyst Finds Users of Flexible Work Arrangements Maintain Career Momentum," news release, Catalyst, New York, June 16, 1993.

[16]*Parent Post*, Parent Action, Baltimore, Winter 1993, p. 3.

[17]Ellen Galinsky, James T. Bond, and Dana E. Friedman, *The Changing Workforce: Highlights of the National Study* (New York: Families and Work Institute, 1993), p. 71.

[18]K. McCartney and D. Phillips, "Motherhood and Child Care," in Beverly Birns and Dale Hay, *The Different Faces of Motherhood* (New York: Plenum Press, 1988), p. 172.

[19]Susanna Rodell, "Do You Work? Are You Guilty?: A Mother's Day Present for Working Mothers," *New York Times*, May 8, 1994, p. 16.

[20]A. M. Farel, "Effects of Preferred Maternal Roles, Maternal Employment, and Sociodemographic Status on School Adjustment and Competence," *Child Development*, vol. 51, 1980, p. 1185.

[21]Michael E. Lamb, "Maternal Employment and Child Development: A Review," in Michael E. Lamb (ed.), *Nontraditional Families: Parenting and Child Development* (Hillsdale, NJ: Lawrence Erlbaum Assoc., Publishers, 1982), p. 57.

[22]Lois Wladis Hoffman, "Effects of Maternal Employment in the Two-Parent Family," *American Psychologist*, February 1989, pp. 283-292.

[23]Zvia Breznitz and Sarah L. Friedman, "Toddlers' Concentration: Does Maternal Depression Make a Difference?" *Journal of Child Psychology and Psychiatry,* vol. 29, no. 3, pp. 267-279.

[24]Lois Wladis Hoffman, "Effects of Maternal Employment in the Two-Parent Family," *American Psychologist,* February 1989, p. 285.

[25]Kyle D. Pruett, "Consequences of Primary Paternal Care: Fathers and Babies in the First Six Years," in S. Greenspan and G. I. Pollock (eds.), *The Course of Life, Vol. III, Middle and Late Childhood* (Madison, CT: International Universities Press, 1991).

[26]Ronald J. D'Amico, R. Jean Haurin, and Frank L. Mott, "The Effect of Mothers' Employment on Adolescent and Early Adult Outcomes," in Cheryl D. Hayes and Sheila B. Kamerman (eds.), *Children of Working Parents: Experiences and Outcomes* (Washington, D.C.: National Academy Press, 1983), p. 144.

[27]Ibid, p. 150.

[28]Ibid.

[29]Ibid, p. 163.

[30]Cheryl D. Hayes and Sheila B. Kamerman (eds.), *Children of Working Parents: Experiences and Outcomes* (Washington, D.C.: National Academy Press, 1983), p. 6.

[31]Ibid.

[32]Michael E. Lamb, "Maternal Employment and Child Development: A Review," in Michael E. Lamb (ed.), *Nontraditional Families: Parenting and Child Development* (Hillsdale, NJ: Lawrence Erlbaum Assoc., Publishers, 1982), p. 58.

[33]Wendy A. Goldberg and M. Ann Easterbrooks, "Maternal Employment When Children Are Toddlers and Kindergartners," in A. E. Gottfried and A. W. Gottfried (eds.), *Maternal Employment and Children's Development: Longitudinal Research* (New York: Plenum Press, 1988), p. 142.

[34]"Speaking of Kids: A National Survey of Children and Parents," National Commission on Children, Washington, D.C., 1991.

[35]Michael E. Lamb, in Michael E. Lamb (ed.), *The Father's Role: Applied Perspectives* (New York: John Wiley & Sons, 1986), p. 3.

[36]Mary Maxwell Katz and Melvin J. Konner, "The Role of the Father: An Anthropological Perspective," in M. E. Lamb, *The Role of the Father in Child Development* (New York: John Wiley & Sons, 1981), p. 172.

[37]Kyle D. Pruett, "Consequences of Primary Paternal Care: Fathers and Babies in the First Six Years," in S. Greenspan and G. Pollock (eds.),

The Course of Life, Vol. III, Middle and Late Childhood (Madison, CT: International Universities Press, 1991), p. 85.

[38]Michael Lewis, Candice Feiring, and Marsha Weinraub, "The Father as a Member of the Child's Social Network," in M. E. Lamb, *The Role of the Father in Child Development* (New York: John Wiley & Sons, 1981), p. 271.

[39]Jacqueline V. Lerner and Nancy L. Galambos, "The Influence of Maternal Employment Across Life: The New York Longitudinal Study," in A. E. Gottfried and A. W. Gottfried, *Maternal Employment and Children's Development* (New York: Plenum Press, 1988), p. 76.

[40]Carolyn Cowan and Philip A. Cowan, "Men's Involvement in Parenthood: Identifying the Antecedents and Understanding the Barriers," in P. Berman and F. A. Pedersen (eds.), *Fathers' Transitions to Parenthood* (Hillsdale, NJ: Lawrence Erlbaum Assoc., Publishers, 1982), cited in Arlie Hochschild, *The Second Shift* (New York: Viking, 1989), p. 237.

[41]Mitch Golant and Susan Golant, *Finding Time for Fathering* (New York: Fawcett Columbine, 1992), pp. 95-96.

[42]Ibid, p. 61.

[43]Ibid, pp. 56, 97.

[44]Ibid, p. 93.

[45]Ibid, pp. 99-103.

Chapter Seven

[1]Joseph Pleck, "Are 'Family-Supportive' Employer Policies Relevant to Men?" prepared for Jane C. Hood (ed.), *Work, Family and Masculinities*, in press.

[2]K. D. Pruett, "Father's Influence in the Development of Infant's Relationships," *Acta Paediatrica Scandinavica*, Supplementum vol. 77, no. 344, 1988, pp. 43-53.

[3]J. Jacobson and D. Willie, "Influence of Attachment and Separation Experience on Separation Distress at 18 Months," *Developmental Psychology*, vol. 20, 1984, pp. 477-484.

[4]Marylou Tousignant, "When Nursing Moms Go Back to Work," *Washington Post*, Nov. 6, 1993, p. A13.

[5]Ibid.

[6]Daniel Goleman, "Infant in Need of Psychotherapy? A Fledgling Field Is Growing Fast," *New York Times*, March 23, 1989, p. B13.

[7]Dorothy Coniff, "Day Care: A Grand and Troubling Social Experiment," *Utne Reader,* May/June 1993, p. 67.

[8]Barbara Morgan Wilcox, Phyllis Staff, and Michael F. Romaine, "A Comparison of Individual and Multiple Assignment of Caregivers to Infants in Day Care," *Merrill-Palmer Quarterly,* vol. 26, no. 1, 1980, pp. 53-62.

[9]Annette Axtmann, "The Center for Infants and Parents at Teachers College, Columbia University: A Setting for Study and Support," *Zero to Three Child Care Anthology, 1984-1992* (Arlington, VA: National Center for Clinical Infant Programs, 1992), pp. 29-34.

[10]Michael E. Lamb, "The Changing Role of Fathers," in Michael E. Lamb (ed.), *The Father's Role: Applied Perspectives* (New York: John Wiley & Sons, 1986), p. 87.

[11]Ibid, pp. 18, 20.

Chapter Eight

[1]Susan Kontos, *Family Day Care: Out of the Shadows and Into the Limelight* (Washington, D.C.: National Association for the Education of Young Children, 1993), p. 6.

[2]David Elkind, *Miseducation: Preschoolers at Risk* (New York: Alfred A. Knopf, 1987), p. 165.

[3]Ellen Galinsky, Carollee Howes, Susan Kontos, and Marybeth Shinn, *The Study of Children in Family Child Care and Relative Care: Highlights of Findings* (New York: Families and Work Institute, 1994), p. 59.

[4]*Safe & Sound: Choosing Quality Child Care* (Urbana, IL: Baxley Media Group, 1991).

[5]David Elkind, *Miseducation: Preschoolers at Risk* (New York: Alfred A. Knopf, 1987), p. 141.

[6]*Safe & Sound: Choosing Quality Child Care* (Urbana, IL: Baxley Media Group, 1991).

[7]Stanley Turecki and Leslie Tonner, *The Difficult Child* (New York: Bantam Books, 1985).

[8]David Elkind, *The Hurried Child* (Reading, MA: Addison-Wesley Publishing Co., 1981), p. 106.

[9]Lilian Katz, "Multiple Perspectives on the Quality of Early Childhood Programs," *Childhood Education,* Winter 1992, pp. 66-71 (Eric Clearinghouse, ERIC Digest EDO-PS-93-2).

[10]"Innocence Lost: The Verdict," produced by Ofra Bikel, aired on PBS, July 20, 1993.

[11]*The Demand and Supply of Child Care*, National Child Care Survey 1990, p. 18.

[12]National Child Care Staffing Study, 1990, p. 12.

[13]Sharon Lynn Kagan and James W. Newton, "For-Profit and Non-profit Child Care: Similarities and Differences," *Young Children*, November 1989, pp. 4-10.

[14]Dan Belm, "The McChild-Care Empire," *Mother Jones*, April 1987, p. 36.

[15]Susan Kontos, *Family Day Care: Out of the Shadows and Into the Limelight* (Washington, D.C.: National Association for the Education of Young Children, 1993) pp. 4, 6.

Chapter Nine

[1]Penelope Leach, "Say What You Mean, Mean What You Say," *Parenting*, April 1989, p. 54.

[2]Marguerite Kelly and Elia Parsons, *The Mother's Almanac* (New York: Doubleday, 1975), p. 141.

[3]David Elkind, *Miseducation: Preschoolers at Risk* (New York: Alfred A. Knopf, 1987), p. 185.

[4]Ellen Hock, "The Transition to Day Care: Effects of Maternal Separation Anxiety of Infant Adjustment," in Ricardo C. Ainslie (ed.), *The Child and the Day Care Setting: Qualitative Variations and Development* (New York: Praeger Publishers, 1984), p. 186.

[5]Ibid.

[6]E. Mark Cummings and Jessica Beagles-Ross, "Toward a Model of Infant Day Care: Studies of Factors Influencing Responding to Separation in Day Care," in Ricardo C. Ainslie (ed.), *The Child and the Day Care Setting: Qualitative Variations and Development* (New York: Praeger Publishers, 1984), p. 173.

[7]Ibid, p. 171.

[8]T. Field, J. L. Gewirtz, P. Cohen, R. Carcia, R. Greenberg, and K. Collins, "Leavetaking and Reunions of Infants, Toddlers, Preschoolers and Their Parents" (1983), in *Child Development*, vol. 55, 1984, pp. 628-635.

[9]Louise Tutelian, "Mommy When Are You Coming Back?" *Working Mother*, January 1991, pp. 29-34.

[10]Ibid, p. 29.

[11]Lennard J. Davis, "Helping Your Child Cope with Change," *Child,* November 1992, p. 60.

Chapter Ten

[1]National Study of Before and After School Programs, Final Report, U.S. Department of Education, Office of Policy and Planning, 1993, p. 63.

[2]Ibid, p. 54.

[3]Linda L. Creighton, "Kids Taking Care of Kids," *U.S. News & World Report,* December 20, 1993, pp. 26-33.

[4]National Study of Before and After School Programs, Final Report, U.S. Department of Education, Office of Policy and Planning, 1993, p. 4.

[5]Ibid, p. 35.

[6]David Savageau and Richard Boyer, *Places Rated Almanac* (New York: Simon & Schuster, 1993), p. 167.

[7]National Study of Before and After School Programs, Final Report, U.S. Department of Education, Office of Policy and Planning, 1993, p. 14.

[8]Karen Levine, "Should I Stay Home?" *Parents' Magazine,* vol. 63, no. 1, January 1988.

[9]Juliet B. Schor, *The Overworked American* (New York: Basic Books, 1991), p. 29.

[10]Ibid.

[11]Stanley Turecki, lecture, Lowell School lecture series, Washington, D.C., February 8, 1994.

[12]Andree Aelion Brooks, *Children of Fast-Track Parents* (New York: Viking, 1989), p. 88.

[13]Earl A. Grollman and Gerri L. Sweder, *The Working Parent Dilemma* (Boston: Beacon Press, 1986), p. 124.

[14]Ibid, p. 127.

[15]Edward F. Zigler and Mary E. Lang, *Child Care Choices: Balancing the Needs of Children, Families, and Society* (New York: The Free Press, 1991), p. 124.

[16]Betsy A. Lehman, "When *Can* a Child Be Left Home Alone?" *Boston Globe,* Jan. 1, 1993, pp. 29-30.

[17]National Study of Before and After School Programs, Final Report, U.S. Department of Education, Office of Policy and Planning, 1993, p. 5.

[18]L. Steinberg, "Latchkey Kids and Susceptibility to Peer Pressure: An Ecological Analysis," *Developmental Psychology*, vol. 22, 1986, pp. 433-439.

[19]Edward F. Zigler and Mary E. Lang, *Child Care Choices: Balancing the Needs of Children, Families, and Society* (New York: The Free Press, 1991), p. 126.

Bibliography

Ainslie, R. C. (ed.). *The Child and the Day Care Setting*. New York: Praeger Publishers, 1984.

Arent, Ruth P., M.A., M.S.W. *Parenting Children in Unstable Times*. Golden, CO: Fulcrum Publishing, 1993.

Atkinson, Alice M. "Stress Levels of Family Day Care Providers, Mothers Employed Outside the Home, and Mothers at Home." *Journal of Marriage and the Family*, May 1992, pp. 379-386.

Axtmann, Annette, Ed.D. "The Center for Infants and Parents at Teachers College, Columbia University: A Setting for Study and Support." *The Zero to Three Child Care Anthology, 1984-1992*. Arlington, VA: National Center for Clinical Infant Programs, 1992.

Balaban, Nancy. "Mainstreamed, Mixed-Age Groups of Infants and Toddlers at the Bank Street Family Center (February 1991)." *The Zero to Three Child Care Anthology, 1984-1992*. Arlington, VA: National Center for Clinical Infant Programs, 1992.

Barglow, P., B. Vaughn, and N. Molitor. "Effects of Maternal Absence Due to Employment on the Quality of Infant-Mother Attachment in a Low-Risk Sample." *Child Development*, vol. 58, 1987, pp. 945-954.

Baydar, Nazli, and Jeanne Brooks-Gunn. "Effects of Maternal Employment and Child-Care Arrangements on Preschoolers' Cognitive and Behavioral Outcomes: Evidence from the Children of the National Longitudinal Survey of Youth." *Developmental Psychology*, vol. 27, no. 6, Nov. 1991, pp. 932-945.

Belm, Dan. "The McChild-Care Empire." *Mother Jones*, April 1987, pp. 32-38.

Belsky, Jay. "Parental and Nonparental Child Care and Children's Socioemotional Development: A Decade in Review." *Journal of Marriage and the Family*, vol. 52, no. 4, Nov. 1990, pp. 885-903.

Belsky, Jay. "Infant Day Care: A Cause for Concern?" (Sept. 1986). *The Zero to Three Child Care Anthology, 1984-1992*. Arlington, VA: National Center for Clinical Infant Programs, 1992.

Belsky, Jay, and Michael J. Rovine. "Nonmaternal Care in the First Year of Life and the Security of Infant-Parent Attachment." *Child Development*, vol. 59, 1988, pp. 157-167.

Belsky, Jay, and Michael J. Rovine. "Temperament and Attachment Security in the Strange Situation: An Empirical Rapprochement." *Child Development*, vol. 58, 1987, pp. 787-795.

Belsky, Jay, and L. D. Steinberg. "The Effects of Day Care: A Critical Review." *Child Development*, vol. 49, 1978, pp. 929-949.

Belsky, Jay. "The 'Effects' of Infant Day Care Reconsidered." *Early Childhood Research Quarterly*, vol. 3, no. 3, Sept. 1988, pp. 235-272.

Belsky, Jay. "Mother-Father-Infant Interaction: A Naturalistic Observational Study." *Developmental Psychology*, vol. 15, no. 6, 1979, pp. 601-607.

Belsky, Jay. "Parental and Nonparental Child Care and Children's Socioemotional Development: A Decade in Review." *Journal of Marriage and the Family*, vol. 52, no. 4, Nov. 1990, pp. 885-903.

Benn, Rita K. "Factors Promoting Secure Attachment Relationships between Employed Mothers and Their Sons." *Child Development*, vol. 57, 1986, pp. 1224-1231.

Berg, Barbara J. *The Crisis of the Working Mother.* New York: Summit Books, 1986.

Berry, Mary Frances. *The Politics of Parenthood.* New York: Viking Penguin, 1993.

Beyond Rhetoric: Final Report of the National Commission on Children. Washington, D.C., 1991.

Birns, Beverly, and Dale F. Hay. *The Different Faces of Motherhood.* New York: Plenum Press, 1988.

Bond, J. T., E. Galinsky, M. Lord, G. Staines, and K. Brown. *Beyond the Parental Leave Debate*. New York: Families and Work Institute, 1991.

Boston Women's Health Book Collective. *The New Our Bodies Ourselves*. New York: Simon & Schuster, 1984.

Boston Women's Health Book Collective. *Our Bodies Ourselves*. New York: Simon & Schuster, 1976.

Bowlby, John. *Attachment and Loss*. Vol. 2. New York: Basic Books, 1973.

Bowlby, John. *Child Care and the Growth of Love*. First edition. New York: Penguin Books, 1953.

Brazelton, T. Berry. *Touchpoints*. Reading, MA: Addison-Wesley Publishing Co., 1992.

Brazelton, T. Berry. "Infant Day Care: Issues for Working Parents." *American Journal of Orthopsychiatry*, vol. 56, no. 1, Jan. 1986, pp. 14-25.

Brazelton, T. Berry. *Working and Caring*. Reading, MA: Addison-Wesley Publishing Co., 1985.

Breznitz, Zvia, and Sarah L. Friedman. "Toddlers' Concentration: Does Maternal Depression Make a Difference?" *Journal of Child Psychology and Psychiatry*, vol. 29, no. 3, pp. 267-279.

Bronfenbrenner, Uri. *The Ecology of Human Development*. Cambridge, MA: Harvard University Press, 1979.

Brooks, Andree Aelion. *Children of Fast-Track Parents*. New York: Viking, 1989.

Burchinal, Margaret R. et al. "Early Day Care, Infant-Mother Attachment, and Maternal Responsiveness in the Infant's First Year." *Early Childhood Research Quarterly*, vol. 7, no. 3, Sept. 1992, pp. 383-396.

Caruso, David A. "Quality of Day Care and Home-Reared Infants' Interaction Patterns with Mothers and Day Care Providers." *Child & Youth Care Quarterly*, vol. 18, no. 3, 1989, pp. 177-191.

Chase-Lansdale, Owen. "Maternal Employment in a Family Context: Effects on Infant-Mother and Infant-Father Attachments." *Child Development*, vol. 58, no. 6, pp. 1505-1512.

The Child Care Action Campaign. "Choosing Quality Child Care: Topline of Findings." Prepared by EDK Associates, New York, for the Child Care Action Campaign, Sept. 1991.

The Children's Foundation. *1993 Child Day Care Center Licensing Study.* Washington, D.C.: The Children's Foundation, 1993.

The Children's Foundation. *1993 Family Day Care Center Licensing Study: Family Day Care Advocacy Project.* Washington, D.C.: The Children's Foundation, 1993.

Clarke-Stewart, K. Alison. "Infant Day Care: Maligned or Malignant?" *American Psychologist,* vol. 44, 1989, pp. 266-273.

Clarke-Stewart, K. Alison. "The 'Effects' of Infant Day Care Reconsidered: Risks for Parents, Children and Researchers." *Early Childhood Research Quarterly,* vol. 3, no. 4, March 1988, pp. 293-318.

Clarke-Stewart, K. Alison. "Predicting Child Development From Child Care Forms and Features: The Chicago Study." In Deborah Phillips (ed.), *Quality In Child Care: What Does Research Tell Us?* Washington, D.C.: National Association for the Education of Young Children, 1987, pp. 21-41.

Clarke-Stewart, K. Alison, and Christian P. Gruber. "Day Care Forms and Features." In Ricardo C. Ainslie (ed.), *The Child and the Day Care Setting: Qualitative Variations and Development.* New York: Praeger Publishers, New York, 1984, pp. 35-62.

Cochran, Moncrieff M., and Lars Gunnarsson. "A Follow-Up Study of Group Day Care and Family-Based Childrearing Patterns." *Journal of Marriage and Family,* May 1985, pp. 297-309.

Coniff, Dorothy. "Day Care: A Grand and Troubling Social Experiment." *Utne Reader,* May/June 1993, pp. 66-67.

Creighton, Linda L. "Kids Taking Care of Kids." *U.S. News & World Report,* December 20, 1993, pp. 26-33.

Crosby, Faye. *Juggling.* New York: Free Press, 1991.

Dally, Ann. *Inventing Motherhood: The Consequences of an Ideal.* New York: Schocken Books, 1982.

Davis, Lennard J. "Helping Your Child Cope with Change." *Child,* November 1992, pp. 60-67.

Dombro, Amy Laura, and Patty Bryan. *Sharing the Caring.* New York: Simon & Schuster/Fireside, 1991.

Doyle, A. "Infant Development in Day Care." *Developmental Psychology,* vol. 11, 1975, pp. 655-656.

Dynerman, Susan B., and Lynn O. Hayes. *The Best Jobs in America for Parents.* New York: Rawson/MacMillan, 1991.

Easterbrooks, M. Ann, and Wendy Goldberg. "Toddler Development in the Family: Impact of Father Involvement and Parenting Characteristics." *Child Development,* vol. 55, 1984, pp. 740-752.

Eheart, Brenda Krause, and Robin Lynn Leavitt. "Family Day Care: Discrepancies between Intended and Observed Caregiving Practices." *Early Childhood Research Quarterly,* vol. 4, no. 1, March 1989, pp. 145-162.

Ehrenreich, Barbara, and Deirdre English. *For Her Own Good: 150 Years of Experts' Advice to Women.* New York: Doubleday, 1978.

Elkind, David. *Miseducation: Children at Risk.* New York: Alfred A. Knopf, 1987.

Elkind, David. *The Hurried Child.* Reading, MA: Addison-Wesley Publishing Co., 1981.

Etzioni, Amitai. "Children of the Universe." *Utne Reader,* May/June 1993, pp. 52-61. Excerpted from Amitai Etzioni, *The Spirit of Community: Rights, Responsibilities and the Communitarian Agenda.* New York: Crown Publishers, Inc., 1993.

Eyer, Diane E. *Mother-Infant Bonding: A Scientific Fiction.* New Haven: Yale University Press, 1992.

Faber, Adele, and Elaine Mazlish. *How to Talk So Kids Will Listen & Listen So Kids Will Talk.* New York: Avon Books, 1980.

Fallows, Deborah. *A Mother's Work.* Boston: Houghton Mifflin Company, 1985.

Faludi, Susan. "The Kids Are All Right." *Utne Reader,* May/June 1993, pp. 68-70.

Faludi, Susan. *Backlash: The Undeclared War Against American Women.* New York: Crown Publishers, Inc., 1991.

Farel, A. M. "Effects of Preferred Maternal Roles, Maternal Employment, and Sociodemographic Status on School Adjustment and Competence." *Child Development,* vol. 51, 1980, pp. 1179-1186.

Ferber, Richard. *Solve Your Child's Sleep Problems.* New York: Simon & Schuster, 1985.

Field, Tiffany. "Quality of Infant Day Care and Grade School Behavior and Performance." *Child Development,* vol. 62, no. 4, Aug. 1991, pp. 863-870.

Field, T., J. L. Gewirtz, P. Cohen, R. Garcia, R. Greenberg, and K. Collins. "Leavetaking and Reunions of Infants, Toddlers, Preschoolers and Their Parents." *Child Development,* vol. 55, 1984, pp. 628-635.

Field, T., W. Masi, S. Goldstein, S. Perry, and S. Parl. "Infant Day Care Facilitates Preschool Social Behavior." *Early Childhood Research Quarterly,* vol. 3, 1988, pp. 341-359.

Finkelstein, Neal W. "Aggression: Is It Stimulated by Day Care?" *Young Children,* vol. 37, Sept. 1982, pp. 3-12.

Fraiberg, Selma. *Every Child's Birthright.* New York: Basic Books, 1977.

Fraiberg, Selma. *The Magic Years.* New York: Charles Scribner's Sons, 1959.

Galinsky, Ellen. *Work and Family: 1992 Status Report and Outlook.* New York: Families and Work Institute, 1992.

Galinsky, Ellen. *The Cost of Not Providing Quality Early Childhood Programs.* New York: Families and Work Institute, 1988.

Galinsky, Ellen, James T. Bond, and Dana E. Friedman. *The Changing Workforce: Highlights of the National Study.* New York: Families and Work Institute, 1993.

Galinsky, Ellen, and Judy David. *The Preschool Years.* New York: Ballantine Books, 1988.

Galinsky, Ellen, Carollee Howes, Susan Kontos, and Marybeth Shinn. *The Study of Children in Family Child Care and Relative Care: Highlights of Findings.* New York: Families and Work Institute, 1994.

Galluzzo, D., C. Matheson, J. A. Moore, and C. Howes. "Social Orientation to Adults and Peers in Infant Child Care." *Early Childhood Research Quarterly,* vol. 3, March 1988, pp. 417-426.

Golant, Mitch, and Susan Golant, *Finding Time for Fathering*. New York: Fawcett Columbine, 1992.

Goleman, Daniel. "Infants in Need of Psychotherapy? A Fledgling Field Is Growing Fast." *New York Times*, March 23, 1989, p. B13.

Gottfried, A. E., and A. W. Gottfried (eds.). *Maternal Employment and Children's Development: Longitudinal Research*. New York: Plenum Press, 1988.

Greenberger, Ellen, and Wendy A. Goldberg. "Work, Parenting and the Socialization of Children." *Developmental Psychology*, vol. 25, no. 1, 1989, pp. 22-35.

Greenberger, Ellen, and Robin O'Neil. "Maternal Employment and Perceptions of Young Children: Bronfenbrenner et al. Revisited." *Child Development*, vol. 63, 1992, pp. 341-348.

Greenspan, Stanley I., M.D., with Jacqueline Salmon. *Playground Politics: Understanding the Emotional Life of Your School-Age Child*. Reading, MA: Addison-Wesley Publishing Co., 1993.

Greenspan, Stanley I., M.D., and Nancy Thorndike Greenspan. *First Feelings*. New York: Viking, 1985.

Grollman, Earl A., and Gerri L. Sweder. *Teaching Your Child to Be Home Alone*. New York: Lexington Books, 1992.

Grollman, Earl A., and Gerri L. Sweder. *The Working Parent Dilemma*. Boston: Beacon Press, 1986.

Haskins, Ron. "Public School Aggression Among Children with Varying Day Care Experience." *Child Development*, vol. 56, no. 3, June 1985, pp. 689-703.

Hayes, Cheryl D., John L. Palmer, and Martha Zaslow (eds.). *Who Cares for America's Children?* Washington, D.C.: National Academy Press, 1990.

Hayes, Cheryl D., and Sheila B. Kamerman (eds.). *Children of Working Parents: Experiences and Outcomes*. Washington, D.C.: National Academy Press, 1983.

Hegland, Susan M., and Mary K. Rix. "Aggression and Assertiveness in Kindergarten Children Differing in Day Care Experiences." *Early Childhood Research Quarterly*, vol. 5, no. 1 (March 1990), pp. 105-116.

Helping Children Grow Up in the '90s: A Resource Book for Parents and Teachers. Silver Spring, MD: National Association of School Psychologists, 1993.

Hewlett, Sylvia Ann. *When the Bough Breaks.* New York: Basic Books, 1991.

Hewlett, Sylvia Ann. *A Lesser Life.* New York: William Morrow, 1986.

Hochschild, Arlie. *The Second Shift.* New York: Viking, 1989.

Hoffman, Lois Wladis. "Effects of Maternal Employment in the Two-Parent Family." *American Psychologist,* Feb. 1989, pp. 283-292.

Holcomb, Betty. "Where's Mommy? The Great Debate Over the Effects of Day Care." *New York,* vol. 20, April 13, 1987, pp. 73-87.

Honig, Alice. *Quality Infant/Toddler Caregiving: Are There Magic Recipes?* Eric Document 288-625, Sept. 25, 1987.

Howes, Carollee (ed.). *Keeping Current in Child Care Research: An Annotated Bibliography.* Washington, D.C.: National Association for the Education of Young Children, 1988, 1990.

Howes, Carollee. "Can the Age of Entry Into Child Care and the Quality of Child Care Predict Adjustment in Kindergarten?" *Developmental Psychology,* vol. 26, no. 2, 1990, pp. 292-293.

Howes, Carollee. "Research in Review: Infant Child Care." *Young Children,* Sept. 1989, pp. 24-26.

Howes, Carollee. "Social Competency with Peers: Contributions from Child Care." *Early Childhood Research Quarterly,* vol. 2, no. 2, 1987, pp. 155-168.

Howes, C., C. Rodning, D. Galluzzo, and L. Myers. "Attachment and Child Care: Relationships with Mother and Caregiver." *Early Childhood Research Quarterly,* vol. 3, no. 4, 1988, pp. 403-416.

Innes, R., and S. Innes. "A Qualitative Study of Caregivers' Attitudes About Child Care." *Early Child Development and Care,* vol. 15, 1984, pp. 133-148.

Ipsa, Jean, et al. "Long-Term Effects of Day Care." Paper presented at the Biennial Meeting of the Society for Research in Child Development. Eric Document 285-694.

Jacobson, J., and D. Willie. "Influence of Attachment and Separation Experience on Separation Distress at 18 Months." *Developmental Psychology,* May 1984, pp. 477-484.

Jaeger, Elizabeth, and Marsha Weinraub. "Early Nonmaternal Care and Infant Attachment: In Search of Process." *New Directions for Child Development,* vol. 49, fall 1990, pp. 71-90.

Kagan, Sharon Lynn, and James W. Newton. "For-Profit and Nonprofit Child Care: Similarities and Differences." *Young Children,* Nov. 1989, pp. 4-10.

Karen, Robert. *Becoming Attached.* New York: Warner Books, 1994.

Karen, Robert. "Becoming Attached: What Children Need." *Atlantic Monthly,* Feb. 1990, pp. 35-70.

Katz, Lilian. "Multiple Perspectives on the Quality of Early Childhood Programs." *Childhood Education,* Winter 1992, pp. 66-71. Eric Clearinghouse, ERIC Digest EDO-PS-93-2.

Kelly, Marguerite, and Elia Parsons. *The Mother's Almanac.* New York: Doubleday & Co., 1975.

King, Donna, and Carol MacKinnon. "Making Difficult Choices Easier: A Review of Research on Day Care and Children's Development." *Family Relations,* vol. 37, no. 4, Oct. 1988, pp. 392-398.

Kontos, Susan. *Family Day Care: Out of the Shadows and Into the Limelight.* Washington, D.C.: National Association for the Education of Young Children, 1992.

Labich, Kenneth. "Can Your Career Hurt Your Kids?" *Fortune,* vol. 123, no. 10, May 20, 1991, pp. 38-56.

Lamb, Michael E. (ed.). *The Father's Role: Applied Perspectives.* New York: John Wiley & Sons, 1986.

Lamb, Michael E. (ed.). *Nontraditional Families: Parenting and Child Development.* Hillsdale, NJ: Lawrence Erlbaum Assoc., Publishers, 1982.

Lamb, Michael E. (ed.). *The Role of the Father in Child Development.* New York: John Wiley & Sons, 1981.

Lamb, Michael E., Carl-Philip Hwang, Anders Broberg, and Fred I. Bookstein. "The Effects of Out-of-Home Care on the Development of Social Competence in Sweden: A Longitudinal Study." *Early Childhood Research Quarterly*, vol. 3, March 1988, pp. 379-402.

Lamb, Michael E., K. Sternberg, and M. Prodromidis. "Nonmaternal Care and the Security of Infant-Mother Attachment: A Reanalysis of the Data." *Infant Behavior and Development*, vol. 15, 1992, pp. 71-83.

Leach, Penelope. *Children First*. New York: Alfred A. Knopf, 1994.

Leach, Penelope. "Say What You Mean, Mean What You Say." *Parenting*, April 1989, pp. 54-59.

Leach, Penelope. *Your Baby and Child*. New York: Alfred A. Knopf, 1984.

Lehman, Betsy A. "When Can a Child Be Left Home Alone?" *Boston Globe*, Jan. 11, 1993, pp. 29-30.

Levine, Karen. "Should I Stay Home?" *Parents' Magazine*, vol. 63, no. 1, Jan. 1988, pp. 58 and ff.

Lusk, Diane, and Bruce McPherson. *Nothing But the Best: Making Day Care Work for You and Your Child*. New York: Quill/William Morrow, 1992.

Macrae, John W., and Emily Herbert-Jackson. "Are Behavioral Effects of Infant Day Care Programs Specific?" *Developmental Psychology*, vol. 12, no. 3, 1976, pp. 269-270.

Marshall, Melinda. *Good Enough Mothers*. Princeton, NJ: Peterson's, 1993.

Marx, Fern. "School-Age Child Care in America: Final Report of a National Provider Survey." Wellesley College Center for Research on Women, Working Paper No. 204, 1990.

Montgomery, Laurel, and Carol Seefeldt. "The Relationship Between Perceived Supervisory Behavior and Caregivers' Behavior in Child Care." *Child Care Quarterly*, vol. 15, no. 4, Winter 1986, pp. 251-258.

National Child Care Staffing Study, Executive Summary. San Francisco: Child Care Employee Project, 1989.

National Institute of Child Health and Human Development (NICHD) Study of Early Child Care: A Comprehensive Longitudinal Study of Young Children's Lives. Available from Sarah L. Friedman, Human Learning and Behavior Branch, National Institute for Child Health and Human Development, Bethesda, MD (unpublished).

National Study of Before and After School Programs, Final Report. Washington, D.C.: U.S. Department of Education, Office of Policy and Planning, 1993.

National Work-at-Home Survey. New York: LINK Resources, 1993.

Osborne, Sandy. "Attachment and the Secondary Caregiver." *Day Care and Early Education*, vol. 13, no. 3, Spring 1986, pp. 20-22.

Phillips, Deborah A. "Infants and Child Care: The New Controversy." *Child Care Information Exchange*, vol. 58, 1987, pp. 19-22.

Phillips, Deborah (ed.). *Quality In Child Care: What Does Research Tell Us?* Washington, D.C.: National Association for the Education of Young Children, 1987.

Phillips, Deborah A., S. Scarr, and K. McCartney. "Child Care Quality and Children's Social Development." *Developmental Psychology*, vol. 23, no. 4, July 1987, pp. 537-539.

Pleck, Joseph. "Are 'Family-Supportive' Employer Policies Relevant to Men?" Prepared for Jane C. Hood (ed.), *Work, Family and Masculinities* (in press).

Powell, Douglas R. "Research in Review: After-School Child Care." *Young Children*, March 1987, pp. 62-66.

Pruett, Kyle D. "Consequences of Primary Paternal Care: Fathers and Babies in the First Six Years." In S. Greenspan and G. Pollock (eds.), *The Course of Life, Vol. III: Middle and Late Childhood*. Madison, CT: International Universities Press, 1991.

Pruett, K. D. "Father's Influence in the Development of Infant's Relationships." *Acta Paediatrica Scandinavica*, Supplementum No. 344, vol. 77, 1988, pp. 43-53.

"Quality Child Care Lasts a Lifetime." Family Day Care Survey Results. Montgomery County, MD: Child Care Connection, 1993.

Reeve, Ronald E., and Ilene J. Holt. "Children and School Entry Decisions." Reprinted in *Student Grade Retention: A Resource Manual for Parents and Educators*. Silver Spring, MD: National Association of School Psychologists, March 1991.

Responses to "Infant Day Care: A Cause for Concern?" Deborah Phillips, Kathleen McCartney, Sandra Scarr, and Carollee Howes; Jay Belsky; Stella Chess; Ross Thompson; Peter Barglow. In *The Zero to Three Child Care Anthology, 1984-1992*. Arlington, VA: National Center for Clinical Infant Programs, 1992.

Richters, John E., and Carolyn Zahn-Waxler. "The Infant Day Care Controversy: Current Status and Future Directions." *Early Childhood Research Quarterly*, vol. 4, no. 3, March 1988, p. 321.

Ries, Paula, and Anne J. Stone (eds.). *The American Woman 1992-1993—A Status Report*. Women's Research and Education Institute. New York: W. W. Norton, 1992.

Robinson, John P. "About Time: Caring for Kids." *American Demographics*, July 1989.

Rodman, H., D. J. Pratto, and R. S. Nelson. "Child Care Arrangements and Children's Function: A Comparison of Self-Care and Adult-Care Children." *Developmental Psychology*, vol. 21, 1985, pp. 413-418.

Rodriguez, D. T., and W. F. Hignett. "Infant Day Care: How Very Young Children Adapt." *Children Today*, vol. 10, 1981, pp. 10-13.

Rubenstein, Carin. "What Pediatricians *Really* Think About Working Mothers." *Working Mother*, April 1990.

Rubenstein, J., and C. Howes. "Caregiving and Infant Behavior in Day Care and in Homes." *Developmental Psychology*, vol. 15, 1979, pp. 1-24.

Rubenstein, J., C. Howes, and P. Boyles. "A Two-Year Follow-up of Infants in Community Based Daycare." *Journal of Child Psychology and Psychiatry*, vol. 22, no. 3, 1981, pp. 209-218.

Safe & Sound: Choosing Quality Child Care. Urbana, IL: Baxley Media Group, 1991. (To order this video, write Baxley Media Group, 110 W. Main St., Urbana, IL 68101.)

Sanger, Sirgay, and John Kelly. *The Woman Who Works, The Parent Who Cares.* Boston: Little, Brown & Co., 1987.

Savageau, David, and Richard Boyer. *Places Rated Almanac.* New York: Simon & Schuster, 1993.

Scarr, Sandra. *Mother Care/Other Care.* New York: Warner Books, 1984.

Schenk, Vicky M., and Joan E. Grusec. "A Comparison of Prosocial Behavior of Children With and Without Day Care Experience." *Merrill-Palmer Quarterly,* vol. 33, no. 2, pp. 231-240.

Schor, Juliet B. *The Overworked American.* New York: Basic Books, 1991.

Shinn, Marybeth, D. Phillips, Carollee Howes, Ellen Galinsky, and Marcy Whitebook. *Correspondence Between Mothers' Perceptions and Observer Ratings of Quality in Child Care Centers.* New York: Families and Work Institute, 1990.

Shreve, Anita. *Remaking Motherhood.* New York: Fawcett Columbine, 1987.

"Speaking of Kids: A National Survey of Children and Parents." Washington, D.C.: National Commission on Children, 1991.

"Special Issue: Infant Day Care." *Early Childhood Research Quarterly,* vol. 3, no. 3, Sept. 1988 and vol. 3, no. 4, Dec. 1988.

Sroufe, Alan L. "A Developmental Perspective on Day Care." *Early Childhood Research Quarterly,* vol. 3, March 1988, pp. 283-291.

"Starting Points: Meeting the Needs of Our Youngest Children." New York: Carnegie Corporation of New York, April 1994.

Steinberg, L. "Latchkey Children and Susceptibility to Peer Pressure. An Ecological Analysis." *Developmental Psychology,* vol. 22, 1986, pp. 433-439.

Stith, S., and A. J. Davis. "Employed Mothers and Family Day Care Substitute Caregivers." *Child Development,* vol. 55, 1984, pp. 1340-1348.

Thacker, Stephen B., M.D., M.Sc., et al. "Infectious Diseases and Injuries in Child Day Care." *JAMA,* vol. 268, no. 13, Oct. 7, 1992, pp. 1720-1726.

Thompson, Ross A. "The Effects of Infant Day Care Through the Prism of Attachment Theory: A Critical Appraisal." *Early Childhood Research Quarterly*, vol. 3, March 1988, pp. 273-282.

Thornburg, Kathy R., et al. "Development of Kindergarten Children Based on Child Care Arrangement." *Early Childhood Research Quarterly*, vol. 5, no. 1, March 1990, pp. 27-42.

Tousignant, Marylou. "When Nursing Moms Go Back to Work." *Washington Post*, Nov. 6, 1993, p. A13.

Turecki, Stanley, M.D., with Sarah Wernick, Ph.D. *The Emotional Problems of Normal Children*. New York: Bantam Books, 1994.

Turecki, Stanley, M.D., with Leslie Tonner. *The Difficult Child*. New York: Bantam Books, 1985.

Tutelian, Louise. "Mommy When Are You Coming Back?" *Working Mother*, Jan. 1991, pp. 29-34.

Vandell, Deborah Lowe, and Mary Anne Corasaniti. "Variations in Early Child Care: Do They Predict Subsequent Social, Emotional and Cognitive Differences?" *Early Childhood Research Quarterly*, vol. 5, no. 4, Dec. 1990, pp. 555-572.

Vandell, Deborah Lowe, V. Kay Henderson, and Kathy Shores Wilson. "A Longitudinal Study of Children with Day-Care Experiences of Varying Quality." *Child Development*, vol. 59, 1988, p. 1286.

Vandell, Deborah Lowe, and Mary Anne Corasaniti. "The Relation Between Third Graders' After-School Care and Social, Academic, and Emotional Functioning." *Child Development*, vol. 59, no. 4, Aug. 1988, pp. 868-875.

Vliestra, A. G. "Full- Versus Half-Day Preschool Attendance: Effects in Young Children as Assessed by Teacher Ratings and Behavioral Observations." *Child Development*, vol. 52, 1981, pp. 603-610.

Weinraub, M., E. Jaeger, and L. Hoffman. "Predicting Infant Outcomes in Families of Employed and Nonemployed Mothers." *Early Childhood Research Quality*, vol. 3, no. 4, 1988, pp. 361-387.

Weissbourd, Bernice, and Judith Musick (eds.). *Infants: Their Social Environments.* Washington, D.C.: National Association for the Education of Young Children, 1981.

Whitebook, M., C. Howes, and D. Phillips. *Executive Summary: National Child Care Staffing Study.* Oakland, CA: Child Care Employee Project, 1989.

Who's Minding the Kids? Current Population Reports. Washington, D.C.: Bureau of the Census, U.S. Department of Commerce, Fall 1991.

Who's Minding the Kids? Current Population Reports. Washington, D.C.: Bureau of the Census, U.S. Department of Commerce, Fall 1988.

Wilcox, B., P. Staff, and M. Romaine. "A Comparison of Individual and Multiple Assignment of Caregivers to Infants in Day Care." *Merrill-Palmer Quarterly,* vol. 26, 1980, pp. 53-62.

Willer, Barbara, et al. *The Demand and Supply of Child Care in 1990.* Washington, D.C.: National Association for the Education of Young Children, 1991.

Willer, Barbara (ed.). *Reaching the Full Cost of Quality in Early Childhood Programs.* Washington, D.C.: National Association for the Education of Young Children, 1990.

Wingert, Pat, and Barbara Kantrowitz. "The Day Care Generation." *Newsweek Special Edition: The 21st Century Family,* Winter/Spring 1990.

The Zero to Three Child Care Anthology, 1984-1992. Arlington, VA: National Center for Clinical Infant Programs, 1992.

Zigler, Edward F., and Meryl Frank (eds.). *The Parental Leave Crisis.* New Haven: Yale University Press, 1988.

Zigler, Edward F., and Mary E. Zigler. *Child Care Choices: Balancing the Needs of Children, Families, and Society.* New York: The Free Press, 1991.

Index

A

Abuse, in day-care centers, 34-35
Academic performance, 317
Accreditation and licensing of day care, 17, 18, 212-16
Adaptation of children to child care, 265-68
Adolescence, self-care in, 330-31
Advocacy groups and organizations, 48-51
Aggression
  in children, dealing with, 261-62
  day care and, 59, 60, 61-63
Ainsworth, Mary, 98, 99
Anxiety. *See also* Stress
  separation, 112, 119-20, 122-23, 171-72
  in working mothers, 107, 145
Assertiveness, day care and, 62-63
AT&T, 121
Attachment
  controversy, 83-110
  in infant development, 172, 174-75
  maternal-deprivation studies, 94-98
  measuring, 98-100
  NICHD study, 90-91
  process, 91-94
  theory, 88-89, 94-95
Au pairs, 16, 216
Authority, day care and, 60
Axtmann, Annette, 198, 199

B

Babies. *See* Infants
Babysitters, 327-28. *See also* Caregivers
Backlash, 147
Baird, Zoë, 27-28
Ballas, Tracey, 294, 299, 304, 305, 306
Becoming Attached, 94, 131
Behavior
  children embarrassing parents, 256-57
  in infants, normal vs. abnormal, 182-83
Behavior problems
  day care and, 56-57, 58, 59-63
  troubleshooting, 286-88
Belle, Deborah, 299, 318, 320, 329
Belsky, Jay, 5, 86, 101-6, 110, 147
Benn, Rita, 108

Benner, Phylis, 223, 227, 262
Bernstein, Neil, 282
Berry, Mary Francis, 9, 162
The Best Jobs in America for Parents, 138
Bonding. *See* Attachment
Bowlby, John, 94, 95
Boys with working mothers, attachment and, 108
Brazelton, T. Berry, 10, 87, 99, 105, 106, 119, 129, 130, 132, 176, 273, 287
Breastfeeding, 178-79
Brimfield, Renee, 330
Bronfenbrenner, Uri, 60, 100
Bryan, Patty, 280
Bush, George, 5, 7
Business. *See* Employers
Businesses owned by women, 143
Business trips, 273-78

C

Caregivers. *See also* Center care; Day care; Family day-care providers; In-home care
  anecdotes, 13-14
  for child-care programs, 42-45
  communication with, 249-51, 305-7
  compensation, 37-42
  credentials for in-home care, 215-16
  dealing with, 288-90
  hiring, 189-92
  interactions with children, 217-19
  interviewing, 191-92
  quality, characteristics, 71-73
  search for, 14
  training, 71, 76-81, 242
  turnover, 28, 32-33, 35-36, 67, 175
Carlson, Nancy, 293, 318
Carnegie Corp., 12, 89
Catalyst, 143
Center care, 32-36
  behavior problems and, 56-57, 58, 59-63
  child development and, 126-27
  employee earnings, 38, 41
  family day care and in-home care vs., 66-68